THE
ANOINTED ONE

THE
ANOINTED ONE

An Inside Look
At Nevada Politics

Jon Ralston

Huntington Press

Las Vegas, Nevada

The Anointed One:
An Inside Look At Nevada Politics

Published by
   Huntington Press
   3687 South Procyon Ave.
   Las Vegas, Nevada 89103
   (702) 252-0655 Phone
   (702) 252-0675 Fax
   e-mail: books@huntingtonpress.com

ISBN 0-929712-01-3

Cover Design: Bethany Coffey Rihel
Interior Design: Bethany Coffey Rihel
Production: Laurie Shaw

Photos reprinted courtesy of the *Las Vegas Sun* and the
Guinn campaign.

Printing History
1st Edition—September 2000

To Maddy,
The only miracle I have ever witnessed.

Contents

AUTHOR'S NOTE

The idea to write this book first occurred to me sometime in 1997; I consider myself fortunate that it has been published.

I had theorized in my newspaper column I've written for 12 years that Nevada's political system is controlled by a small number of men, all of them with access to the money of the gambling industry. But when Kenny Guinn, who had never before sought public office, announced more than two and a half years before the balloting that he wanted to be elected governor in November 1998, the race seemed a perfect case study to prove my thesis.

I conceived of an academic book, one that would tell a good yarn, but would also provide a road map to the state's political system. So, soon after the 1998 balloting, I approached the University of Nevada Press. I told them that a book showing how modern-day Nevada politics functions had never been penned and that I was ready to do it. They were not just receptive; they were enthusiastic about the idea, telling me it was just the sort of book the university press would want to publish.

A few weeks later, I sent an extensive proposal. And then I waited. And waited. And waited. When I finally called to inquire about the prospects in late February 1999, the enthusiasm had evaporated. Apparently, some at the press were now not sure they wanted to publish the book. A few days later, I received the rejection letter; to this day, it astonishes me with its unwitting candor and the conciseness with which it illustrates how incestuous Nevada's political system can be. Here is what my rejection letter of March 3, 1999, written by a high-ranking member of the publishing company, said:

"We have now had an opportunity to study and discuss your book proposal. I am very sorry to say that we have decided—reluctantly, I must confess—against encouraging you to submit the full manuscript to the press.

"This is not to say your project is without merit. Quite the contrary. You have an exciting and timely topic, and you write about it with great insight and real verve. We have no doubts that this would make an engaging and useful book.

"However, we have concluded that this press would not be a suitable outlet for it. Like most publicly supported academic presses, we are dependent on the legislature for some of our support, and to be very candid with you, it would not be appropriate for us to publish a book that comes too close to the political bone, so to speak. ... Even though we cannot work with you, I encourage you to seek another outlet, perhaps with a commercial press that has no connections or obligations to the political establishment. The project certainly has a great deal of appeal, and it should arouse a lot of interest."

I was stunned—as were others to whom I read the letter in subsequent days. Here was the academic press of the state telling me I had a wonderful proposal, but it was too hot for them to handle.

I reeled for quite some time before I sought a commercial publisher. And I will never be able to fully express my gratitude to Anthony Curtis and the folks at Huntington Press in Las Vegas for reading the proposal, liking it, and agreeing to publish this book. Curtis & Co. took a chance on a first-time author with a book that not only had to be written quickly so it could still be timely, but that was sure to be controversial. I salute them.

This book was produced from a variety of sources. I wrote, through columns and two newsletters, a voluminous amount of copy about the 1998 Nevada governor's race throughout the campaign. I also kept a journal for much of the race. But the book would not have been possible without extensive interviews I conducted with the major players shortly after the election. All were generous with their time and most were extremely forthcoming, even those who knew that the book might expose a process that might not seem as swell as some of them believe it to be. Indeed, some of the powers that anoint were torn—between the view that this book would portray them as influential and that this book would reveal too many secrets.

I should tell you that I admire and respect almost all of the men whose stories are contained herein. Some of them are acquaintances, some are friends, and one, Billy Vassiliadis, is like a brother to me. In fact, Vassiliadis told me shortly after the election that as my friend he would be totally supportive of my writing this book, even though he knew he wasn't going to like what it said.

These relationships have been difficult over the years—without these men as sources, I would not have had access to some of the best information I have dispensed. Yet I have also infuriated all of them many times by telling too much or too little of a story, or not telling it the way they would have wished. So be it. Still, relationships of mutual respect have evolved with nearly all of them, which surely have served their interests and mine. Some of them will be happy about parts of this book; some of them will wince as they turn every page. But none will be able to argue that what follows is not true.

This book is not about Kenny Guinn, the man. I believed when he announced his candidacy—and I believe today—that he is a good man, who ran with the sincerest of intentions, but also with a sense of entitlement. He turned out to be even more of a perfect messenger for this book's theme than I had ever thought. He was so naive, so unprepared for what was to come, and such an awkward candidate that he more than made the point of the book: that with the right horses, the quality of the rider is not so critical.

The political process in Nevada may not be much different than it is in California or Mississippi or Washington, D.C. But Nevada's size uniquely lends it to a case study such as this one. This book tells the story of the anointment of Kenny Guinn; however, it is not only emblematic of how power is amassed and doled out in Nevada, but how politics works most everywhere.

Finally, this book would not have been possible without the help of a number of people. I have already mentioned Anthony Curtis and Huntington Press. But I must single out Deke Castleman, my editor at Huntington, for his attention to my manuscript and for molding a lump of clay into an actual book.

Others were unrelentingly supportive of this project, including Jim Mulhall, who prodded me to go forward; Major Garrett, who helped spruce up an early version of the proposal; and especially Jenny Backus, who constantly challenged me to be better and whose suggestions were of incalculable assistance.

I also want to thank the many journalists who covered the governor's race and whose work both jogged my memory and provided insight. They include the two venerable Carson City hands, the *Associated Press'* Brendan Riley and the *Las Vegas Sun's* Cy Ryan, and *Review-Journal* capital reporters Ed Vogel and Sean Whaley. But, most of all, I owe much to the *Review-Journal's* Jane Ann Morrison, who has been a valued friend and a respected colleague for 16 years. She, more than anyone in this state, drives political coverage. In a sense, she is one of the powers that anoint.

A special thanks goes to Lou Cannon, the legendary author and journalist from the *Washington Post*. Cannon not only encouraged me to write this book, but helped with the proposal and gave me invaluable editing assistance along the way. Without him, *The Anointed One* would not exist.

I cannot forget my father, a published author many times over and still the smartest person I have ever met. He has been not just a supportive parent, along with my always enthusiastic and proud mother. But he applied the same firm but gentle hand to my manuscript that he did as a dad to all four of his children.

Finally, my wife, Sarah, who has made me what I am today, has been amazingly supportive of this project. She not only gave me the benefit of her unequaled common sense, but she has put up with an absentee husband while I completed this book. Her patience, her support, and her love have inspired me.

Jon Ralston
September 2000

PROLOGUE:
ECHOES TO THE FUTURE

When he stepped to the microphone at Las Vegas' Mc-Carran International Airport on Oct. 11, 1989, Brian McKay could have embarked on a path to the governor's mansion.

Smart, glib, and telegenic, McKay, Nevada's attorney general, was the Republican Party's golden boy, his perpetually tanned visage like the sunshine he brought to the GOP's gubernatorial ambitions.

To hopeful Republicans, McKay's expected announcement that he was running for governor would change the course of history. It would muck up the best-laid Democratic Party plans that foresaw the election of Bob Miller, the lieutenant governor who had ascended to the governorship when then-Governor Richard Bryan was elected to the U.S. Senate a little less than a year earlier.

McKay, running dead-even in the polls, was all that stood in the way of Miller's extending what already had been eight years of Democratic gubernatorial hegemony, He was the man who could begin the new decade right for the GOP. Today, McKay would make it official.

And indeed, he did make it official. The words Brian McKay spoke into that microphone, though, sounded not a triumphal herald, but the death knell for the GOP's hopes for the following year.

"I just don't want to run," he declared matter-of-factly.

McKay was out. Technically, there would still be an election in 1990 for governor. But with the attorney general's decision, and no other viable GOP candidates, the die was cast. Acting Gov. Miller, filling out Bryan's term, was a shoo-in. The governor's race had become a mirage.

But how? And why?

Miller's anointment began during the summer of 1989, when a small group of men quietly set out to guarantee that there wouldn't be a race. The men, all with keys to the Las Vegas Strip's money vaults, wanted to ensure the doors were shut if McKay knocked. Among those who turned the dead bolts were casino executives such as Golden Nugget chief Steve Wynn, the industry's charismatic self-appointed leader, who was about to open a spectacular megaresort called the Mirage; Circus Circus' Mike Sloan, the silky smooth pol who helped vet gaming appointments for Miller and was arguably the industry's savviest political operative; and John Giovenco, the courtly boss of Hilton who'd become active in the Nevada Resort Association, the industry's chief lobbying group.

These three industry captains had the direct ability to cut off money from three of the state's largest casino companies. Others, whose offices were not on Las Vegas Boulevard but who were in some ways more influential, were also committed to seeing Miller anointed by the casinos: Billy Vassiliadis, a close Miller confidant with a wide interlocking series of connections among the major donors; Kent Oram, who had overseen Miller's 1986 campaign for lieutenant governor and advised Giovenco as part of his Hilton retainer; and Frank Schreck, a gaming attorney and Miller friend who was also the Democratic Party's chief fund-raiser.

The casino industry and its front men were fond of Miller. His stolid style signaled predictability, which was reflected in his policy initiatives. In 1989, the governor left the gamblers alone and instead extracted money from the miners, whom the casinos always felt paid too little. What's more, Wynn and others knew the Mirage was a tremendously risky proposition, that Las Vegas was either on the cusp of a new era or at the beginning of the end. In the Midwest and South, states were on the verge of legalizing gambling. Congress, the previous year, had enacted the National Indian Gambling Regulatory Act to oversee a burgeoning new segment of the casino industry. The Nevadans wanted a piece of the action. Thus many companies were planning to explore other jurisdictions and preparing to lobby state regulators, appointed by the governor, to relax long-standing rules that made it onerous for the locals to invest elsewhere.

The industry assumed Miller would look the other way. The economy was fine now, but who knew what was coming? The casinos were planning to push a business tax during the 1991 Legislature to deflect attention from their bottom lines, and they needed to have someone they could count on to carry their water. The last thing anyone needed, industry insiders calculated, was someone in the governor's mansion who might not go along.

So, led by Giovenco, Sloan, and Wynn, with a little help from Vassiliadis, Oram and Schreck, the word went out: Miller is our man. Exclusively. He gets a blank check: If Brian McKay comes calling, you're not home.

So it was decided; so it was done.

McKay found that industry friends were no longer friendly. Sorry, Strip emissaries told him, we're behind Miller. If he wanted money, he would have to go elsewhere. But in Nevada, there was nowhere else to go.

This closed-door policy toward McKay was a gamble, but a calculated one. In fact, it was a game of brinkmanship—if McKay ran, the anointers knew, the casinos would have to play both sides. It would be expensive and uncertain.

There was another possibility, too, because McKay was one of the state's more mercurial politicians. Would the attorney general decide to run *against* the gambling industry because it was trying to dictate the candidates who would appear on the ballot?

That wouldn't be pretty. So, this small group hoped, the same holy water that anointed Miller would douse whatever fire to be governor flickered in McKay's belly. If he wasn't sure whether he wanted to run, the cold Strip shoulder surely would make him shudder at the thought of entering the contest.

And Vassiliadis and Oram were already imagining the TV spots should McKay challenge Miller—and they made sure their musings wafted McKay's way. The hypothetical commercials would focus on the peripatetic attorney general's taxpayer-funded travels, which had been the subject of news stories and columns, as well as his typically flippant criticism of Governor Miller for his veto of a 300 percent pension increase for state legislators. This would be no game of pattycake, McKay had to know; these guys would play for keeps.

By early October, McKay had gotten the message. He informed the media he would hold a news conference to announce his decision. At first, political observers assumed he was simply confirming what most had concluded a couple of years ago: He was running for governor. Few were aware of the sub-rosa shut-out brutally implemented by the powers that anoint.

But a few days before McKay stepped to the microphone on that October day, word had leaked. The attorney general was actually going to bow out, even though polls showed he could win. It was almost unfathomable: The party's most promising candidate, the only one who could beat Miller, the man destined to lead the Republicans to the promised land would not part the waters.

McKay hung his decision that fateful day on lack of desire. But the trickle that dripped forth when he tried to turn on the financial spigot told him that he would be parched if he tried to drink there.

More than a year before the balloting, the race essentially ended. Sure, there were moments of faux drama, some prominent names floated, some moments of worry for Miller. But ultimately, a deep-pocketed California carpet-bagger named Jim Gallaway, assisted by a boisterous Republican operative by the name of Pete Ernaut, did little more than make noise. Bob Miller, *The Anointed One*, prevailed easily in November, defeating Gallaway in a more than 2-to-1 landslide.

Though, at the time, it was a postscript to that day—October 11, 1989—that changed the course of Nevada political history, the end of one anointment presaged the beginning of another. As McKay was making his announcement, reports filtered out that Miller had corralled a prominent Republican to be one of his co-chairmen for the coming non-campaign, someone who was thought to be a potential GOP gubernatorial candidate himself some day. That man's name: Kenny Guinn.

1

KENNY OF THE THOUSAND DAYS IS BORN

Kenny Guinn shifted in his chair and looked plaintively at the man sitting next to him, Sig Rogich. Uncertainty was etched on Guinn's handsome visage, his physiognomy a portrait of tentativeness, his large frame rigid. Rogich, who like his friend had retained his good looks into his mid-50s, squirmed slightly, too, feeling Guinn's eyes upon him.

The pair of Republicans were sitting next to each other in a conference room inside Rogich's office suite, ensconced on the fifth floor of a bank tower a few blocks from the Las Vegas Strip. A few days earlier, Rogich, one of the state's foremost political consultants, had announced Guinn's candidacy for governor. The occasion for Guinn's present discomfort was a question I had posed about his stance on abortion. For several seconds, the room was silent as Guinn stole glances toward Rogich, his eyes pleading for guidance. It was unclear who would answer, as if they were straining to make a telepathic connection, to respond as one.

Finally, Rogich spoke. "I think he feels about that the way we all feel," he began, elaborating that he and Guinn were pro-choice. Guinn, almost with a sigh of relief, nodded, his body momentarily relaxing.

Anyone witnessing the scene would have been hard-pressed to discern which man was running for governor and which man was his confidant. They even looked alike. Both men had turned completely gray; both were distinguished and fit. Guinn, the former football player, was beefier than Rogich, but either one could have posed for a portrait of a prototypical governor.

Nearly every question I asked of Guinn, Rogich tried to answer. And he didn't have to interrupt Guinn, who seemed all too willing to defer to his handler. Both men talked in the first-person plural, and Guinn answered a question about why he was running for governor by motioning to Rogich and declaring, "We didn't see anyone with our beliefs and our principles."

Guinn had insisted that Rogich sit in on the meeting and asked that it take place at his longtime friend's office— Guinn would later move his office into the Rogich Communications Group warren, his name on the door below the company principal. Both men wanted Rogich there that day for a reason. Guinn, the candidate for governor of Nevada, had little grasp of issues and needed Rogich to run interference.

Issues, it turned out, had little to do with why Guinn was seeking to succeed Democrat Bob Miller, who would be term-limited after an unprecedented 10-year tenure. He was, he said that day, more concerned with "day-to-day operations, management more than philosophical debates." A pragmatist, not a philosopher. He sounded much like a Rogich client of yore, George Bush, who was similarly all about his resume and often had trouble with syntax. Most importantly, Guinn asserted, after years of being wooed and years of flirting with elective office, "For the first time, I'm willing to be seriously considered."

In other words, it was his turn. He had spent three and a half decades in Las Vegas preparing for this moment— serving Republican and Democratic governors as chairman of blue-ribbon panels, appearing on television as the helmsman of various bond campaigns for more schools and policemen, and achieving financial security after stints as chairman of a utility, Southwest Gas, and a bank, Nevada Savings. He had cultivated an amiable and dedicated persona, one that seemed to reflect the motto of the bank he once served—Big, Safe, and Friendly.

He may not have been prepared for questions or well-versed on too many issues, but Kenny Guinn was ready to be governor. And the men who could make it happen, led by Rogich, were ready, too. The date was Feb. 29, 1996. The election was still more than two and a half years away. But that week, a plan was set in motion that would attempt to eliminate all elements of chance. Kenny of the Thousand Days was born on that Leap Year Day. The quadrennial calendar event heralded a process that had become de rigueur in Nevada politics, occurring in one form or another in every election cycle. Leap Year Day 1996 it may have been, and November 1998 may have seemed far off. But this felt like an a priori coronation, with one small step from here for Guinn to arrive at the mansion.

You've heard of company towns. Nevada is a company state.

Here politics is much like any table game offered by the casinos. But nowhere is the deck more stacked; and, in the long run, the house always wins.

This state of affairs has remained relatively unchanged for decades, despite an influx of tens of thousands of new residents that has dramatically affected Nevada's demographics, though not its politics. The mob may have lost its grip, but the corporate titans who run the Las Vegas Strip maintain a stranglehold over the political system that the capos of La Cosa Nostra would envy. Despite the state's phenomenal growth, power continues to repose in a handful of men, who through their access to the Strip and its economic and political might are able to anoint—and un-anoint—candidates for public office. And they do so now at a time of lleled external threats to the state's economic well-from a federal gambling inquisition and Indian gaming in California to the real possibility that the Las Vegas boom is about to go bust.

Never was their exercise of power as blatant as it was with the anointment of Kenny Guinn. And, at the time, he seemed like the perfect vehicle. Guinn was the epitome of the Nevada establishment. Not only was he a regular honoree as man of the year for some civic group, but he was a board member of Boyd Gaming and Del Webb, representing the most powerful (gaming) and second most powerful (development) industries in the state. When Guinn decided to enter the fray, the powers who anoint assembled behind him.

This is the story of how they cleared the way for Guinn using a potent synergy of ruthless and relentless fundraising and the harnessing of the best talent available in an attempt to make the election result inexorable in November 1998. This is the story of who these men are and how, through their talents and the state's incestuous power structure, they were able to take a tabula-rasa and graft onto his candidacy their hopes and dreams—for the state and for themselves. And, as you will see, this is not a new story. While the names of the candidates change, the process and those manipulating and exploiting it are nearly immutable.

For much of 1995, Sig Rogich was telling friends and associates that he wanted to run for governor himself. Many thought the spinmeister extraordinaire, whose attentiveness to shaping his own image often superseded fashioning facades for his clients, was just puffing. But it was hard to be sure. Rogich was like the neon signs of the Las Vegas Strip—he sparkled from a distance, glowing with promise. But even in the light of day and viewed close-up, where the allure of neon fades, Rogich somehow maintained his incandescence.

One of his longtime associates once said of Rogich that he erected a virtual reality around himself—and then believed it was real.

No one, though, could argue with the record of success that Rogich's networking abilities and serial self-promotion had wrought. His Italian suits, beautiful homes, and multifarious business interests were testament to how he had translated his innate smarts and myriad relationships into success. And in a town where superficiality is supreme, Rogich also had depth. He could converse about Manchester's biography of Winston Churchill as easily as he could rant about the Dodgers' latest personnel move. He didn't need much sleep, so he read voraciously and had plenty of time to concoct advertising campaigns and political stratagems. Thus he could ingratiate himself equally well with presidents as he could with city councilmen—he always knew what people wanted to hear, what buttons to push. He had a reputation for being as smooth as a newly paved road, and his career had few potholes—at least none that he couldn't make disappear almost as quickly as they formed.

Sig Rogich was the classic case of local kid making good. He grew up poor in Henderson, an industrial town next door to Las Vegas. He parlayed an instinct for salesmanship, carefully nurtured relationships, and a fierce native intelligence into a successful business career in Southern Nevada. Eventually, he would move to Washington, D.C., where he was an adviser to two presidents, Ronald Reagan and Bush.

After attending the University of Nevada-Reno, Rogich spent the 1970s building an advertising empire through his creative wellspring and community contacts. He was instrumental in electing Republican Attorney General Bob List as governor in 1978. That outcome gave him a direct pipeline to the mansion, which he used to help friends garner state appointments. A notable example was his high-school classmate, Bruce Woodbury, whom List appointed in 1981 to a vacancy on the Clark County Commission, the government body that oversees the Strip and virtually every aspect of Southern Nevada life. Today, Woodbury is the longest-serving elected official in Las Vegas and one of the more influential and respected politicians in Southern Nevada.

Rogich's company, R&R Advertising, came into its own in the early 1980s when the man closest to the new governor obtained the lucrative contract for the Las Vegas Convention and Visitors Authority. The LVCVA markets the city to tourists and conventions and is funded by room taxes paid by the hotel-casinos. It is overseen by a melange of politicians and casino and business executives, some of whom know Rogich or were elected with his help. The contract became the foundation of Rogich's business. Thanks to the convention authority's close ties to the most powerful special interest in the state—the casino industry—and because so many elected officials cycled through the LVCVA's board of trustees, the contract also helped Rogich cement his political clout.

The campaigns helped, too. Rogich, a Republican, was involved in 1982 in electing a Democrat, Harry Reid, to a newly created second Nevada seat in the House of Representatives. Reid and Rogich both were close to Reid's mentor, former Gov. Mike O'Callaghan, who remained influential in Democratic politics and who then, as now, helped run the *Las Vegas Sun* afternoon daily newspaper. That same year, Rogich also assisted the state's only congressman, Jim Santini, in what would prove to be a disastrous primary bid against Democratic Sen. Howard Cannon. Because Santini wounded but did not kill Cannon in the primary, Rogich inadvertently helped the Republicans take the Senate seat when an unknown clothier named Chic Hecht swooped in and finished off the incumbent in November.

Rogich recovered from that loss, though, and played a role in Reid's 1984 re-election to the House. The two parted ways in 1986. Even though Rogich promised Reid over breakfast shortly before that campaign season began that he would never run a candidate against him, the consultant eventually sided with his old friend Paul Laxalt, the retiring U.S. senator. Laxalt had anointed Santini to replace him in the Club of 100 and tabbed Rogich to oversee the race. Reid prevailed and, ever flexible, Rogich soon became cozy with him again. Thanks to his relationships with Capitol Hill Republicans and Reagan, he even helped the senator pass an important piece of legislation, a wilderness-preservation bill for Nevada.

In 1984 Rogich left the state for Washington, D.C., to become part of Reagan's celebrated team of admen, leaving R&R Advertising in the hands of his lieutenant, Billy Vassiliadis. Rogich was essentially a Washington resident for the next eight years. He counseled Presidents Reagan and Bush, and was appointed ambassador to his home country of Iceland. He then returned from that oblivion to help rearrange the deck chairs on the S.S. Bush '92. That move was choreographed in classic Rogich fashion—he made it sound as if an SOS had gone out across the waves to get him to save the day. He was like Red Adair sailing in to put out the oil rig fire. Image was everything.

But even Rogich couldn't douse the flames of Bush's self-immolation at the hands of Bill Clinton. After the 1992 disaster, the prodigal son returned, hoping to resume his standing as the state's most successful political consultant. It didn't go well.

First, the pupil had all but surpassed the teacher. Billy Vassiliadis was in the kitchen Cabinet of Gov. Miller, playing a similar role that Rogich had for List. Vassiliadis had also ascended to the role of consigliere for as many pols as Rogich had ever been Svengali to in the old days. Vassiliadis had also taken the Convention Authority contract to another level, both creatively and financially. By 1993, Rogich had worked out the details of selling R&R to Vassiliadis, a deal that provided him with a guaranteed seven-figure income for the near future.

Second, the Rogich touch had turned from gold to lead. In his first forays back into state politics in 1994, he sustained a hat trick of crushing defeats. He handled Secretary of State Cheryl Lau's candidacy for governor and succeeded in getting her blessed by the state GOP. But Lau proved to be an inept and inarticulate candidate who was shredded in the primary by a Reno assemblyman, Jim Gibbons, a formidable and energetic campaigner. Rogich also handled John Mason, a wealthy entertainment lawyer from Lake Tahoe who hoped to become lieutenant governor. Not only did Mason lose, but he finished a poor second to an eccentric university regent named Lonnie Hammargren. Finally, Rogich was deeply involved in former Sheriff Ralph Lamb's attempted comeback. Lamb was a relic from Las Vegas' small-town days, a prototypical Western tough guy. Lamb ran against an archetype of the modern cop, Jerry Keller, a voluble glad-hander who could also talk the sheriff talk. It wasn't even close. Keller won with 68 percent of the vote. The new sheriff's campaign manager and most trusted adviser: Vassiliadis.

Rogich's star as a campaign guru had dimmed and he began thinking more about running for office himself, perhaps for governor or the U.S. Senate. Still, he spent much of 1995 reasserting himself as a consultant, sidling up to various public officials, especially at the local level, and securing a number of advertising and public-relations contracts for his new company, the Rogich Communications Group.

"I realized at one point [at the end of 1995] that I was just kidding myself [about running]," Rogich would later recall. "I just had too many conflicts, with city, state, and county contracts. I came to the realization that it was just not a practical thing for me to do."

Surely, part of Rogich's calculus was his desire to maintain his lifestyle and his fear of stepping from behind the scenes into the foreground. By year's end, he had decided not to run. Besides, as he had discovered with Bob List two decades earlier, he knew that the next best thing—and sometimes even better—to being there was being close to the one who was.

Those thoughts inevitably crossed his mind in early 1996 when he went to lunch with his friend, Kenny Guinn, at Cafe Nicolle, a popular eatery on Sahara Avenue a couple of miles west of the Strip. Guinn told him that he was seriously thinking of running for governor. Rogich knew Guinn was the perfect package. He looked gubernatorial, with his rugged face, broad shoulders, and gray mane. Guinn also had nearly as many contacts as Rogich, albeit not as many on the Strip. "If I could utilize the relationships I had to raise money for him, he would be tough to beat," Rogich mused at the time. Rogich told Guinn that if he were to run, he would be there at his side. They didn't know it then, but that day marked the beginning of the longest campaign for elective office in Nevada history.

Kenny Guinn moved to Nevada in 1964 at the age of 28 after growing up in Exeter, a small town in central California. He had received undergraduate and graduate degrees in physical education from Fresno State University.

Guinn started low in the hierarchy of the Clark County School District, as a planning specialist. But he moved up fast: After only five years, the 33-year-old was named superintendent. During his time at the school district, Guinn obtained a doctorate in education from Utah State University. His dissertation, "A Case Study of School Air Conditioning Operating Cost," was emblematic of what was to come from Guinn, a man who loves to crunch numbers. It was a mind-numbingly detailed discussion of various air-conditioning systems in Clark County schools, with calculations done to decide which ones were most efficient.

But Guinn had no accountant's personality—he may have been the most gregarious niumbers-cruncher in history. Guinn's affability and accessibility made him a favorite among the city's social elite and the local media. He got to know many of the power brokers in the then-relatively small metropolitan area, which had just passed a quarter of a million people. If he wasn't signing diplomas for the children of important Las Vegans, he was coaching their kids in Pop Warner football.

When he left the school district in 1978, he was only 42 and embarked on a second career as a bank executive, starting out as an administrative vice president for Nevada Savings and Loan—an institution that later became PriMerit Bank. In less than a decade, Guinn had ascended to chairman of the board. By 1987, he was president of the company that owned the bank, Southwest Gas, and he became chairman of the Las Vegas natural-gas utility in 1993. By 1994, Guinn, having become a millionaire, began phasing out of his private-sector career.

In his public life, Kenny Guinn had become a Las Vegas icon by virtue of his willingness to help raise money for a wide range of causes, from myriad charities to school and public-safety bond issues. If an organization or a government entity wanted credibility, it came to Guinn. And he was always there, ready to lend a hand in everything, from awful tragedies to management challenges. As far back as 1980, Guinn had helped sort out the damage after a devastating fire swept through the original MGM Grand Hotel. New retrofitting laws were needed—the cost to the hotels versus the need to appear safer was the conflict—and Guinn oversaw that effort. Ten years later, when Gov. Miller wanted to reorganize state government and needed someone to chair a blue-ribbon panel, Guinn answered the call.

So it was no surprise in 1994 that Guinn was enlisted to bring his coalition-building skills to the riven campus of the University of Nevada-Las Vegas, where a conflagration between legendary basketball coach Jerry Tarkanian and President Robert Maxson had resulted in the sequential departure of both men.

Guinn accepted only $1 as his salary. He didn't need the money. But he couldn't resist the opportunity, as usual, to exercise his characteristic combination of ego and altruism. It was typical Guinn: He saw himself as a problem-solver, especially with budgets, and UNLV's was in disarray.

This, though, did not go as smoothly as Guinn's past endeavors, where the establishment had embraced whatever cause he took up. Nothing so inflamed passions, and so divided friends, as the Maxson-Tarkanian war and its detritus. It was a tumultuous time for Guinn, who became embroiled in controversy when he authorized a nearly $2 million buyout of Tarkanian's disastrous replacement, Rollie Massimino, then brought in Tarkanian acolyte Tim Grgurich as his replacement. Many of the community doyens and members of the private fundraising group, the UNLV Foundation, who had supported Tarkanian's ouster were furious. They saw Guinn's hiring of Grgurich, his estimable coaching credentials notwithstanding, not just as a huge step backward, but as a betrayal of what they had accomplished. When Grgurich abruptly left after only a few months, citing emotional and physical ailments, Guinn, for the first time in his career, had egg on his face.

But it wasn't there long. By the time Guinn left in June 1995, he had righted the university's financial ship and helped soothe the Las Vegas community, which despite its growth, still had a small-town-like devotion to its college basketball team. After 30 years of amassing a fortune in political capital, the little he lost during the UNLV experience was small change.

In fact, Guinn had been talked about as a political candidate ever since the 1980s. He seemed to have all the requisite credentials—he was handsome, popular, presumably camera-friendly, and well-connected. And he was one of the best-liked men in the state.

The thought had occurred not just to others, but to Guinn himself. As far back as 1977, when he was still superintendent of schools, Guinn thought about seeking public office. He even hired Richard Wirthlin, the national Republican pollster, to conduct a survey to gauge his chances of becoming governor. It cost him $2,700, which was no pittance in those days. When he got the results of the poll, Guinn remembered, "I didn't even know how to read it." So he asked a friend to interpret the numbers and discovered that he was well-known in Las Vegas, but was a cipher outside Clark County. Guinn realized he had wasted his money; anyone could have told him the same thing. He ultimately decided not to run, especially because Bob List, the attorney general and a childhood friend of Guinn's from California, had declared his candidacy.

In subsequent years, Guinn often mused about running and others encouraged him to do so. One of his admirers was Hank Greenspun, the crusading publisher of the *Las Vegas Sun*. Greenspun tried to push him in the direction of a U.S. Senate seat, but Guinn had just left the school district and was committed to going into the banking business. Four years later, in 1982, Sen. Paul Laxalt, whom Guinn had helped in his campaigns, also felt him out about running for the seat then held by Democratic Sen. Howard Cannon. It didn't come together, though. When Guinn demurred, Laxalt gave him the hard sell, even promising visits by his friend, President Reagan. But Guinn blinked. And the unknown haberdasher Chic Hecht won a crowded GOP primary, then defeated Cannon, who had been badly bruised in his own primary by Rogich's candidate, Jim Santini. If Guinn had beaten Hecht into the race, he surely would have been elected to the Senate back in 1982, changing the course of Nevada history.

Guinn was still thinking about running for high office eight years later. Bob Miller had ascended from lieutenant governor to acting governor after Gov. Richard Bryan was elected to the Senate in 1988. Miller had never been elected to the state's top office, so Guinn might have had a chance. But after conversations with Miller's top consultants, Billy Vassiliadis and Kent Oram, Guinn instead endorsed the governor, crossing party lines to do so. Besides, for Guinn, personal relationships always trumped both partisan considerations and his own ambitions—he had known Miller for years.

It also helped that there were no Republicans on the horizon Guinn might be pressured to support. Those close to Miller needed a front man to make their case that the acting governor was a moderate, just as the bank, the gas company, and countless bond-issue proponents had used Guinn's face for their causes. After Miller won, Guinn told friends that he might be interested in running in 1994 if the incumbent wasn't on the ballot.

In June 1991, in a special edition of its newsletter, *The Advocate*, the Nevada State Education Association listed the state's most powerful figures and included Guinn in a category titled, "Working Behind The Scenes." In the sketch, the teachers union praised Guinn for supporting a broad-based business tax that the group had proposed to get more money into education, which passed through the 1991 Legislature. "Guinn, a Republican, was instrumental in the Miller election campaign in 1990," the piece said. "Speculation continues that when Miller leaves office, Guinn could ... finally go for the gold." It was a prospect, at that time considering Guinn's public support for more education funding, that seemed to please the teachers, his party affiliation notwithstanding.

Guinn had reason to be hopeful that 1994 would be his year. Legal questions arose after Miller won a full gubernatorial term in 1990 about whether he could run in 1994—Republicans hoped that those last two years of Bryan's tenure would be construed as a whole term, thus activating a state constitutional prohibition against a third term.

But Attorney General Frankie Sue Del Papa, a fellow Democrat, issued a controversial opinion in December 1992 that Miller could serve another term, and Guinn's hopes of running began to fade. The state Supreme Court validated Del Papa's opinion in July 1994, so Miller ran—and won—again.

But there was another major race in Nevada in 1994—Bryan's Senate re-election—in which Guinn was also interested. He was, in the words of one of his friends, "a little more tempted than people thought."

It almost happened, too, thanks to Steve Wynn. The mercurial founder of Mirage Resorts, nominally a Democrat, had oscillated since Bill Clinton's inauguration between playing golf with and publicly demonizing the president. In November 1993, Wynn called a meeting at his exclusive golf course called Shadow Creek.

The main purpose of the gathering, which included many key Strip executives, as well as Republican National Committee Chairman Haley Barbour, was to discuss making six-figure contributions to the national Republicans to help them take over Congress so they could blunt Clinton's policies. Wynn invited Guinn to the meeting. Guinn remembered Wynn telling him he wanted him to meet with John Moran. Guinn mistakenly thought Wynn meant the outgoing sheriff of Clark County, but the man of the same name to whom the Mirage Resorts chief was referring was the finance director of the national Republican Party. At the meeting, Wynn sprayed Bryan with his anti-Democratic venom and suggested that perhaps his colleagues in the industry—"the fellas," as he called them—should persuade Guinn to challenge the first-term senator. The idea didn't get much traction, though, especially when, shortly thereafter, Guinn took the UNLV job.

By mid-1994, national publications were suggesting that Bryan might be vulnerable, even though the GOP's hopes rested with a little-known candidate named Hal Furman. So Wynn began pushing the Guinn candidacy again. He raised the idea after a meeting of prominent casino executives at the Las Vegas Hilton. The meeting had been convened to discuss setting up a national gaming association. Bryan participated in a conference call during the meeting and refused to commit when Wynn asked him about a striker replacement bill. The Mirage Resorts boss saw his chance. After the meeting, Wynn suggested to some of the others, including well-known anti-union types such as the MGM Grand's Bob Maxey, that they should start calling Guinn to try to persuade him to enter the contest.

Guinn did receive calls, including some from national Republican strategists suddenly sensing a winnable Nevada race in their quest to take the Senate. Among those who called were Barbour, who gave Guinn the hard sell.

But Guinn received other phone calls, too. University supporters, including members of the board of regents, were upset that Guinn was considering a quick exit after committing himself to clean up the mess at UNLV. After mulling the prospects, Guinn ultimately elected not to run—and Bryan obliterated Furman in a landslide.

As the 1996 election cycle began, as usual in the middle of the previous year, it seemed Guinn was precluded from taking part—at least as a formal candidate. The governorship was not up until 1998 and there was no Senate race. With only legislative and local contests on the ballot, there was nothing that suited Guinn. But he and Rogich talked often during 1995, and after that lunch at Cafe Nicolle in early '96, the two were virtually inseparable. Rogich still had quite an aura at that time. At home, he was The Teflon Man, with nary a shred of tarnish from his 1994 defeats. His entrenched relationships still conferred access and his powers of persuasion and promotion remained unmatched. Finally, he was still the local success who had acted on the national stage as a consultant to presidents and could help guide Guinn to victory.

By early February 1996, Guinn and Rogich were quietly talking to friends and potential campaign contributors about a race that was still one cycle away. Guinn concentrated on informing friends that he was getting ready to run—and he had plenty of them to tell. Guinn knew that because of the history of his name being floated, and then his letting the air out of the balloon, he had to sound decisive when he told people about his plans—and he did.

Guinn's strongest relationships weren't in gaming, although he had contacts on the Strip—he was on the board of Boyd Gaming, which owned the Stardust and a few downtown properties, and he was still friendly with Steve Wynn, although his wife, Elaine, a rabid Tarkanian-hater and Maxson-booster, was disillusioned after the UNLV experience. But outside the Strip, Guinn seemingly knew everyone, from Andy Anderson, the president of the police union, and Terry Wright, a business leader and head of Nevada Title, to political types, developers and a raft of elected officials. As one longtime political observer remembered it: "He had put a lot of capital in the bank over the last thirty years, with an incredibly diverse group of people."

What Guinn lacked, Rogich had in spades. And like Willie Sutton, he went where the money was, up and down Las Vegas Boulevard. Rogich confided in men like Wynn, Circus Circus Enterprises' Mike Sloan, MGM's Terry Lanni. He even ran into Lanni's boss, MGM Chairman Kirk Kerkorian, in a restaurant and told him about Guinn's incipient candidacy. His pitch was simple: "Kenny Guinn is going to run for governor. He's going to be very formidable. And we need someone who is fiscally sound."

Hardly a gaming executive was less than enthusiastic in early 1996, with the notable exception of the Rio's Tony Marnell. Marnell had gone to high school with Attorney General Frankie Sue Del Papa, who was a possible contender on the Democratic side. Rogich remembers Marnell being disparaging toward Guinn: "What's he ever done that he should be governor?" It was a question Rogich hoped he would never have to answer.

Rogich was hoping to operate underneath the radar screen for much of 1996, but it was not to be. Las Vegas, despite its population explosion, is still very much a small town when it comes to politics and power, and word began to course through the community that Guinn was serious this time. Though some dismissed the rumblings as the biennial Hamlet performance, Rogich and Guinn had talked to too many people by late February.

On February 23, after getting wind of what was happening, I wrote about the possibility in my biweekly newsletter, *The Ralston Report*. "Like the swallows returning to Capistrano, the Guinn for Governor chirping has begun," I wrote. "It's an open seat, he would have broad support, and the race is wide open. Might the swallows be staying over this time?"

Three days later, after Guinn had chatted with his old friend, *Las Vegas Sun* executive editor Mike O'Callaghan, the emerging phenomenon was officially unmasked in the newspaper. The banner headline was "Guinn To Run for Governor." Emblazoned on the front page, above the fold, were two, large, equally sized photos—one of Guinn and the other of Rogich. The story, penned by *Sun* reporter/columnist Jeff German, was effusive.

"At 59, Guinn already has crammed in more than a lifetime of public service," German wrote, later referring to a "hero's stint" by the candidate when he served as interim president of UNLV. "And his devotion to civic affairs and local charities has become legendary." Near the end of the announcement piece, Rogich stated matter-of-factly: "He's an unusually talented candidate."

Rogich, ever the man with the vision, had a game plan that he had presented to Guinn, one that he later laughably claimed did not include that splashy announcement in the *Sun*. Rogich wanted the news to break reasonably early, but he wanted it on his own terms and, he would say later, certainly not in the afternoon paper with its limited circulation of 35,000 or so. It's hard to imagine, though he was quick to deny it, how Rogich could have gotten better coverage for his man—or himself.

"I sure as hell didn't want my picture in the paper with Kenny Guinn," Rogich insisted. "It was his day, not mine."

Still, Rogich reflected, having his picture in the story gave it more credibility because people would know he was involved. "If nothing else, it was viewed as a neutralizing factor with Billy [Vassiliadis]," Rogich said. "At least he would not work against me."

Indeed, Vassiliadis, who had run both of Miller's gubernatorial campaigns and was still a loyal Democrat, was also a friend of Guinn's. And R&R Advertising was the agency of record for the bank and the gas company. If Vassiliadis were not involved on the Democratic side of the race, Guinn would have a tremendous advantage.

Rogich's initial strategy was two-fold.

First, he took a page from the playbook another successful Republican pol, Richard Nixon, had used during the 1960 presidential campaign. Rogich recalled that Nixon, then not well-known across the country, pledged to visit all 50 states. He wanted Guinn, who similarly was little-known outside Clark County, to visit the other 16 counties in rural and northern Nevada. Rogich told Guinn that he would go to places that are rarely talked about anymore in Nevada campaigns, burghs such as Winnemucca, Tonopah, and Ely. Sparsely populated rural Nevada is heavily Republican, and Rogich believed that if Guinn could carry the so-called cow counties by a substantial enough margin, he could not lose the race. Guinn would have a head start over any Democratic opponent, who would not announce for months, even years. So Guinn would be able to devote the time to glad-handing and cementing the ties that bind in small towns.

Guinn, who relished glad-handing, embraced that part of the strategy without hesitation. He was a full-time traveler for the rest of 1996, quietly visiting rural towns and meeting scores upon scores of residents. He attended the annual Cowboy Poetry gathering in Elko, where he also rode in his first parade after being invited by a few county commissioners. Democratic county commissioners, in fact. Few people were really paying attention yet, but the man with the common touch was building lists that proved critical later.

The second page of Rogich's playbook was about money—$5 million, to be exact. Miller had raised $3.2 million in 1994; Guinn would need a lot more. Television costs had gone up, and the candidate would have to put a lot of money into increasing his name recognition because he was relatively unknown.

Rogich calculated that if Guinn were willing to put in $1 million of his own money, he could raise $2 million to $3 million altogether fairly quickly. No one else could match that kind of war chest, and constant press leaks of how successful the fundraising was going would be like notes of a dirge for any prospective opponents.

Timing, they say, is everything in politics. And the situation in early 1996 could not have been more propitious for Guinn and Rogich.

First, there hadn't been an open governor's seat in Nevada since 1978. No incumbent meant no obligation from the major donor community. That gave Rogich and Guinn a golden opportunity to fill the breach—and get the cash.

Indeed, Rogich found few doors closed to him as he began seeking financial commitments. Rogich had always been known as a successful adman and political consultant. But during the next two and a half years, he would establish himself as the state's most prolific fundraiser as well.

Two more factors also played to his benefit. First, the Democrats' almost-unbroken string of mansion occupancy for 40 years would surely energize Republicans, who would see Guinn as their ticket to power. Nevada had elected only two Republican governors since 1956—Paul Laxalt in 1960 and Bob List in 1978. Since 1982, when List lost to Richard Bryan, there had been no Republican in the mansion. It would be 20 years, by the time the election occurred in 1998, since a Republican had been elected.

Miller, thanks to Bryan's successful senatorial bid and

the state Supreme Court opinion, was on his last leg as the longest-serving governor in Nevada history. Republicans had endured a decade of frustration, even more so because during those 10 years they had never controlled both houses of the Legislature at the same time. They'd had their victories, but they were evanescent because of Miller. His veto pen during the biennial legislative sessions, along with his ability to raise money and organize support during campaign years, was a source of constant chafing by Republican leaders. They had controlled the state Senate since 1993, but the best they could do in the Assembly, since controlling the lower house in 1985, was a tie (21-21) in 1995. The Republicans were in the political wilderness in state politics, and Guinn was their Moses.

Rogich, who fondly remembered the good old days of List nearly two decades past, knew that Republican longings for a winner at the top of the ticket would be potent. He knew something else, too: The state's demographics were changing. For the first time in modern Nevada history, Republicans had more registered voters statewide than Democrats (as of October 1995). The number of independent voters was burgeoning, too—hovering at about 15 percent. And they tended to be more conservative, which also would help Guinn. Clark County, which encompasses Southern Nevada and Las Vegas, remained heavily Democratic. But, Rogich figured, Guinn had a base there—albeit, only among the insider elite—and if he could hold his own in Southern Nevada, Guinn would do well in the rurals and the Republican North.

The other major factor slanting the odds toward Guinn was Miller. The departing governor was almost a Democratic version of Guinn—a steady pragmatist whose don't-rock-the-boat mentality had helped galvanize the state's economy since shortly after he took office, with only one downturn in late 1991. Like Guinn, Miller looked the part. He cut a gangly figure, and while not exactly Lincolnesque, he could be imposing. Also, Miller was no Cicero, often morphing nouns into verbs and occasionally disgorging syntactical nightmares. But his verbal mangles were almost endearing, and his Guinn-like common touch was emphasized by his regular basketball playing and stories about how he wanted people to "just call me Bob."

Miller was a classic middle-of-the-road Democrat, a man who was at home in the centrist Democratic Leadership Council and who, not coincidentally, had developed a close relationship with DLC icon Bill Clinton when the latter was also a governor. Like Guinn, he had long-held connections to the Las Vegas power structure. And like Guinn, Miller was an eminently likable man, not known for partisanship or stridency, who had been a capable steward of the state.

The gaming industry loved Miller. Early in his administration, in 1989, Miller lead a move to tax the casinos' arch-nemeses, the miners. The mining industry is extremely difficult to tax because of prohibitions written into the Nevada Constitution by a mining-dominated group of state founders. But Miller found a way, and aided and abetted by the casinos, along with outspoken Assembly Ways and Means Chairman Marvin Sedway, he extracted more money from the industry. That session, Miller also signed a bill sought by the casinos to limit punitive-damage awards. The genesis of that measure did not involve any pressing concerns in casino boardrooms for tort reform. It had come about because of a huge judgment against Circus Circus Enterprises after a patron was mugged in the parking garage of its Reno property. The trial lawyers fought the damages limit, but eventually had to concede.

Miller's major initiative after being elected to a full term in 1990 was to propose the number-one item on the industry's agenda—a broad-based business tax, which was designed to do two things. First, it would create an avenue of taxation other than the gross gaming levy, which made up close to half the state budget. And second, it would take the bull's-eye off the casinos, which had not had their gross taxes raised since 1987. Miller did sign a business tax bill in 1991, but not the one he proposed. That one withered in the face of GOP opposition. The one that became law was presented as an administration initiative just before the session ended by the casino industry's main lobbyist, Harvey Whittemore. Whittemore cleverly snuck a tax break for his clients into the bill as it whooshed through the Legislature and was ratified by the governor.

In 1993, the industry's primary goal was reforming the State Industrial Insurance System. The workers' compensation behemoth was hemorrhaging millions every year. The reforms were carried out in such a way as to save the gambling industry, the state's biggest employer, millions of dollars by slashing benefits the resorts had to pay to injured workers. Once again, their lobbyists had won the day, swaying lawmakers and Miller to their point of view. Like the trial lawyers a session before, the union advocates wailed about unfairness, but eventually had to wave a white flag.

So Miller rarely bucked the industry, which had helped fund his campaigns and whose lobbyists were members of his inner circle. He adhered to the principle that what was good for the industry was good for the state. Occasionally, however, if the industry blatantly overreached, Miller had to step in. A prime example occurred in 1995, when Whittemore tried to pass a law that would have erased a $5.2 million jury verdict against the Las Vegas Hilton for the infamous Tailhook convention. Tailhook is an annual gathering of naval aviators that had a tradition of male aviators groping female aviators. Paula Coughlin, an unwilling participant in the 1991 hazing, won the judgment in that case, but the Hilton folks hoped to get refunded from the political system what the courts had cost them. This was not unprecedented. Whittemore had tried retroactively to make a multi-million verdict disappear in 1987, also for the Hilton, when the company lost an age-discrimination lawsuit. That effort failed when he could not get support. His move to deny Coughlin her victory also withered when the media picked it up, Coughlin traveled to Carson City to lobby against it and Miller informed Whittemore, one of his close advisers, that he would not sign the measure.

Generally, though, Miller wasn't one to surprise the industry. With men such as Whittemore and fellow gaming lobbyist Richard Bunker in his inner circle, Billy Vassiliadis as his close friend and confidant, and even Rogich as his sometime adviser, the industry was fairly well protected. Miller also relied on Circus Circus' Mike Sloan and gaming attorney Frank Schreck for advice—in fact, the two often recommended to Miller candidates for the state's two casino regulatory panels, the Gaming Control Board and the Gaming Commission.

Rogich knew that Guinn would be seen as a near-mirror image of Miller. The candidate knew all the players, was trusted by most of them, and projected a similarly steady-as-she-goes mien. No one else out there would have that ability—to provide the casinos with a comfort level that the tax man would not cometh, and if he did show up, it would be to knock at another industry's door. Guinn was the safe choice, Rogich knew, and if he could persuade his friends on the Strip that his man was all but impregnable, nobody else would be able to get any money—or even much traction on a slope greased with Guinn's green.

So who else was out there? After all, 1,000 days stretched before the balloting. Surely, both parties had viable alternatives to Guinn, especially elected officials who would find an open governor's race irresistible.

Surveying the lay of the land, Rogich was further heartened that the time was right for a Guinn candidacy. He knew that none of the possible contenders had the kind of drawing power—as a fundraising magnet, that is—as his man. Looking at the rosters, or so it seemed to Rogich, gave the impression that Guinn was a major leaguer compared to the Triple A talent—at best—that could step up to the plate.

On the Republican side, the pickings were slim. The most likely gubernatorial aspirants were Lt. Gov. Lonnie Hammargren, Secretary of State Dean Heller, and state Senator Mark James. All of them, in one way or another, had problems Guinn did not.

Lonnie Hammargren, though he was the state's highest elected Republican official and a practicing neurosurgeon, was considered an erratic accident of political history. He cut a good figure—he could have played Teddy Roosevelt in a movie, but his performance would have been more like the nutty uncle in "Arsenic and Old Lace" who imagined himself as TR charging up San Juan Hill. This former university regent, who once sent a double to pose as him in a parade, had emerged unexpectedly from a four-way GOP primary in 1994, then faced a Democratic candidate, former Las Vegas Mayor Bill Briare, who overestimated the public's memory of his tenure and underestimated Hammargren's willingness to spend money. Hammargren still had personal wealth, but his fortune had been greatly diminished since 1994. Even if he did run, and the lieutenant governor was murmuring to friends about it, he would not be a factor.

Mark James was one of the stars of the Legislature. An attorney from Southern Nevada, only 36 in early 1996, he was considered one of the state's most precocious lawmakers in many years. He was handsome and articulate, although he had developed an early reputation for arrogance that eventually saddled him with the nickname, "King James," courtesy of his Democratic adversaries. He was also widely seen as having a thin epidermal layer—as one elected official used to say about overly sensitive pols, "His bones were showing."

James had quickly risen to become chairman of the Senate Judiciary Committee, through which many gaming bills were vetted. He had developed relationships with the casino lobby, and he clearly had his eye on higher office. As chairman of judiciary, he'd also have access to fundraising sources. But he would have to give up his Senate seat, and he was not seen as a risk-taker. Challenging the powers-that-be in Nevada politics didn't seem to fit his profile.

Dean Heller was a true wild card, almost the anti-Guinn. He had a fondness for populist rhetoric and liked to portray himself as an outsider within his own party, taking on un-popular causes, such as campaign finance reform. He was sometimes seen as shamelessly playing to the media and using the party elite as a punching bag to further his own political ambitions. He was young, good-looking, and ambitious. He would provide a striking contrast to Guinn, too, on the stump—he was half Guinn's age, tall, and athletic (he played basketball regularly). His blond locks and radiant smile al-most gave him a look of a model, a perfect contrast to the grandfatherly Guinn in a TV debate.

Heller also had the potential to spend money—his in-laws were millionaires. However, he had a decided disad-vantage—he lived in Carson City, an inadequate base from which to run a statewide campaign. Mostly because of the southern surge in population and the Democratic-domi-nated demographics in the South, no northern Republican had won a top-of-the-ticket statewide contest since Laxalt prevailed in his last Senate race in 1980.

Still, Heller had legislative experience—he was part of an impressive GOP freshman class of 1990. When he ran for secretary of state after just two terms as an assembly-man, he crushed a veteran Democratic state senator, Tom Hickey, by a nearly 2-to-1 margin, garnering more than 204,000 votes statewide, second that year only to Treasurer Bob Seale, who ran essentially unopposed. Heller clearly had his sights set even higher, and his ambitions were being fueled by Don Carlson, a political Svengali in Nevada's capi-tal. Carlson's day job was as a community-college professor, but at night, he was a fixture at a capital haunt called Adele's, where legislators often supped and imbibed during the ses-sion. Sipping Hennessy's, his white, Einstein-like curls askew,

Carlson was willing to impart his wisdom to anyone who asked, but everyone knew that Heller was his main protégé, almost the living embodiment of an academic experiment. What's more, despite some friendships with elected and private-sector leaders, Carlson relished the opportunity to take on the state's political powers-that-be.

The odds, though, said Heller would not run, and that Carlson was just having fun. Heller was not likely to jeopardize a promising career and give up a safe post as secretary of state to risk elective-office unemployment by challenging Guinn. Was he?

The only other possibility on the Republican side was that a wealthy recent California transplant would run for governor. It had almost become a trend in Nevada politics. Jim Gallaway, a millionaire from Lake Tahoe, took on Miller in 1990 and funded his own campaign; he lost in a landslide. John Mason, the entertainment lawyer from Southern California who moved to Lake Tahoe, found a similar fate when he ran for lieutenant governor in 1994. Charles Woods, another wealthy entrepreneur who was horribly scarred from a World War II plane crash, also ran a couple of times in Nevada—once for governor and once for the U.S. Senate—and was creamed both times. But no one fitting that profile had surfaced so far, so it didn't seem to be much of a threat in early 1996.

The pickings on the Democratic side were even slimmer. Attorney General Frankie Sue Del Papa was the most likely contender, followed by Las Vegas Mayor Jan Jones. Beyond those two, though, no one would have any chance. Sure, there were a few legislators who might be interested in running someday, but none were ready, personally or politically.

Frankie Sue Del Papa was the Democrats' best bet. She was a longtime elected official, having been a regent, secretary of state, and now a second-term attorney general. Del Papa was still young—in her early 40s. And her business-like appearance—short brown hair, conservative dress—was set off by her seemingly unquenchable, even childlike enthusiasm. She called almost everyone "Hon" and breathlessly offered platitudes to any audience such as, "Democracy is not a spectator sport." No one loved politics and government more than Del Papa.

Del Papa also had statewide ties—she was born in rural Hawthorne, raised in Tonopah in the middle of the state, went to junior high and high school in Las Vegas and received her political science degree from the University of Nevada-Reno. She had cut her political teeth in Washington, D.C., working for Sen. Alan Bible in the early 1970s as she attended George Washington University for law school. She sandwiched in time working for Sen. Howard Cannon between practicing law in Reno in the late '70s. Del Papa embarked on her own public career in 1980 when she was elected to the board of regents.

Del Papa also could make a gender appeal as the potential first female governor—she had been the first Nevada woman elected secretary of state and attorney general—and she was an enthusiastic and peripatetic campaigner. The only question was whether she had the will to run. She'd seriously considered leaving public life behind before her last campaign for attorney general in 1994, and she had never endured a tough race. Rogich knew she could be competitive, but he also remembered telling her friend, the Rio's Tony Marnell, that he thought she'd ultimately not enter the race. Even if she did, Del Papa would probably not be able to match Guinn in fundraising. Also, he had locked in key consultants and insiders; the talent pool was thin.

Jan Jones had run for governor in 1994; she had actually decided to run within the first year of her first term as mayor. Jones was a flamboyant character—an athletic-looking fortysomething with mounds of ash-blond hair who had made a name for herself hawking cars on TV commercials for the Fletcher Jones dealerships started by her father-in-law. She appeared in outrageous outfits such as Little Bo Peep, always with her trademark smile and signature line, "Nobody's cheaper than Fletcher Jones."

But this TV pitchwoman was no dummy—a Southern California native, schooled at Stanford with an English degree, she was as quick and quick-witted as any elected official in the state. Jones had come to Las Vegas in 1981 after 10 years in the restaurant business and working for a family-owned company called Thirftymart, which sent her to Las Vegas from Los Angeles to target Hispanic customers. It was a typical Las Vegas story—she never left, married her second husband, Ted Jones, and by 1986 she was working for Fletcher Jones. She eventually became president of the Fletcher Jones Management Group, but this was not just nepotism. Jones knew what she was doing; she introduced a centralization plan of all the company's business functions, which she had completed when she ran for mayor in 1991 and won in a landslide.

Jones was an immensely popular leader of Las Vegas, projecting charisma and energy that had rarely been seen in that office. But she quickly felt constrained by the job—the city did not have a strong-mayor form of government, and she disdained the task of having to play insider politics with her four council colleagues to gain majorities. She wanted more authority, just as she had in that former incarnation as an executive with the auto conglomerate her husband's family owned. So after a few months, she looked toward Carson City. But Miller had the power structure, the money and the inside players. Eventually, Jones' challenge to her fellow Democrat became a disaster: She picked the wrong time, she couldn't articulate a message, and her campaign dissolved into paranoia and recriminations. Miller destroyed her in the primary by 35 percentage points. Jones managed to resurrect herself and win another term as mayor in the spring of 1995, with no credible opponents standing in her way.

But a year later, she remained unhappy with her political lot and undoubtedly would look at the open governor's seat. Jones, though, couldn't relish a second confrontation with the same power structure she took on in 1994. That had cost her dearly personally and politically. Rogich had developed a relationship with her, and he felt confident she would not run. History was against her, too—mayors had run for governor before, and not one had been successful in Nevada.

None of the prospective candidates for Miller's job publicly acknowledged that Guinn's declaration in early 1996 had cowed them. But in politics, the public face is often just a mask, covering private worries and fears. Such was obviously the case when the potential opponents were contacted within days of Guinn's announcement on the front page of the *Sun*. The possible contenders were queried by the *Las Vegas Sun's* Cy Ryan, the dean of Nevada reporters. Their responses ran the gamut: dismissive, brave, even borderline petulant.

Lonnie Hammargren tried to sound as if he were already in a race no one gave him any chance to win, Guinn or no Guinn. "It just means I've got to campaign harder," he said, adding with an uncharacteristic braggadocio: "I think any other Republican should be scared out. There is nobody else who will be able to get significant financing for this race."

Frankie Sue Del Papa injected a subtle thrust at Guinn into her own expected brand of political happy talk: "I'm keeping my options open. My decision whether to run for governor will not be determined on what Kenny Guinn does. He has always supported Democrats. I never run against anybody. I always run for an office. It's too early to begin a race for nineteen ninety-eight."

Jan Jones was unexpectedly candid, offering Ryan an almost visceral reaction, saying Guinn's announcement "wouldn't change my plan if I knew what my plan was. Kenny Guinn has long been floated as a potential candidate and it's always positive to have somebody from the private sector willing to get involved." It sounded almost like an endorsement from the mayor, after all but saying she had no idea what she was going to do in 1998. And that clearly was true, as the future would bear out.

29

Rogich believed with good reason that the path would not exactly be clear for Guinn. But with all of the candidate's inherent advantages, and the shallowness of the opposition talent pool, the road to Carson City would much more likely be littered with pebbles rather than obstructed by boulders.

In the wake of Guinn's announcement, Rogich's plan appeared to be working perfectly. The splash had, as he'd hoped, frozen everyone else in place. While prospective candidates felt a chill, Guinn was just warming up. For the next six months, everything proceeded according to plan, with Guinn picking up plenty of publicity for his charitable works and Rogich carefully letting out word of their fundraising successes.

Guinn soaked up kudos for his role in championing a bond issue designed to pay for a new regional justice center—just one of many signs of how the Las Vegas Valley's needs were outstripping its current infrastructure. The issue proved to be immensely popular, passing with 67 percent of the vote. And it didn't hurt Guinn with a few key constituency groups, either, such as law enforcement unions.

Stories also appeared intermittently about Guinn being the honoree for one group or another, something that had been occurring seemingly on a monthly basis for years, but now had more political resonance. In June, for instance, Guinn and his wife, Dema, were honored by the American Jewish Committee. In accepting the award from none other than Bob Miller, Guinn offered the kind of platitude that would later become the hallmark of his campaign, the kind of warm, but occasionally cloying, line that he had given so many times before: "Looking out across the room, I don't see any hatred," Guinn told the crowd at Caesars Palace. "And I believe that all of us working together can make a difference." One of the co-chairs of the dinner was Brian Greenspun, the editor of the *Las Vegas Sun*, which would prove, along with the other daily, the *Las Vegas Review-Journal*, to be consistently supportive of Guinn's candidacy.

It also didn't take long for Rogich to begin spreading word of Guinn's expanding war chest. By the end of May 1996, two months after the candidate's announcement, the *Sun's* Jeff German was writing that Guinn had amassed $1 million in commitments and that he and Rogich were the toast of rural Nevada. The kicker to German's column read: "All the while, Guinn keeps picking up momentum, enjoying politics the way a candidate for governor should."

But there were rumblings of discontent. Jones, who had won re-election with 72 percent of the vote that spring, appeared fully recovered from her 1994 gubernatorial debacle. Yet even though she had just asked Las Vegas voters to elect her to a second term as mayor, Jones couldn't get her mind off the only job in politics she really wanted. She'd heard the whispers of Guinn's invincibility from Rogich and others, and she was irked. How could Kenny Guinn, who had never run for anything, be unbeatable? After all, he was relatively unknown and she had recently run a statewide race. So, after some prodding by friends, Jones commissioned a poll.

The survey was conducted in late September by Mike McGuire, a Reno pollster experienced in Nevada. The results validated Jones' instincts. She was ahead of Guinn by almost 2-to-1 (32 percent to 18 percent) and was crushing him in Clark County by 43-25. Del Papa's numbers were just as strong in the McGuire poll—she led Guinn 41-24.

The results didn't mean much; they were purely a reflection of the two elected officials' stronger name recognition. Guinn hadn't yet spent a dime on television ads to get himself known to the electorate. But the release of the poll in late October at least sent a message to the Guinn campaign that Jones might be interested in the race.

Around that same time, Guinn decided to pay a visit to Secretary of State Dean Heller, possibly the most threatening primary candidate. They met in Heller's Carson City office on Sept. 30 for two hours. "He wanted me to be aware that he was running," Heller said at the time. And, Heller added, "He wanted me to know that anybody who is anybody in politics [was supporting] him. There wasn't a name that didn't come up. And [Guinn said] any dime that was available for statewide campaigns, they [had] signed onto him, too. He was sitting there, talking, saying this is the way it is." During the meeting, Guinn also raised the possibility of Heller running for lieutenant governor, a scenario he had also raised with another prospective opponent, state Sen. Mark James, who had decided to pursue the safe course to re-election. Heller recalled Guinn telling him that during his career, he had "always had young lieutenants and had always given them a lot of responsibility. And he was always willing to turn over the mantle when he left. ... He said he'd love to see one of these bright young Republicans be lieutenant governor." Ah, yes, he was just mentoring the young lads.

Heller gave no ground, though. He told Guinn he would wait until after the 1997 Legislature to make up his mind. He wanted to see if the 1996 elections signaled that voters were ready for an anti-establishment populist messenger.

Shortly after the meeting, word leaked out that Guinn had called on Heller. Guinn was furious. Although some on his team believed Rogich was the source, Guinn suspected Heller had leaked the conversation to make himself look good. He would not forget it.

Even though Jones and Heller were clearly not willing to let the Guinn steamroller flatten them just yet—they were still undecided about what to do—the anointment was proceeding apace behind the scenes. By October, thanks to Rogich's whispers, I was reporting that the Guinn machine was chugging along, having developed a list of 2,000 supporters in Clark County alone. In retrospect, the number seems exaggerated; but I, too, was romanced by the Rogich-created steamroller.

But Rogich had accomplished something much more

significant. He had recruited two of the state's most prodigious fundraisers to the cause—gaming attorney Frank Schreck and physician Elias Ghanem. They, not coincidentally, had been the money men for the previous gubernatorial anointee, Bob Miller. Schreck was an intense, connected advocate who had raised millions over the years for a slew of candidates up and down the ticket. Ghanem, the so-called "physician to the stars" and erstwhile Elvis Presley caregiver, had also raised money for many local and national candidates, often hosting events at his house. And even though the election was two years away, they had seen the phenomenon before. That was the real beauty of what Rogich had accomplished: Ghanem and Schreck, both Democrats and key figures in the anointment of Miller in 1990 and 1994, wanted to be with the man they thought would win.

Guinn maintained his lifestyle as if nothing had changed. Despite his candidacy, he continued to serve on those two prominent boards—Boyd Gaming and Del Webb. Guinn felt he didn't have to give up serving on those boards, thus relinquishing the sizable yearly fees, until he officially became a candidate in 1998. In fact, he even took on another board duty in September, when he agreed to become a director of Norwest Bank of Nevada. A couple of months earlier, Norwest had merged with Guinn's former employer, PriMerit Bank.

Guinn occasionally surfaced when he gave speeches, which were not getting the most flattering reviews, even from his friends. He almost always rambled, and occasionally took bizarre positions. One such instance, and the first that received any newspaper coverage, occurred on Oct. 17 when he addressed a Nevada Development Authority forum at the Rio Hotel. In introducing Guinn, the moderator read his long resume and concluded by intoning his name and adding, "who I'm told is the next governor of the state of Nevada." In a serpentine speech to the high-level group of business executives, Guinn proposed taking 5,000 acres of federal land in Southern Nevada and giving them to private developers as a way to help ameliorate growth problems. Growth was—and remains—the single most pressing issue in Las Vegas because of the skyrocketing population. Every growth-related problem has manifested during the last decade—clogged roads, worsening air pollution, and commercial encroachment into residential areas, to name a few.

What seemed strange about Guinn's proposal was that he was suggesting that vacant land from the Bureau of Land Management be developed. And while it would create millions of dollars in property-tax revenue as the land was put onto the rolls, which could be used to offset growth costs, it could also conceivably cause even more crowded roads, polluted air, and haphazard zoning. Guinn also didn't specify whether he thought the BLM should donate the land or whether it should be purchased, which is how the process usually works. The moderator's immediate assessment of Guinn's speech—"sounds like the next governor"—belied how amateurish it was. It was not an auspicious beginning to Guinn's political speaking career.

The Nevada Development Authority had given the event some advance publicity. It turned out that Guinn was one of two speakers at the forum touted in the flyer for the event. In fact, the pair was listed as though they were an inseparable act. And, indeed, they were. The other speaker on the forum announcement was Guinn's shadow campaign manager. Sig Rogich got top billing.

2

THE POWERS
THAT ANOINT

If political guru Jim Joyce were alive in 1996, he surely would have been a key cog in the Kenny Guinn machine. Joyce, reared in Nevada politics during the 1970s alongside his friend, Sig Rogich, was a dominant force. In many ways, Joyce, more than Rogich, more than anyone, epitomized power in modern-day Nevada. During his heyday in the late 1970s and the 1980s, Joyce was the anthropomorphic evidence of anointment, the progenitor for a process that has become imbued in the state's political fabric. If one measure of a man's power is the myths that surround him, even as he lived, then Joyce was nearly omnipotent.

Jim Joyce was a gangly, courtly adman and political consultant with a distinctive bass voice who loved to operate in the background and turned self-deprecation into an art form. "If only I had all this 'power' people say I have ..." he would intone, gazing down on whomever happened to be listening, a wry smile creasing his face. Privately, he would chuckle when friends came to him, upset that someone in the media had suggested that it might be too cozy an arrangement for him, that he had the power to both run campaigns and then turn around and lobby the very people he helped elect. "Oh, not that," Joyce would reply. "Don't tell me they're saying I have a lot of power. Now, *that* can't be good for business."

Oh, he had power all right. One oft-repeated bit of apocrypha about Joyce is that during the 1970s he sat down with Rogich and Kent Oram, like the other two an adman and political consultant, and divided up the state. Joyce wanted the Legislature, Oram coveted the local governments, and Rogich could have all the big-ticket items—especially governor and U.S. Senate. They would never, without permission, encroach on each other's turf—there was plenty to go around. But neither Rogich nor Oram, their successes after that legendary meeting notwithstanding, could match what Joyce achieved in the system he himself perfected.

Joyce handled the campaigns of any number of legislative candidates—sometimes having a say in most of the campaigns for the 42-member Assembly and the 21-seat Senate. And he wouldn't just plot strategy and craft mail pieces. He'd also raise money, much of it from the gaming industry, and personally deliver the checks. A portion of those checks, of course, would eventually be redirected his way for campaign expenses. Ah, but even that wasn't the real payoff.

After Joyce's candidates won—and they almost always did, until late in his career when he took a few high-profile losses—they were indebted to him not just for shepherding them to victory, but also for providing them the money to fuel their campaigns. And when they subsequently traveled to Carson City for their biennial bivouac to make laws, guess who was strolling the hallways asking for votes for his clients? Yes, the same Jim Joyce who had recently raised money for them and ran their campaigns. Joyce drew a ruthlessly tight circle and those who weren't inside were out in the cold.

And that was what most important Nevada businesses, including gaming and development, knew when they went to Carson City looking for legislation: If you hired Joyce, you had a leg up. Joyce rarely lost a major vote in Carson City, exercising his brilliant strategic mind while trading in his campaign connections for votes. And he never did it with bravado or bluster—he just did it. Some old-timers tell tales of how Joyce used to stand in the back of committee rooms and flash a thumbs up or thumbs down to signal to lawmakers which way to vote on legislation. But he hardly needed to do even that—many of the Gang of 63 knew that if they went against him, the thumbs-down Joyce would give them during the next campaign year would be the equivalent of the sign Roman emperors once gave to unfortunate gladiators in the Coliseum.

Joyce's influence was quantified in 1990 when a study of campaign-contribution reports showed that Joyce, then in the midst of running many legislative races, was the prime lobbyist for four of the top contributors—Summa Corp., the company started by Howard Hughes and the largest development player in Southern Nevada; America West, the airline company seeking to protect its turf in the state; Arco, enmeshed in a constant battle against so-called divorcement legislation designed to stop the oil giant from becoming a monopolist in the Nevada market; and Sierra Health Services, the state's largest managed-care provider, always trying to protect its bottom line.

For a man who must have occasionally had trouble keeping all his clients, candidates, and agendas straight, Joyce's equanimity was legendary. In all the years I knew him, I only saw him lose his temper once. That was during the 1991 Legislature, at a meeting he was having in the Assembly majority leader's office. He was there with his fellow gaming lobbyist Richard Bunker talking to a state senator from Las Vegas named Bob Coffin. Coffin had been hemming and hawing about where he stood on a bill and he wondered aloud whether Joyce and Bunker had enough votes to pass the legislation. Joyce turned toward Coffin, his voice rising to an uncharacteristically high and furious level, and roared: "When we count 'em, they stick!" Coffin said nothing. Joyce later won, of course.

Joyce took over as the lead gaming lobbyist in 1987. It was hardly a surprising development, considering his track record. He rarely lost an issue he took on, including unpopular causes, such as the legalization of Laetrile and acupuncture. He helped the industry win some important fights, including capping punitive damages in 1989. With Bunker constantly at his side—I once referred to the pair as the Siamese gaming lobbyist—Joyce bestrode the Legislative Building like a Colossus, with the rest of the lobbying crew peeping about his long legs as mere underlings. The fault was not in their talents, but in their lack of IOUs, which provided the access and, ultimately, that endemic Nevada commodity, juice, that made Joyce the gentle giant.

With the casinos now on his lobbying resume, Joyce was a one-man anointing crew—sprinkling holy water on those who bowed at his altar, and consigning to oblivion nearly all who came up against him and his flock.

There were a few black marks—a devastating defeat by his friend, U.S. Sen. Howard Cannon, fatally weakened in a primary by Rep. Jim Santini, and a couple of state Senate losses during his last election cycle in 1992. But Joyce could always adjust and never failed to have a drop of anointing fluid left to apply retroactively.

Only a few days after the 1992 balloting, when a newcomer named Lori Lipman Brown stunned Joyce's candidate, Assemblyman John Norton, Joyce was on a panel at UNLV to analyze the results. He waited for his moment and when it came, a question about the unpredictability of elections, he was ready. If anyone wondered whether the voters could upset conventional wisdom, Joyce said, they should take a look up in the audience at a woman sitting in the back who had run a wonderful campaign to upset an incumbent assemblyman. And surely she would make a wonderful state senator, too. Joyce never mentioned the vanquished assemblyman's name, nor his own affiliation with the failed campaign. But sitting far in the back of the auditorium, Lori Lipman Brown beamed. He had her.

Joyce died during the 1993 session, succumbing to emphysema. The void was gaping and immediate. But while he had set the standard, he also left behind a road map with the path to power that others would follow. And those gentlemen were starting their engines as Kenny Guinn's incipient anointment came to light.

After Guinn's candidacy became public in early 1996, Rogich's plan was two-pronged: get the men and get the money. And they were inextricably linked. Rogich didn't need a new playbill to see which actors to put on the marquee to ensure that the ending of this production, as with the conclusion to most sequels, was foreordained. During the rest of 1996, with varying degrees of success, Rogich and Guinn persuaded many of the powers who anoint, the men who filled the vacuum left by Joyce, to join up. Even those who initially were coy eventually signed on. This was about solving a math problem that involved addition and subtraction. Rogich didn't just want to ensure certain people augmented Guinn's inner circle; he also wanted to put out the word that critical Democratic players would not be available to anyone who considered running against Guinn. Rogich's task might have seemed daunting, but in many ways, it wasn't at all. After all, he was only looking for a few good men. In Nevada, that's all it takes.

During the 1988 U.S. Senate race, then-Lt. Gov. Bob Miller, who wasn't even running, became the focal point of the contest. Miller was in line to succeed then-Gov. Richard Bryan, who was challenging incumbent Chic Hecht for the Senate seat. Hecht began to question whether Miller was fit for the governorship, playing off a serendipitous *San Jose Mercury News* story that highlighted the organized-crime associations of Miller's father and the boasting of one mobster that he could influence the younger Miller when he was Clark

County district attorney. Hecht asserted that an "organized-crime cloud" hung over Miller's head, insinuating that if Bryan won, the mob would return.

Soon thereafter, though, a spectacular news conference was held. Among those present were Clark County Sheriff John Moran and District Attorney Rex Bell, as well as several former U.S. attorneys. The reason: These law-enforcement luminaries were there to attest to Miller's integrity. The most memorable moment came when Moran told reporters that Miller was no closer to organized crime "than the Pope." It helped defuse the issue. Bryan went on to victory. And Miller eventually became the state's longest-serving governor. The mob issue never surfaced again.

Only one man in Nevada at that time could have put together all those people and choreographed that news conference so beautifully. His name is Billy Vassiliadis and he is the only Nevada pol who ever approached—and perhaps exceeded—Jim Joyce's breadth of connections, ability to raise money, and prowess at lobbying and dealmaking.

Vassiliadis is the man schooled by Rogich at R&R Advertising, and who eventually took over the business. Vassiliadis is also the personality antithesis of Rogich. Where Rogich is glib and slick and effortless, Vassiliadis is straightforward, often blunt, and utterly unaffected. If Rogich is always calm and in control, Vassiliadis can be emotional, occasionally volcanic. If Rogich has taken self-promotion to new heights, Vassiliadis is almost egoless, balking at public praise and pooh-poohing tales of his power in a Joyce-like fashion.

He also shares common traits with Rogich, though they often manifest differently. He has a tremendously fertile and creative mind—he helped craft some of Las Vegas' most successful marketing campaigns, as well as some of Nevada's most effective recent political strategies. And like Rogich, he came from a working-class background, but had the drive and intellect to rise above his roots and prosper. A native Chicagoan and an All-State basketball player in high school,

Vassiliadis idolized Mayor Richard Daley and President John F. Kennedy. His athletic days behind him, Vassiliadis, now 44, has put on weight and his black hair is now almost all gray. He came to Las Vegas in 1975 and attended UNLV. He was active in the Young Democrats and after graduation hooked up with Rogich at R&R.

By the early 1980s, Vassiliadis was beginning to establish his own identity. First, unlike his mentor, he was a Democrat, so he naturally gravitated to different politicians and candidates. Second, he became an indispensable adviser to the most powerful man in Clark County—Sheriff John Moran—whom he helped elect in 1982 and re-elect in 1986. When Rogich left in 1984 to go to Washington, Vassiliadis took over the company and began to thrive. With Rogich essentially absent from the state for the next eight years, Vassiliadis filled his shoes—then grew out of them.

Rogich returned briefly in 1986 to run Jim Santini's Senate campaign and enlisted Vassiliadis to the cause. Santini was trying to fill the opening left by the retirement of Paul Laxalt, who had asked Rogich to get involved. Laxalt had brutally snubbed his loyal lieutenant, Barbara Vucanovich, a congresswoman who coveted the Senate seat, but whom Laxalt felt couldn't win. Instead, Laxalt persuaded Santini, a Democrat, to switch parties on the last day he was eligible to do so and run for the seat against the state's other congressman, Democrat Harry Reid. A loyal Laxaltite, Ace Robison, was Santini's nominal campaign manager, but this was a Rogich-Vassiliadis operation. And it was one of the few during those years that came up short. Santini was never comfortable in his GOP garb. Not even Laxalt fronting for him for the last month and three last-week appearances by President Reagan could save him. Harry Reid won by five percentage points.

But the Santini campaign wasn't the only one Vassiliadis was involved in that year. Also in 1986, Governor Richard Bryan ran for a second term, but he had his eyes less on his own noncompetitive race than on the one below him, for lieutenant governor. Bryan was most concerned about getting a Democrat elected to the state's number-two post because he was already considering a run for the U.S. Senate in 1988; he knew that without a Democrat to ascend to the governorship, he could not attempt to become a member of the Club of 100. So Bryan helped recruit Miller, the popular Clark County district attorney, to run for the normally dead-end job, but one that was now being seen as an audition to be Bryan's successor. Miller's decision to run thrust Vassiliadis into a statewide campaign, managed by another longtime Las Vegas consultant, Kent Oram, for what would be one of the year's most closely watched contests. Miller won in a landslide.

Bryan, as expected, ran for the U.S. Senate in 1988 against the vulnerable Republican incumbent Chic Hecht. Hecht, whom *The Wall Street Journal* once dubbed a "human gaffe machine," was that rarity among Senate incumbents—a heavy underdog, with early polling showing him 40 points behind. Hecht took the offensive most of the campaign. That's how the Miller-and-the-Mob angle started, first through whispers, then overtly through the *Mercury News* piece and Hecht's comments.

The subsequent news conference with law-enforcement row and its aftermath was classic Vassiliadis—an unbeatable mix of access and creativity. He also followed the timeless sports/political maxim that a best defense is a good offense, by helping to disseminate to the media materials indicating Hecht's campaign manager, Ken Rietz, had been tangled up in the Watergate scandal as a Republican Party operative. Vassiliadis' facility with the media was, and is, one of his abiding talents. Like Rogich, he cultivated key players at all levels—reporting, commentary, and management of newspapers and TV stations. One of his close friends in the 1980s was the most influential newspaper columnist in the state, Ned Day, who was also a frequent contributor to the CBS affiliate.

The story of Rietz's past eclipsed any second-day stories

about Miller and the mob (which was Vassiliadis' goal, of course) in every media outlet except one—the most important, the *Las Vegas Review-Journal*. Going with contemporaneous, rather than 15-year-old, information about a campaign consultant, I wrote a piece about Hecht's pushing the mob issue, with a fresh quote from the candidate. I relegated to the second paragraph the information about Rietz's ties to Nixon's Waterloo.

Early the next morning, my phone rang in the *Review-Journal* newsroom. It was Vassiliadis, calling from his car phone. His voice had already reached a high level: "You wrote another Miller story!" he screamed, then went on for five minutes berating my news judgment. Finally, I interjected, "You're entitled to your opinion."

"And I expressed it!" he yelled, then hung up. Later, however, he called to apologize—"Do you still love me?" That was Vassiliadis in a nutshell—a canny and innovative strategist whose passion always bubbled right below the surface, and occasionally erupted.

Bryan survived a Hecht rally that year, but only after Vassiliadis joined his campaign team and did what he does best—both troubleshooting and (almost always) fixing whatever the trouble is. Bryan believes he would not be a U.S. senator today (he was re-elected in 1994) if Vassiliadis had not boarded his sinking ship and given it buoyancy.

After the 1988 cycle, Vassiliadis' star was ascendant. He had plenty of campaign experience. He was the closest confidant to the acting governor (Miller). And he was about to embark on his first statewide contest as campaign manager when Miller ran in 1990. He didn't, however, relish having a competitive race, so he set about winning a full term for Miller long before the campaign began. Along with a few others, Vassiliadis ensured that the only man who could have beaten Miller, Attorney General Brian McKay, did not enter the fray. McKay's fire may not have burned as brightly as Vassiliadis and the others feared, but they wanted to make sure it was extinguished before any Republicans stoked it.

They did that, efficiently and ruthlessly, and Miller defeated that GOP sacrificial lamb, Jim Gallaway, in a landslide.

So Vassiliadis was the closest man to the most powerful elected official in the state. As Rogich toiled in Washington, Vassiliadis reached the upper echelon of influence back home. And in the early 1990s, it began to pay off as candidates solicited his services and clients, looking for PR help or lobbying clout, knocked on his door.

During this time, slowly but surely, Vassiliadis followed the model set by one of his mentors, Jim Joyce. He cultivated relationships with critical players in the House Joyce Once Ruled in Carson City. No one since Joyce, with the possible exception of his partner, Richard Bunker, has been able to attract the level of trust, confidence, and even friendship from the Legislature's major domos that Vassiliadis has. By virtue of his blunt style and his thoughtful, often penetrating, analyses of situations, he induced people to confide in him and trust him. By 1993, he'd become a consummate inside player in the state capital. He not only was in Miller's kitchen Cabinet, but he had entree to the offices of the two most powerful players among the Gang of 63—Republican Senate Majority Leader Bill Raggio and Democratic Speaker Joe Dini. Both men relied on Vassiliadis and listened to his counsel. In turn, he helped them on their pet issues, especially pork projects for Dini's native Yerington or Raggio's hometown of Reno. They knew he could get it done for them, and he knew they could get it done for him. If either man were asked today to name the lobbyists they most trust, both would put Vassiliadis high on the list. And both would call him a trusted friend.

But Vassiliadis went below the top tier in making friends and influencing people. He was an adviser to Democratic Senate Minority Leader Dina Titus, who once taught him at UNLV and is one of the strongest-willed and most outspoken members of the Legislature. Vassiliadis also became friendly with two of the Legislature's up-and-coming political prospects—Democrat Richard Perkins and Republican Pete Ernaut. Those two would share floor-leader duties in the 1995 Legislature during an unprecedented session when the lower house was populated by 21 Republicans and 21 Democrats. Vassiliadis now is godfather to one of Ernaut's boys and his phone number is at the top of Perkins' Rolodex.

These relationships paid off for Vassiliadis' clients—whether gaming or utilities or health care, all of which he represented—and himself. His role soon metamorphosed into one well beyond a lobbyist. He became the indispensable closer of the legislative sessions, the diplomat shuttling back and forth between the houses, between the partisan leaders of the Assembly and Senate and across the courtyard to the governor's office. Vassiliadis loved the excitement, the thrill of helping to make the deal, whether it was on the redrawing of legislative boundaries during contentious reapportionment negotiations in 1991 or during the reforming of the State Industrial Insurance System in 1993. He was the one man in the building who could go to all the major backroom players and have credibility. Only Joyce in his prime could have approached his reach.

By the end of the 1993 session, Vassiliadis was recognized as the state's foremost campaign manager and one of Nevada's pre-eminent lobbyists. He was the central insider in this still-small universe, and nearly every major politician and major business and gaming executive was in his orbit.

Vassiliadis' relationship with Miller—as his foremost adviser and campaign aide—was one reason the governor was considered such a heavy favorite for re-election in 1994. But Vassiliadis also knew that, because of the 1993 legislative session, Miller now had problems with the Democratic Party's core constituency—labor. The workers-compensation reform package he had helped craft was seen by the unions as being overly skewed toward the benefit of management (i.e., the casinos). Benefits had been cut while companies, especially gaming companies, stood to save millions of dollars. Combining labor's anger with rumblings that popular Las Vegas Mayor Jan Jones might challenge Miller in a Democratic primary led observers to speculate the governor might be in political trouble.

But Jones, who indeed was getting ready to run, underestimated two things. First, the ability of Vassiliadis and the rest of Miller's kitchen Cabinet, including gaming executive Mike Sloan, gaming attorney Frank Schreck, fundraiser Elias Ghanem, and political consultant Kent Oram, to create a financial tourniquet on the Strip when Jones came calling. Oh, she might get a pittance here and there, but Miller would have geometrically more money shoveled his way from the Strip vaults. Second, she didn't understand that the Millerites control of the inside game was so absolute that, led by Vassiliadis, they would be able to turn what seemed like a sure thing—the AFL-CIO endorsement for Jones—into a lock for Miller, even though he'd supported what the unions saw as the most anti-labor bill in Nevada history. The endorsement was not about policy decisions, though; it was about relationships. And Vassiliadis, with help from Miller's titular campaign manager Gary Gray, a long-time Democratic Party insider, had them with labor leaders; Jones had almost none.

With all of the political capital Vassiliadis had amassed by early 1996—and the fact that he was in a class by himself as a statewide campaign manager—Rogich knew he had to recruit his old protégé to the Guinn campaign. Or at least prevent him from working for any prospective opponents. Rogich figured that might be slightly problematic— after all, Vassiliadis was a Democrat and had a close relationship with Jones, despite the 1994 gubernatorial race. But Rogich also calculated that if he raised enough money and created an aura of inevitability, no Democrat would have much chance. And Vassiliadis would want to remain as close to the next governor as he'd been for 10 years to Miller. Not only that, but Rogich and Vassiliadis had known each other for two decades, and Rogich knew it would be uncomfortable for Vassiliadis to oppose him in a campaign.

Finally, Miller wasn't anointing anyone as his successor—he was politically loyal to Del Papa, but not especially close to her personally, and he certainly had no great love for ex-foe Jones. So Rogich figured Vassiliadis was a likely team member.

Vassiliadis' relationship with Guinn would also be part of Rogich's calculus in deciding what to do in the campaign. Guinn and Vassiliadis had known each other for years and were quite friendly. Vassiliadis had worked for Guinn when the latter was at the bank and it had been a fruitful relationship. Guinn's involvement in school and police bond campaigns, which Vassiliadis helped shepherd, and his willingness to be used by various candidates running for office also brought him into contact with Vassiliadis. Nonetheless, Vassiliadis was not eager to march in the Guinn parade so early, when Rogich first approached him in early 1996. Guinn also talked to him a couple of times and Vassiliadis told him it was too early—both for Guinn to be a formal candidate and for Vassiliadis to commit.

His reasons were sound, too. Vassiliadis would be donning his legislative hat during 1997—a full year before the actual campaign cycle—and he had to be concerned about how becoming a Guinnite would be viewed in Carson City. State Sen. Mark James, who at that time was still mulling a run for governor, chaired the critical Judiciary Committee. Vassiliadis didn't want to lobby James on behalf of his clients while wearing a scarlet "G" for Guinn on his chest. Vassiliadis also didn't want to commit so early against Del Papa and especially Jones, whom he knew might want to run. Rogich badly wanted Vassiliadis publicly on board because he knew it could help dissuade any serious challengers. But Vassiliadis wouldn't sign up. Yet.

In late 1989, Gov. Miller was looking for a replacement for Dennis Amerine, who had just left the Gaming Control

Board for a private-sector job. The Control Board is the most important regulatory body in the state. It's three members act as gatekeepers for the state's lifeblood industry. It grants and revokes licenses, must approve key employees, and is responsible for maintaining the integrity of the industry. Over the years, the Board has been considered much tougher than the part-time Nevada Gaming Commission, which has the power to overrule Control Board decisions, but rarely does so. Naturally, the Control Board and the Gaming Commission have been seen as susceptible to political influences.

Those most concerned with Dennis Amerine's replacement were, of course, those who would be regulated by him—the casinos. As Miller looked for a new member, two former members of the Control Board had a name they wanted considered. Guy Hillyer, who was working at accounting behemoth Arthur Anderson, and Mike Rumbolz, who had been plucked by Donald Trump to explore Nevada investments, suggested that Tom Roche, an accountant they both knew and respected, would be a fine choice. They passed the word to Frank Schreck, the prominent gaming attorney, and Mike Sloan, the Circus Circus Enterprises executive, whom they knew were members of Miller's inner circle. Sloan and Schreck set up a breakfast meeting with Roche and quizzed him about his interest in the job. Afterwards, as if acting as an ad hoc screening committee, Schreck, whose clients would appear before Roche should he get appointed, called gubernatorial chief of staff Scott Craigie to inform him that he and Sloan approved of Roche.

Craigie was furious, knowing that if word got out about the meeting, it would look as if the casino industry was selecting its own regulator. Sloan and Schreck insisted that Craigie was overreacting. Schreck comically described the meeting in an interview: "It was so innocent, it's unbelievable." A few weeks later, even after the meeting became public, Miller appointed Roche.

If Jim Joyce was the public embodiment of the anointment process in Nevada, Mike Sloan is the private facilitator who helps make much of it happen. Slim, always dressed impeccably in tailor-made suits, his hair thinning, the 55-year-old Sloan is one of the smartest and most cunning men in Nevada. He speaks in a rat-a-tat-tat staccato, his verbal effusions often illustrating his searing wit, expansive vocabulary, and broad knowledge. He's as smooth as he is ruthless, concocting more schemes and stratagems in the shower every morning than most people do in a year. At least one Nevada insider routinely refers to him as "Machiavelli." He has a history of playing the cutthroat game of politics, deftly wielding a sharp blade that more often than not cuts all the way through—whether he's clearing the way for a favored appointee or candidate, or slashing forward for the often-backward casino industry.

But Sloan's reach goes beyond simply being a political operative in Nevada. He's the least parochial of any major player in the state. He was operating on the national stage long before gambling was on Capitol Hill's radar screen. Indeed, Sloan is one of the few members of the industry who can rightly be dubbed a visionary—a man who sees problems in their incipient stages and prophesies troubles long before they actually manifest. Sloan long ago identified what may be the two greatest threats to the Nevada economy's continued prosperity—a traffic tourniquet stanching travel from Southern California on Interstate 15 and the metastatic spread of Indian casinos, now poised to expand in California.

Sloan was one of the first gaming executives to understand the utility of not just locking up the political system in Nevada, but of harnessing the casinos' vast wealth to buy access to national elected officials. By inviting congressional speakers and majority leaders and powerful committee chairmen to Las Vegas, Sloan knew he could educate them about the industry they would inevitably be asked to regulate or tax. The most important lesson, though, as Sloan knew too well, would be how many zeros would appear on the end of the total campaign cash the Washington pols extracted from their visits. And as various entombed regulatory and taxing proposals and a watered-down federal gaming report attest, the strategy has paid off like a loose slot machine.

Sloan is steeped in the Nevada political establishment. He moved to Las Vegas as a teen and his Las Vegas High School class of '62 included several people who would evolve into political animals—Clark County Commissioner Bruce Woodbury, political consultant Sig Rogich, and Clark County Manager Dale Askew. Sloan actually started as a journalist, working part-time for the *Review-Journal* during his senior year at the University of Nevada-Reno. After school, he worked for a variety of Nevada Democratic pols, including a stint as Ralph Denton's press secretary during his unsuccessful bid against Congressman Walter Baring in a 1966 primary. Sloan was later hired by U.S. Sen. Alan Bible to run his Las Vegas office; he moved to the nation's capital and attended George Washington Law School while working in the Senate Post Office.

Sloan returned home after becoming a lawyer and worked briefly in the district attorney's office and in private practice before his high-school friend, Rogich, helped land him a job with Attorney General Bob List. Even though Sloan had worked against List on behalf of Richard Bryan in the 1974 attorney general's race (Bryan lost by only 701 votes), Rogich helped persuade the victor to hire his pal. After a couple of years there, Sloan took up electoral politics and got himself elected as city attorney for Las Vegas. He later won a couple of appointments to the state Senate, filling vacant seats for Bryan (1979) and Floyd Lamb (1981).

As the decade turned, Sloan went back into private practice, working for a series of prominent firms, including ex-Gaming Commissioner Frank Schreck's in 1983. Sloan handled a number of gaming clients, coming into contact with a few notorious types, as he did work for the likes of Moe Dalitz and Ed Torres. In 1985, the chairman of Circus

Circus Enterprises, William Bennett, offered Sloan a boat-load of money to come to work for him. If he was looking for a lawyer who understood politics, Bennett had his man in Sloan.

Now Sloan truly began to make his mark. Given access to Bennett's bank account, Sloan started spending money on local and national politicians as no Nevadan ever had. But he quickly realized money can't buy everything he wanted from politicians. So he used the national contacts he was building through fundraisers for congressional leaders to begin hiring renowned pollsters. From Peter Hart and Doug Schoen, two of the country's foremost Democratic pollsters, to Lance Tarrance, a renowned Republican public opinion expert, Sloan retained the best. These experts helped him gauge where races stood so he could make informed decisions on where to spend company money. He'd often share the results with favored politicians and candidates to curry favor. Sloan also used the pollsters to measure the company's, and the industry's, standing with the public.

Sloan is a Democrat, and his contacts, both locally and nationally, have always been with his own party. In that, his timing has matched his insight. From 1982 until 1998, only two men inhabited the governor's mansion—Richard Bryan and Bob Miller. Both were Democrats. Both relied on Sloan. The Clark County Commission, responsible for zoning and licensing issues critical to the industry, was dominated by Democrats. In fact, the only Republican commissioner for many years was Woodbury, Sloan's high-school classmate.

His Democratic ties and his acute sense of political re-alities also enabled him to begin forming organized-labor connections in Las Vegas and in Washington, especially af-ter a devastating strike in 1984 during which pictures of Strip picketers were beamed across the world. Sloan real-ized the importance of a symbiotic arrangement with the Culinary Union, which represents most of Las Vegas' hotel workers. Sloan knew that if the industry maintained cordial relations with union leaders at home, those bosses would return the favor in Washington by helping to kill onerous proposals. Sloan began cultivating relationships with key union personnel, including up-and-coming Culinary boss John Wilhelm, who today is the secretary-treasurer of the international union.

The Culinary's parent organization, the Hotel Employees and Restaurant Employees International Union, had immense clout on Capitol Hill. Thanks to the union's access to House Ways and Means czar Dan Rostenkowski, burdensome IRS and Treasury regulations aimed at the casinos during the 1980s were squelched. By the early '90s, the interrelationships were growing as Sloan, casino lobbyist Richard Bunker, and ex-Attorney General Brian McKay were all serving as trustees of the union's health-and-welfare fund.

In many ways, Sloan has been much more influential in developing the industry's political power than the man known far and wide as the casinos' most active player—ex-Mirage Resorts Chairman Steve Wynn. Yes, Wynn is a much more public and dynamic figure and his former corporation was the first to set up a sophisticated political operation in the early '90s. But Sloan, more than Wynn, has been better able to build consensus in the industry for critical initiatives, from derailing tax threats in Carson City or on Capitol Hill to extra-Nevada competitive threats. The two share a paradoxical respect and disdain. When the gaming industry decided to form a national lobbying arm, some thought Sloan would be the perfect person to lead the group. But Wynn scotched that idea before it got aloft.

Sloan has other enemies, too, to be sure. His affinity for black-bag tactics and his flashes of abrasive arrogance have alienated some of his compatriots. And he's had his occasional failures, especially when he's been too clever or too vindictive toward pols he sees as having challenged the industry. For instance, Sloan was exposed by the California media in the mid-1990s for helping to set up a front group in that state designed to oppose Indian gaming. And in 1988 when he and Joyce and other gaming operatives tried to erase an anti-casino legislator named Bob Price, the assemblyman ran against the industry and was re-elected overwhelmingly.

But those are isolated cases. And most people—including me—often have no clue as to when Sloan's fingerprints are on some public policy initiative or backroom shenanigans or when he had no role.

Sloan's longtime relationships with Nevada politicians—from senators to county commissioners—and his access to money and polling make him an essential component of any major campaign. He approaches Vassiliadis in the breadth of his relationships and the depth of his strategic mind, and when the two have worked together—the Miller campaign and a panoply of gaming lobbying issues—they've been virtually unstoppable.

Sloan had almost unfettered access to Miller during the governor's 10-year tenure and, as Miller's term waned, he recognized that he, and the industry, needed the same kind of reliable steward at the helm. He had known Guinn for years and his friendship with Rogich went back to high school. Rogich knew what a devastating sign it would send to any Democratic aspirants if the word went out that Sloan was on board. Rogich didn't expect Sloan to do much more than help with the fundraising and stay out of the race on the Democratic side. Sloan, having been part of an anointment or two, recognized and admired the single-mindedness of what Rogich was doing, So when he saw the Guinn parade forming, it was only a short step for Mike Sloan to get to the front.

Even before she formally announced her candidacy for governor in 1994, Las Vegas Mayor Jan Jones had signaled that she planned to puncture the state's political Establishment. In an outdoor news conference near the downtown Las Vegas courthouse in November 1993, Jones unleashed some harsh and unprecedented rhetoric. It was not directed at her opponent, incumbent and fellow Democrat Bob Miller, but at a man named Frank Schreck, generally unknown to the electorate, but one of the state's most influential pols. Schreck, an attorney specializing in gaming law, doubled as the chief campaign fundraiser for many important elected officials, including Gov. Miller. Jones insisted that this cozy arrangement, where Schreck raised money for the governor, then represented clients before the Miller-appointed Gaming Control Board, was wrong. He was, in Jones' words, a "juice attorney," cashing in his campaign chips to help his clients. Later in her quest for governor, Jones repeated and honed the allegation. It was, she implied, a form of legalized extortion on the front end—give to the governor because I can help you later, and an insider trading scheme on the back end—I'm the governor's guy so I get all the important clients.

Schreck, an intense advocate, responded forcefully and thoroughly to Jones' charges. After she repeated her broadsides on public television, Schreck sent a lengthy manifesto to the show's moderator, defending himself and assailing Jones. He didn't show anger; he was simply relentless and comprehensive in his approach, just as he'd always been in all things. The issue never came up again, so Schreck's defense memo never aired; but he had made his point.

Schreck built one of the state's most impressive gaming-law practices, with the crown jewel being Steve Wynn's business, by combining his involvement in the political process with a reputation for ferocious advocacy. He raised millions of dollars for the men and women who would make multi-million-dollar decisions for his clients: county commissioners and governors who would select state gaming regulators.

Beginning in the mid-1990s, it became a tradition for incumbent county commissioners to have a fall campaign event at Schreck's house, designed to raise several hundred thousand dollars, and thus, scare off any challengers in the upcoming campaign cycle. For instance, in fall 1995, Schreck hosted an event for Commissioner Yvonne Atkinson Gates, which was sponsored by seven major casino companies. Gates won easily the following November. Two years later, Schreck saved time by combining an event for commissioners Myrna Williams and Lorraine Hunt, building six-figure war chests for both at a single fundraiser at his home in the posh southwest Las Vegas community called Spanish Trail. Schreck later appeared before the commissioners on behalf of a range of clients from prominent gaming companies seeking zoning or licensing approvals. Similarly, he frequently brought casino clients before the state regulatory boards appointed by his friend, Gov. Miller. For many years, he and his clients appeared before a Control Board headed by a man named Bill Bible, a friend of many years. Tom Roche, whom he recommended Miller appoint to the Board, also voted on issues Schreck brought before the Board. He has access to the power structure no other gaming attorney in the state can claim, thanks to his fundraising and relationships.

Like his good friend, Mike Sloan, Schreck grew up in Southern Nevada. He attended Henderson's Basic High School, where he met a man who would become his mentor, a teacher named Mike O'Callaghan, the future governor. Schreck's mother worked for the school district, where she met a man named Kenny Guinn, the schools superintendent. Schreck attended Yale, majoring in history and political science, a prelude to law school at Berkeley, from which he graduated in 1968.

Schreck established himself early on as a rabble-rousing leftist—he calls himself the "William Kunstler of Nevada" in those days—before delving into politics. Schreck helped O'Callaghan in his successful gubernatorial campaign in 1970 and a year later was rewarded with an appointment to the Nevada Gaming Commission. He spent four years as a regulator before leaving to practice law full-time. During the mid-1970s, Schreck was active in school district business, assisting in the assembly of the desegregation plan and working for the Teachers Union. Schreck jousted with Guinn during those days, establishing a relationship of mutual respect. "When he told you something, you could count on it," Guinn remembered.

As he built his law firm, accumulating gaming clients and hiring his friend, Mike Sloan, Schreck kept his hand in politics. He raised money for a variety of candidates—some of the cash came from his clients—as disparate as Sloan when he ran for city attorney and Bob Miller when he sought the governorship.

Schreck also helped form the International Association of Gaming Attorneys, which became populated with some of the state's most successful lawyers, and served as a useful political tool. For many years, the organization was overseen by Schreck's assistant, Judy Klein, a Democratic Party activist with many of her own relationships with elected officials. Schreck and Klein often invited elected officials, especially county commissioners, to the annual IAGA meeting, which usually took place in exotic locales, such as Monte Carlo and Prague. The organization picked up all the expenses. Schreck used the organization as a way to enhance his access to the elected elite, until scandal befell IAGA in 1999, with Klein eventually pleading guilty to charges resulting from tens of thousands of dollars in missing funds—money some IAGA members believed had been used to wine and dine the politicians.

Schreck is not shy about his access—for years some of his fellow lawyers have privately wondered whether he doesn't flaunt it and abuse it. Schreck sloughs off such charges and they certainly haven't cost him any business. Quite the contrary. He's had only one long-term frustration: Rival firm Lionel, Sawyer & Collins has had the lion's share of the legal business from the industry's lobbying arm, the Nevada Resort Association. Schreck has calculated that if he can get at least some of the major companies into his fold, he would be the NRA's practitioner. But the organization's respect for longtime Lionel, Sawyer partner Grant Sawyer, a former governor, and Bob Faiss, once named as the country's pre-eminent gaming attorney, has prevailed for years. Sawyer passed away in 1996, though, and Schreck gradually has made some inroads into the association's business, despite NRA President Richard Bunker's continued loyalty to Faiss. And his share of the work is expected to increase in coming years, especially with the new leadership of the NRA: His crony Sloan is now the chairman of the organization. What's more, the choice of the man to succeed Bunker sprung from Schreck's brain. He knew this person would not only be perfect for the job, but he also happened to be one of his good friends. Bunker's successor? Bill Bible.

During 1996, as he was building support, Guinn sent his friend, Terry Wright, the head of Nevada Title, to Schreck. Everyone in Guinn's corner knew that Schreck was aligned with Democrats and that bringing him into the campaign would be a coup. He was the chief fundraiser, after all, for the previous Democratic governor. As with Sloan, Rogich was practicing the politics of subtraction. Yes, Schreck could raise some money from his gaming clients. But more importantly, if prospective Democratic opponents knew that Schreck wasn't available, it would give them pause.

For his part, Schreck could read the tea leaves. Motivated by his lengthy association with Guinn and the Establishment's imperative of continuity, Frank Schreck readily signed on.

In 1995, the Nevada Legislature embarked on a plan to save money in the troubled workers-compensation system. Part of the strategy was to impose "managed care" on the State Industrial Insurance System, which had been hemorrhaging red ink for years.

Assembly Majority Leader Gene Porter, a Democrat,

didn't care too much about the issue, but he did have one concern about the outcome. He would do everything he could, resisting the plan proposed by his fellow Democrat, Gov. Bob Miller, to stop one man from getting too large a slice of the reformed-system's pie. Indeed, Porter held up the negotiations on the legislation until he received assurances from the governor and his aides that this one doctor would not be too enriched by the reorganized system. Porter's animus toward the physician had strange roots: He blamed the doctor for the death of one of his heroes, Elvis Presley. The part of the law Porter inserted designed to hurt the doctor became known as the "Elvis Provision."

That doctor was Elias Ghanem, who had parlayed a contract with the Culinary Union and relationships with community leaders into a Las Vegas medical empire. Porter was taking on no political pygmy, either. Ghanem is one of the state's largest and most consistent contributors to candidates for Nevada offices, as well as the U.S. Congress. He has hosted fundraisers and contributed to a variety of national politicians, especially Democrats. Among those who have benefited from his largess are senators Frank Lautenberg, Chuck Robb, Ted Kennedy, and Jay Rockefeller. He's also written soft-money checks, usually to a Democratic national PAC. His donations have increased each year, reaching $44,000 in soft and hard money during the 2000 cycle. He's even become a key supporter and friend of President Clinton and was invited to his inaugural ball. A few years ago, after Ghanem had been diagnosed with cancer, Clinton gave him a ride on Air Force One to get treatment at Walter Reed Medical Center.

Ghanem occasionally gives money to Republicans, but there has to be a good reason. One such occasion was the 1996 Southern Nevada race for Congress, which neatly epitomized the marriage between the good doctor and the powerful union, as well as the incestuous nature of the state's political structure. Rep. John Ensign, a Republican and scion of a prominent gaming executive, was running for re-election to the House of Representatives. The Democrats had no impressive candidate willing to step forward, even though the district was heavily Democratic and Ensign had only been elected in 1994 by 1,436 votes. So Ghanem hosted an event for Ensign and persuaded his Culinary business partners to pony up with a $5,000 check. The amount was not nearly so significant as the signal it sent from both Ghanem, a prominent Democratic fundraiser, and the Culinary, a prominent Democratic interest group.

That's not to say Ghanem doesn't occasionally take on lost Democratic causes, too. Later that cycle, partly as a favor to Sen. Harry Reid, Ghanem co-hosted an event for Spike Wilson, a former state senator engaged in a quixotic campaign against GOP Rep. Jim Gibbons in Nevada's other congressional district. Ghanem's co-hosts at the function were his two good friends, Mike Sloan and Frank Schreck.

Because of his illness, Ghanem would not be as much of a factor in the Guinn anointment as he had been for others. But he still made phone calls, and he did what he could. And, after he joined his friends Schreck and Sloan on the Guinn team late in 1996, he would not be making any fundraising entreaties for whomever the Democratic candidate turned out to be.

With Sloan, Schreck, and Ghanem in the fold, and his belief that Vassiliadis would soon be, too, Rogich already had a fundraising foundation for Guinn that would be difficult to shake. But more importantly, the Democrats were, in poker parlance, drawing dead. That is, all the cards they needed to make their hand—the four Democratic aces— were in the Republican's hand. Others, too, would become concrete players—for instance, Guinn's close friend, Mark Brown, an executive with the largest development company in the state, Howard Hughes Corp.; and Kent Oram, the veteran political consultant who had handled many local and a few statewide campaigns. But with himself (the state's pre-eminent Republican operative) and the others (the backbone of the team used by the current Democratic governor), Rogich had Kenny Guinn's anointment well underway.

And while it was quite some time before the election, it wasn't long before the money began to roll in. Or so Rogich told people.

3

PLAYING
THE MONEY GAME

In late November 1996 Clyde Turner, chairman of Circus Circus Enterprises, picked up the phone in his Las Vegas Strip office. On the other end of the line was Sig Rogich, a friend from the old days who had hired Turner, when he was a CPA, as his personal accountant. New campaign spending limits were going into effect in just a few days, he told Turner, which would prohibit corporations from giving any candidate more than $10,000, as opposed to the old ceiling of $20,000. Would Turner consider maxing out to gubernatorial candidate Kenny Guinn for each of Circus Circus' corporate entities?

Wasn't that unusual? Turner asked his friend. Not at all, Rogich replied; in fact, companies had done the same thing in the past for then-Gov. Bob Miller. Indeed, the current governor had received six-figure contributions from major gaming companies, bundling money from various affiliates. But Rogich was asking Turner for a heretofore unprecedented outpouring of cash support, double anything that had come before. I'll get back to you, Turner told Rogich.

Turner had been chairman of the giant casino corporation for about two years but had never been active in campaign contributions. He called in the company's political expert, Mike Sloan, and asked him if the donations would be illegal. Sloan feared such a large amount would bring unwanted attention to the company, but he assured Turner they were breaking no laws.

Turner called Rogich and told him that he was authorizing every corporate affiliate to give $20,000 to Guinn, who had never before run for office. Fifteen Circus Circus outlets—the company had properties in Laughlin, Reno, and Jean, as well as Las Vegas—would give the maximum donation; the total would be $300,000, the largest contribution ever reported by one company in Nevada political history. (It's hard to know what happened in the mob days when some contributions were alleged to have been delivered in cash.) Nearly two years loomed until the election, and no Democrat had even announced a candidacy yet.

For most of 1996, Rogich and Guinn didn't collect a penny for the governor's race. Guinn was busy traveling the state, trying to lock up rural support per Rogich's strategy. At the same time, Rogich was trying to create a statewide network, an unassailable wall of support from elected officials in all areas of Nevada. He had one person in his office calling every elected Republican in the state to try to get them to sign on, and he was helping to fuel media reports that Guinn had seven figures in commitments. Putting the word out was designed to induce politicians, who would want to be with a winner, to sign on. Rogich and Guinn tried to close the deal fast—after the phone call, they sent a follow-up letter asking if it was OK to use the politician's name in campaign materials.

By the time November 1996 rolled around, Guinn had met plenty of new people, from Jackpot to Pahrump. But he had hardly anything in the bank, even though Rogich's spinning through the media made it sound as if he had a bulging war chest. Though *Las Vegas Sun* columnist Jeff

German wrote in a Nov. 9 piece that Guinn "already has more than $1 million in cash and commitments," the candidate's coffers were hardly well-stocked.

Dates of contributions that were later reported on his disclosure reports showed that Guinn had collected only $92,000 before the election in 1996. So he didn't even have six figures in hand, much less seven. And a significant percentage of the actual cash would become problematic. Of those early funds, nearly a third—$30,000—came from a woman named Margaret Elardi and two companies affiliated with the Strip hotel-casino she owned, the Frontier. At that time, Elardi was the bane of organized labor in Las Vegas. Culinary Union picketers had been outside the Frontier every day since 1992. If it had been known then that Elardi had ponied up so much for Guinn, it might have given labor serious pause and even encouraged the unions to court a Democratic contender. But the first public disclosure for the race was not due until August 1998 (although Guinn would acknowledge the contributions from the Frontier in 1997). So Rogich wasn't concerned about such minutiae as 1996 waned. He was just trying to create that aura of inevitability. It's not that he wasn't sure the money was coming—he had the commitments. There was just no rush to collect it—or so he and Guinn thought at the time.

Election Day 1996 in Nevada was uneventful. For the second consecutive presidential cycle, Bill Clinton took the state, this time by 4,700 votes over Bob Dole. The state's two congressmen, Republicans John Ensign and Jim Gibbons, won easily. The news media—and the public—were much more fascinated with interminable election-day lines at the balloting locations. A tempest swept through the city when ever-impatient Las Vegas Mayor Jan Jones cut to the front at the polling venue, rather than endure the hours-long wait. Almost unnoticed was the passage of a group of do-gooder ballot questions, including a term-limits proposal sponsored by Rogich, of all people, and a lowering of the campaign-contribution ceiling to $10,000 from $20,000 for statewide races.

The campaign-contribution initiative, Question 10 on the Nov. 5 ballot, passed overwhelmingly, garnering 71 percent of the vote. It received more than 300,000 votes, one and a half times what the term-limit questions received and just under what an anti-tax proposition attracted. Question 10 mandated that statewide candidates could now receive only half as much per election cycle as they had before.

The initiative provided Secretary of State Dean Heller, who was still considering a bid against Guinn and relished his anti-Establishment credentials, with a political opportunity. Heller had to rule on when the new limits would take effect. The exact language stipulated that "the Legislature shall provide by law" for the new caps, but state lawmakers weren't due to convene until January 1997. Heller inquired of the Legislative Counsel Bureau, then crossed his fingers. Twenty days after the election, legislative attorney Brenda Erdoes ruled that because the ballot question language contradicted the law then on the books, the new law took precedence. Attorney General Frankie Sue Del Papa, who had also not ruled out a gubernatorial bid and, like Heller, was watching Guinn's fundraising prowess, agreed with the legislative counsel's opinion. So the new $10,000 cap would take effect in only a few days when the Supreme Court officially canvassed the election. Heller publicly downplayed any notion that he was taking his position to hurt Guinn. But privately, he was thrilled.

Over at Guinn Central, the edict engendered a sense of urgency. Heller's and Del Papa's motivations notwithstanding (especially since they were backed up by the legal opinion), the real concern for Rogich and Guinn was that the cap was about to take effect before they had collected any major contributions. You know, the ones they were claiming they already had. They had five days to work the phones. And they did.

Heller's ruling that contributions would be limited, as of

Nov. 30, to $10,000 per corporation came down on Nov. 25. The Guinnites had five days. The next day, according to a campaign disclosure report Guinn filed later, Circus Circus and its affiliates wrote those 15 checks totaling $300,000. Four other $20,000 checks also came in on that prosperous day for the Guinn campaign—two from Palace Station and Boulder Station, courtesy of the Fertitta family, majority shareholders in Station Casinos, a company that caters to the Las Vegas locals market. Combined with $40,000 received a month earlier from companies run by the patriarch, Frank Fertitta, Jr., Station Casinos had an $80,000 early investment in Guinn. That amounted to only a fraction of the Circus Circus wager, but that was only the beginning for Station Casinos, which would become Guinn's second-largest contributor. One other Station affiliate, Southwest Gaming, gave $10,000, bringing the company's Nov. 26 total to $50,000.

The other $40,000 was from two companies linked to Gary Primm, the man behind Primadonna Resorts, which has three casinos in Primm, Nevada, on the California-Nevada border and named for his family. (Gary Primm also partnered up with MGM Grand to erect the New York-New York megaresort on the Strip.) Primm, not coincidentally, is a friend of Rogich, who at the time sat on the Primadonna board.

So Nov. 26, 1996, turned out to be a pivotal day for the Guinn campaign, perhaps the largest successful fundraising day in state history. Guinn raked in $390,000, which provided a solid financial foundation for his gubernatorial campaign.

Two other $20,000 contributions not withdrawn from casino vaults arrived at Guinn Central in November, even before the Circus Circus and Station money. Two days after the 1996 balloting had concluded, two companies tied to a man named Billy Walters contributed the maximum amount to Guinn. Walters, a gambler and golf-course developer, was in the process of becoming one of the largest campaign contributors in Nevada. Walters frequently came before local governments for zoning approvals, and he was looking for as much goodwill as he could buy from the political system. At the time, he was also under threat of indictment for his sports-betting activities, which authorities continually alleged violated an obscure part of the criminal code. Indeed, Walters later became the source of a brouhaha in the campaign, when *The New York Times* ran a piece about him. Though a Guinn aide defended Walters in the *Times* story, the campaign nevertheless returned what by then had amounted to a $50,000 contribution from the gambler's companies. Much later, however, Walters, who would be indicted three times for the same allegations, quietly reinvested the returned contributions in Guinn.

Despite the winter of his contented fundraising exploits, by the end of 1996, Guinn had not reached the seven-figure mark that Rogich repeatedly claimed they'd eclipsed. Records show that in contributions of more than $500, the campaign had amassed $597,000, with more than 70 percent of it raised on that one day, Nov. 26. Others who clambered on board early were members of a prominent GOP-aligned law firm, Jones, Jones, Close & Brown, which would soon become Jones Vargas, one of the more politically influential law firms in Nevada. Lawyers from the firm, including politically active members Joe Brown and Greg Jensen, gave a total of $7,000 and the firm donated $3,000. Other Guinn supporters that winter included Jim Chaisson, a longtime car dealer who gave $5,000; Steve Comer, a partner in Arthur Anderson who did work for the casino industry; and several well-known physicians, including M. Nafees Nagy, whose Nevada Cancer Center gave $5,000.

Finally, the first $20,000 contribution to the campaign actually came in August, when Independence Mining, representing Nevada's second-largest industry, began what would become a gold rush for Guinn. And, according to Guinn's disclosure form, the first contribution to the campaign that would eventually raise the most money for a state race in Nevada history was for $1,000. It arrived on June 18 and was from Prime Cable, which dominates the Las Vegas market and was owned by the Greenspun family, the publishers of the *Las Vegas Sun* newspaper.

So of the all the money the Guinn campaign reported raising during that first year, the gaming industry accounted for more than 70 percent of the total. Four companies—Circus Circus, Station Casinos, the Frontier, and Primadonna—combined for $420,000 out of the $597,000 Guinn raised in 1996. Add in $5,000 from Reno casino pioneer Warren Nelson, and the total came to $425,000. That amount was nowhere near what Rogich was telling people, but it was still impressive, considering Guinn had never before run for office and there were more than 700 days until the election. Nearly $600,000 wasn't bad seed money, and more fertile ground awaited to be plowed along Las Vegas Boulevard.

Noticeably absent from this list was the state's most visible gaming executive, Steve Wynn. As Wynn goes, so goes the casino industry, or so the conventional wisdom went. But not only is that not often true—Wynn is much more of a maverick and polarizing force in the industry than people realize—but he was not getting on board the S.S. Guinn with two years to go for several reasons.

First, as mentioned, Wynn, and even more so his wife Elaine, were not thrilled with Guinn's performance as interim president of UNLV. But Wynn's initial reluctance to write a check went beyond the rubble of the local basketball program. Unlike previous contenders, especially Bob Miller, Wynn thought, Guinn had no track record in public office that merited such a large and exclusive commitment. Besides, the Wynns were fond of both Attorney General Frankie Sue Del Papa and Las Vegas Mayor Jan Jones. They had plenty of time to decide where to put their stamp of approval—and their money. The proverbial eternity loomed before the election when Guinn would be on the ballot.

❖ ❖ ❖

The practice of committing to candidates long before an election—and trying to scare out prospective challengers—was not new in Nevada. The casinos don't like to gamble on the games they offer to their customers; they always want the odds in their favor. Even more so, they try to take the element of chance out of the electoral process. It's a technique that has paid dividends—literally and figuratively. The industry has played favorites up and down the ticket—from critical statewide contests to legislative races to municipal tussles. And when there is no clear choice—which happens occasionally—the casinos are only too happy to hedge their bets.

Ten years ago, a study conducted after one primary election revealed that the gaming industry had contributed $1.65 million to candidates—far outdistancing any other industry and about half the money disclosed on all the campaign reports.

The debate back then was the same as it is today: How much of this is expected because gaming is Nevada's largest industry and drives the economy? And how much is a blatant purchase of political influence, subverting the democratic process? The conflict between the need to protect gaming—which makes sense for elected officials from a policy and political standpoint—and the pandering to an industry that has near-omnipotent control of the system is always difficult to gauge.

The industry needs protection. Since 1990, the casinos have been threatened by multifarious external threats—from a proliferation of gaming in other jurisdictions and on tribal lands to a federal government eyeing the casinos' profits more closely. Some of the threats were of the industry's own making. Ten years ago, for example, the industry started pushing to make it easier for the corporations to explore opportunities elsewhere. It's unclear if the state could have stopped the casinos from exploring the global gambling frontier, from Biloxi to Sydney. But the state didn't even try. So companies began investing around the country and in other countries, making money for their shareholders in most cases, but also tickling the antenna of the federal government money machine and catalyzing the anti-gambling forces, which ultimately resulted in the creation of the federal gambling study in 1997, a product of the industry's wanderlust and success.

So the desire for safety and security was never more acute than it was as Miller's tenure wound down. But it wasn't only the national scene that concerned them. State Sen. Joe Neal was talking about proposing a casino tax increase in the Legislature and taking it to the ballot if it failed. So the industry could not afford to take chances with the election for governor.

The problem was that while Guinn was busy consolidating his support on his way to the mansion, the industry itself was less cohesive than ever. Even as Strip resorts were devouring each other—with takeovers and mergers almost a monthly event—the Balkanization of the gamers was continuing. Competition across the country, combined with one-upmanship at home had caused distrust, even hostility among the properties. The Guinn anointment would be even more difficult to accomplish, theoretically, if another prominent candidate surfaced. Thus, Rogich & Co. had to move swiftly to ensure that didn't happen.

The early money coming to Guinn would surely give Frankie Sue Del Papa second thoughts. But Rogich also knew that even if Guinn could count on the gamers all but shutting out any Democrat, it would be trickier to dissuade a candidate with personal wealth. Only two prospective contenders qualified: Jan Jones and Dean Heller.

Jones had some history, though, that Rogich and others thought might make her reluctant to spend money she had banked from her time married to Ted Jones, part-owner of a huge car dealership. Jones had helped build the franchise as an executive and still retained part of the company despite getting divorced from her husband.

She had money in 1994, too, when she was the first mainstream candidate who whispered that she would make the anointment process an issue in her insurgent challenge to Miller. Her campaign had actually imagined a TV spot in which Miller was riding in a jalopy with several of his confidants—Billy Vassiliadis, Frank Schreck, and others—and using the theme of "The Beverly Hillbillies" to satirize how inbred the political system is. But Jones never went through with it. And even though she put $250,000 of her own money into the race, she couldn't keep pace with Miller, who raised $3 million, nor with his crew's ability to lock up key special-interest groups, from gaming to labor.

As for Heller, at the end of 1996 he was threatening to be the Jan Jones of the next gubernatorial cycle—the rebel from within who would take on the Establishment candidate from his own party and run an outsider campaign. He also had something that Jones had and made her a threat to Miller—family money. Heller, having developed a reputation for campaign-finance reform and prodded by his adviser Don Carlson, relished opportunities to tweak the Guinn folks on how they were playing the money game. Carlson figured that putting Heller as the paladin of campaign-finance reform against Guinn, who was exploiting the current Swiss-cheese system, had all kinds of possibilities.

So when Heller issued his decree, soon after the election, that candidates had to abide by a new money cap, it's understandable why the Guinn campaign thought he was targeting them. But Heller went even further. In late December 1996, the secretary of state saw an opportunity when a city council in Southern Nevada decided to adopt stronger campaign-finance-reporting procedures. Heller hopped a plane and traveled to Henderson to testify on the matter and congratulate the council for following his lead in forcing candidates who have raised $5,000 to disclose those contributions annually. "The concern we have in the secretary of state's office now is we have some announced candidates for governor who have claimed to have raised a million dollars up to this point for the ninety-eight race," Heller told the council. "And what if they choose not to run? Have they raised a million dollars, and are they allowed to keep it?"

Heller knew his remarks would be reported in the media and that there would be no mystery to whom he was referring. But was this a prelude to a gubernatorial candidacy? He wasn't saying.

Of course, Guinn didn't have a million dollars. But with more than a half-million in the bank, Rogich felt confident as 1996 slipped into 1997. If Heller were at mid-term, giving him a free shot at Guinn, Rogich might have been more worried. But the secretary of state, Rogich believed, was unlikely to give up his safe re-election in 1998. If he did, and lost, his career might be over. As for Lt. Gov. Lonnie Hammargren, no one in the campaign took him seriously. He would be easily marginalized if he did run; a few commercials showing his greatest gaffes would do the trick.

On the Democratic side, the only possibilities with any chance were Las Vegas Mayor Jan Jones and Attorney General Frankie Sue Del Papa. Jones had been stung so badly by her 1994 demolishment at Miller's hands, and had worked so assiduously to rebuild Establishment relationships, that it seemed inconceivable she would run again.

As for Del Papa, she had to talk herself into running for re-election as attorney general in 1994. She'd briefly flirted with the job of chancellor of the university system before relenting. And she would hardly be willing to give up her assured re-election in 1998 to take on a quixotic campaign against someone many of her longtime supporters were likely to back. Del Papa told some friends during those days that she was irked by the Guinn steamroller, but she was also inclined to seek personal fulfillment. One marriage had already gone by the wayside, and as she approached middle-age, she wouldn't have much chance for a personal life if she stayed in public service. On the other hand, government was in her blood, and she could hardly draw oxygen without the sustenance of elective office. And might the prospect of becoming the first female governor in Nevada history prove irresistible? The answer would come sooner than the Guinn people ever thought.

4

THE SHORT,
UNHAPPY CANDIDACY
OF FRANKIE SUE DEL PAPA

It was Christmas, 1989, and Secretary of State Frankie Sue Del Papa was basking in the spirit of the season. And why not? Her political career was thriving. She was a shoo-in for a second term, thus guaranteed to stay on track for a congressional or gubernatorial bid during the coming decade. She might even be the state's first female governor someday.

Following a tradition practiced by many elected officials, she stopped by political consultant Jim Joyce's annual holiday party at his downtown Las Vegas office. It was the place to be seen during that time of year—partly a courtesy, partly a ring-kissing. Joyce was the most powerful political consultant in Nevada, and he surely would be involved in Del Papa's re-election bid. What the secretary of state didn't know, though, was that Joyce had another agenda when she walked into the Christmas party. Indeed, he and Mike Sloan, the Circus Circus vice president and one of the gaming industry's most active political operatives, wanted expressly to talk to her that day.

Joyce and Sloan had quaffed a few beers before the party and hatched an idea. They had plans for Del Papa, which had nothing to do with the secretary of state's race. That office was insignificant to men such as Joyce and Sloan—

and to the gaming industry. But the attorney general's office was not. The present occupant, Brian McKay, was retiring from public life. The only announced candidate was Jim Spoo, the little-known mayor of Sparks, a bedroom community of Reno. He was unfamiliar to most Southern Nevadans, and generally unfamiliar to Sloan and Joyce. Not so with Del Papa, who had long relationships with both men, as well as powerful figures such as Steve Wynn, who had just opened the Strip's first megaresort, the Mirage.

Joyce and Sloan told Del Papa that attorney general was a much better stepping stone to higher office than secretary of state—a natural stopover on the path to the mansion or Capitol Hill. Spoo had no base of financial support, and Sloan and Joyce could all but guarantee Del Papa that the industry would back her, just as it had in the past.

Del Papa was stunned, but intrigued, by the proposition. In fact, the two men talked her into it as others sipped egg nog and munched on gingerbread cookies around them. By the following week, the news was out that she was considering a bid. Shortly thereafter, Spoo saw his chances of raising money disappear as the cash flowed to the Anointed One, Frankie Sue Del Papa. He soon withdrew from the race. Del Papa coasted to victory in November 1990, brushing aside second-tier primary and general-election opponents who had no campaign cash. She had climbed another rung on the political ladder. And better yet, she had confidence that the men who had helped put her there would give her a push up to the next level when the time was right.

On paper, Frankie Sue Del Papa was Kenny Guinn's worst nightmare. Beyond her gender, which made her inherently strong in any race, she was also a proven statewide vote-getter. She also possessed the best name in Nevada politics, unforgettable and resonant. She may have ostensibly been the most daunting candidate against Guinn—his team certainly thought so. But Del Papa also had some weaknesses. Although she was an enthusiastic and effective retail campaigner, Del Papa was not known as a good debater or for being especially quick on her feet, as was Jan Jones. And while women's groups had enormous affection for her, Del Papa had never built political relationships with critical people and interest groups. She considered it a sign of her independence; others saw it as stubbornness. She also had never experienced a truly difficult contest, one in which raising money would be a problem. Del Papa had always found fundraising repellent—or, as some saw it, she was just lazy. But she was almost always either a heavy favorite or unopposed, so she had no problem gliding to the front in the money race.

Del Papa had also been experiencing second thoughts about whether to continue in public life. She had just spent several years consumed by a controversial conflict with the state Supreme Court over a Washoe County judge, Jerry Whitehead, who had been accused of inappropriate ex parte communications. Whitehead eventually left the bench, but not before the legal community witnessed an unprecedented cataclysm. Whitehead and his allies on the Supreme Court, including Tom Steffen and Charlie Springer, were pitted against Del Papa, her friends in the bar, and a relentless investigator, Don Campbell, a Las Vegas attorney who signed on as a special detective for the attorney general. The episode was debilitating for everyone involved.

Del Papa, who had considered not running for re-election in 1994, still wasn't even sure she wanted to seek a third term as attorney general, much less run for governor. She'd read and heard tales of the Guinn fundraising machine and knew what she would be up against. Her longtime friends might not be so friendly if she entered the race. Some of her associates were not so sure she should get in, no matter what the odds. Bill Prezant, a Reno attorney and Democratic activist who had known Del Papa since high school, warned her that she would age five years if she ran.

The political side of Prezant relished the idea of Del Papa taking on the Establishment and its candidate; but as a friend, he worried about her.

By the time 1997 came around, though, Del Papa was thinking about the race fairly seriously. One of her deputies and close friends, Gordy Fink, loved the idea of Del Papa running and urged her to do it. Fink, whom Del Papa thought of as a brother, believed in the attorney general and prodded her at the 1996 staff Christmas party. She had also been encouraged by various party folks and people on the street, which meant a lot to her. "Everywhere I went I was receiving encouragement," she later recalled. "There was very little discouragement. So I decided to take a more serious look at it."

Del Papa had been invited to President Clinton's 1997 inauguration ceremonies, so she decided to use the trip to Washington to take the fundraising temperature. She knew that major in-state fundraisers were backing Guinn, so if she ran, out-of-state money would be critical. She needed to know if groups such as Emily's List, which supports pro-choice female Democrats, would pony up. Del Papa also consulted with similarly situated pols she knew from other states.

By the time she returned to Carson City from Washington, Del Papa was leaning toward the race. A few days later, she received an invitation to lunch from two Democratic legislative leaders—Assembly Majority Leader Richard Perkins and Senate Minority Leader Dina Titus. Accompanied by Lindsey Jydstrup, who ran the political operation for legislative Democrats, Titus and Perkins laid the hard sell on Del Papa, urging her to challenge Guinn. She had to run, they told her, for the good of the party and the state. Privately, both believed that Guinn was still the favorite even if Del Papa entered the contest. They told Del Papa that despite the picture being painted by Guinn spinmeister Sig Rogich, money would free up if she ran. The casinos couldn't afford to gamble on the governor's race, and Del Papa was a viable candidate, sure to trounce Guinn in the polls because of her high name recognition.

"I don't like the anointing process," Perkins asserted a few days later. "This is an election, not an appointment." Titus, too, spoke of partisan imperatives and anointment: "The Democratic Party shouldn't just roll over in the race for governor. Frankie Sue certainly is the heir apparent and we wanted her to hear that not everyone is supporting Kenny Guinn."

Those high-minded words concealed a baser motivation for their entreaties, though. Titus and Perkins fretted that without a strong Democrat at the top, the entire ticket would wither. The Democrats needed a competitive candidate or the grass roots would suffer, and legislative candidates would be at risk. Titus and Perkins were confident Del Papa would run after that luncheon sit-down, but they would have to wait a couple of weeks to find out.

Guinn was not just standing around. He continued his peripatetic odyssey through Nevada, occasionally popping onto the public radar screen. For instance, he was the guest of honor at the Latin Chamber of Commerce's Valentine's Day banquet. He seemed unconcerned about Del Papa's prospective bid or Secretary of State Dean Heller's consideration of a primary challenge. He hardly noticed publicity about an ex-Hollywood producer named Aaron Russo, a former boyfriend/manager to Bette Midler and producer of films such as *Trading Places*, who appeared at a GOP meeting declaring his intentions to run for governor. Russo distributed a video titled "Mad as Hell," which featured him ranting on stage about government abuses. His candidacy was being promoted by Pat McMillan, an anti-government fulminator. Russo also reportedly had called the Excalibur Hotel on the Strip, owned by Guinn's primary financial benefactor, Circus Circus Enterprises, to see if he could establish residence there for the campaign. But this was all comic relief that had no impact on Guinn's campaign or Del Papa's decision to run.

By late February 1997, after consulting with friends and supporters in Nevada and Washington, the attorney general had made up her mind: She was going to run. Plans were drawn up to announce the proverbial exploratory committee—a device used to keep her candidacy unofficial and shield her from criticism as she pursued her elective agenda during the legislative session that had commenced a month earlier.

The news broke on Feb. 26, 1997, that Del Papa was forming the exploratory committee. The next day, Del Papa got the first sense of what she would be in for in the contest. *Sun* columnist Jeff German wrote a piece declaring the attorney general "isn't exactly getting her campaign off to a roaring start." German had been a relentless critic of Del Papa for years. In fact, the attorney general always knew that the *Sun* would be against her because of German and executive editor Mike O'Callaghan. Del Papa believed that when she, as a regent, argued against giving the presidency of UNLV to anyone who didn't have a doctorate, she created a lifetime enemy in the editor, who was also a larger-than-life Korean War hero and former governor who coveted the presidency. Besides, both O'Callaghan and German were close to Guinn, so German's assault the day after her announcement came as no surprise.

The German column focused on a burgeoning controversy in Del Papa's office: how jailhouse videotapes made of a slot-cheating suspect had found their way into the hands of ABC News. The tapes were sensational—the accused, Ron Harris, alleged conspiracies of political influence stretching all the way to the governor's office and casting doubt on the integrity of the state's gaming regulatory apparatus. Gaming Control Board chairman Bill Bible was furious, especially after having been blindsided with the tapes by ABC in an interview with him. He showed the tapes to industry leaders, who were not happy that they had been leaked. Del Papa denied her office had anything to do with the national story, but the tapes were last in her possession so the circumstantial evidence was all Bible needed.

Worse yet was the news that Del Papa was taking Ron

Harris' allegations seriously and scouring Bible's office for wrongdoing. Bible had never liked Del Papa—he didn't respect her deputies assigned to the Control Board—and he was known to have a direct pipeline to German. Bible, a former budget director and campaign manager for Gov. Richard Bryan, is as cunning and Machiavellian as they come, whether in furthering his agency or personal agendas. He surely would do anything to undermine Del Papa's candidacy—and he had the tools to do it without leaving fingerprints.

That same day, the *Las Vegas Review-Journal's* Jane Ann Morrison also did a story announcing Del Papa's exploratory committee, devoting about a third of the copy to the ABC News flap. If Del Papa hoped for the usual pristine announcement piece candidates hope to obtain from the media, this wasn't it. Morrison also included a statement from Guinn, who said he always believed others would run and rejected the notion that he was the anointed candidate. "If anybody is anointed, I don't know why I've worked so hard the past year," he said.

The first order of business for Del Papa was to assemble members of her exploratory committee. She turned to her close friend, Scott Craigie, an ex-chief of staff to Gov. Bob Miller now working in Reno, coincidentally for Billy Vassiliadis, at R&R Advertising. Craigie advised Del Papa to ask Las Vegas Mayor Jan Jones, the second highest-profile Democratic elected official in the state, to head up the exploratory committee. Jones later remembered that she passed Del Papa in a government building a few days after her exploratory committee was announced. "She was walking into the building and I was walking out," Jones recalled. "'Can I say you're heading up my exploratory committee?'" Del Papa asked her. The Las Vegas mayor agreed, but the "committee" never met.

Soon after Del Papa announced the formation of that committee, she began figuring out where she could raise the money to compete with Guinn. The Guinnites were running a bluff at that time—if polls showed her winning, surely the casinos would play both sides. Del Papa figured early in 1997 that she would need at least $500,000 from out-of-state sources to be competitive. So she called her friend, Patrick Murphy, a Capitol Hill lobbyist, to head up her finance team, and he began working his contacts to shake loose donations. She also hooked up with the Democratic Governor's Association and Emily's List, the women's group in Washington. Her goal was to get on Emily's List's first mailing in January 1998, which would send a message nationwide and seed her campaign with contributions.

In April, the Washington-based *Cook Political Report* published its first take on the Nevada gubernatorial race. Publisher Charlie Cook rated the contest a toss-up, listing Del Papa as the only Democrat and three Republicans as possible nominees—Secretary of State Dean Heller, Lt. Gov. Lonnie Hammargren, and businessman "Kevin Gwinn." Del Papa should have been thrilled—the national folks couldn't even get Kenny Guinn's name right—but the piece didn't mean that much.

Although Del Papa wasn't optimistic about donations from the Strip, she nonetheless began to make calls to see where she stood. The first person she phoned was Elaine Wynn. Del Papa enjoyed a warm relationship with the Wynns, especially Elaine, with whom she'd been involved in education issues. Elaine Wynn told her that she and her husband believed both candidates were qualified and deserved to be supported. Del Papa's casino backing never went much deeper, though. Her high-school chum, Tony Marnell at the Rio, came through. But most casinos didn't give her the time of day. And she didn't work as hard as she might have to find those that would. In the past, when her races were hardly competitive, she didn't have to do the work—the money just flowed in, thanks partly to the likes of Jim Joyce and Mike Sloan.

Now, though, she was the one fighting the Establishment's choice, and she had a revelation about how difficult raising money is for an underdog. She didn't like it. "They tell you you have to sit down for four or five hours a day and make the phone calls," she said. "I don't want to do it." Del Papa had always been described as a tremendous campaigner—enthusiastic and energetic on the stump. But she had never really been tested; she'd never run a first-class media campaign (her ads were always homespun and barebones). This would be a totally new world for her.

Thus, Del Papa was losing the inside game in the early going. A spring poll of legislators and lobbyists showed that 80 percent believed Guinn would defeat the attorney general. On the outside, however, she was doing fine. A Las Vegas Chamber of Commerce survey in April showed that Guinn was unknown by nearly 70 percent of the electorate. No horse race question was asked, but it was clear that Del Papa, whose favorable rating was high, would crush him if the election were held 18 months early.

The Legislature also provided an echo chamber for Del Papa when a measure was introduced designed to force candidates who have been collecting money in off years to disclose their donors. According to the bill, anyone who had received $10,000 in contributions during any year would have to reveal the sources by Dec. 31 of that year. The measure was conceived by Secretary of State Dean Heller and only fueled speculation that he, too, was interested in challenging Guinn. Guinn, for his part, publicly embraced the measure, saying he had collected $1 million.

Del Papa also couldn't have been chagrined when ex-Hollywood producer Aaron Russo, who had been telling people he would challenge Guinn in the GOP primary, declared in May that he would enter the race. It was hard to take Russo seriously—he claimed to have ex-Reagan adviser Lyn Nofziger and ex-JFK press secretary Pierre Salinger on board. Russo sent out a flier telling people he would announce his candidacy on May 10 at the Pioneer Auditorium in Reno. "Freedom Counts!" declared the piece, addressed to voters who were "sick and tried of lying politicians." Inside was the rhetoric of an anti-federalist. Russo made all manner of assertions, including that he would go to the Supreme Court to prevent tips from being taxed, stop the federal government from tapping phones, and make Nevada an "alternative-medicine oasis." In an interview just before his announcement, Russo told the *Las Vegas Sun's* Cy Ryan that Guinn had "been anointed by a few people in the party." He had the patter down, but Russo had been in Nevada for a short time; in fact, he'd only registered to vote a few weeks earlier. And he sounded more like a candidate for federal office—he had helped form the Constitution Party in California a few years earlier—than a gubernatorial contender. But so far as Del Papa was concerned, he was rich and he might make trouble for Guinn.

In midsummer 1997, Del Papa benefited from word that Gov. Bob Miller would endorse her as his successor. This was hardly news. Miller had always said he would support Del Papa. But he also had insisted that he would never say a cross word about Guinn. There was too much history between the men, especially the Republicans-for-Miller efforts in 1990 and 1994, and the role Guinn played in heading Miller's government-reorganization committee.

What happened was that Miller had agreed to co-host, along with a number of other Democrats, a fundraiser for Del Papa on the Strip on Aug. 26. When the governor's name appeared on the invitation, the *Las Vegas Sun* ran the story on page one. The media reaction—and that of the Guinn campaign—was very telling about the state of the race.

Guinn acted as if a childhood friend had spit in his eye. "I'm surprised that he's made up his mind without at least giving me the courtesy of talking to me," Guinn told the *Sun*. "I think longtime friends should sit down and have this discussion." To Guinn, everything in life was about personal relationships; political and partisan loyalty was a foreign concept, indistinguishable from personal fealty. The long years of Miller's association with Del Papa, who wrote the legal opinion that guaranteed Miller a 10-year term, meant nothing to Guinn compared to his friendship with the outgoing governor. He was clearly furious and reacted viscerally when the newspaper called.

Sig Rogich, however, knew that this was not a time for emotion, but for spin: "Saying you're going to support someone and working day and night to help that individual are altogether different things." Indeed, what Rogich knew was that Miller would not work tirelessly to help Del Papa, especially in the fundraising department. And that's all that mattered to him. Rogich surely smiled when *Sun* columnist Jeff German penned a column reminding readers that Miller had hardly helped a Clark County commissioner the previous cycle by appearing in a commercial for what turned out to be a failed campaign.

Del Papa told the *Sun* and the *Review-Journal,* which ran a similar story the following day, that it was 449 days until the election and that she welcomed Miller's backing. Boiler-plate stuff. Del Papa said she had $100,000 and $150,000 more in commitments, compared to Guinn's putative cool million. Del Papa had the governor, but she didn't have all of him and she didn't have much else.

Even though Kenny Guinn had been running since February 1996, more than 15 months later he still didn't have a campaign manager. Rogich was too busy raising money and tending to his myriad business interests to run day-to-day operations. And by the time Del Papa got into the race in early 1997, Rogich knew that Guinn sorely needed a hands-on manager to oversee the campaign. He asked his friend and former partner, Billy Vassiliadis, if he had any ideas. Vassiliadis was not yet officially on board, but he was slowly and quietly sliding into the campaign. He and Rogich discussed going out of state to find a pro who had overseen a previous governor's race.

But then, one day toward the end of the legislative session where he was busy lobbying, Vassiliadis had a thought. That thought, and its eventual metamorphosis into reality, would be the most significant personnel move the Guinn campaign would make. That session, Vassiliadis had been getting to know Pete Ernaut, the assistant Assembly minority leader, a young Republican who had become a key legislative power broker at the precocious age of 32. Ironically, Ernaut had run the campaign of Jim Gallaway against Miller eight years earlier, when Miller had first been anointed. That had been a disaster, although Ernaut had done the good GOP soldier bit by fronting for the party's sacrificial lamb. He had come a long way since then, too.

Ernaut was one of the authentic characters of Nevada politics, a Basque barrel of a man whose combination of bombast and wit made him a favorite of colleagues and lobbyists. He came to Carson City by way of Elko, where he was reared by his mother after she divorced his father when he was a young boy. As a 10-year-old, he felt the awakening of his political soul upon encountering Nevada legends Paul Laxalt and Mike O'Callaghan on Government Day at school. He moved to Reno when he was 10 years old to live with his father, where he played baseball and football before heading to college at UNR.

Ernaut's natural feistiness often went too far in college and he developed a reputation as a brawler. But he was also known for his quick and creative wit and he aspired to become a stand-up comedian. He left the friendly confines of home and transferred to USC, where he worked in comedy clubs and eventually landed a small, recurring role as a nosy janitor on the NBC hit, "L.A. Law." He later appeared in a nationwide Pepsi ad and co-starred in a 1987 movie, *The Gang's All Here*, with Doug McKeon, who had received a boost by playing the kid in *On Golden Pond*.

When the writer's strike hit Hollywood later that year, Ernaut returned to Reno and became a bartender. His interest in politics was rekindled—he had taken a summer off from college to intern for Laxalt on Capitol Hill. In 1988, he was approached by Congresswoman Barbara Vucanovich's organization to run her campaign in the rural counties. After she won re-election, Vucanovich asked Ernaut to come back to Washington, but he turned her down. But when a veteran assemblyman from Carson City suburbs of Gardnerville named Lou Bergevin called and asked him to become the executive director of the Assembly Republican Caucus, Ernaut took the job.

His first session was a doozy. In 1989, legislators were poised to vote themselves a 300 percent increase in their government pensions, shortly after senators and congressmen had voted themselves a controversial pay raise. The deal had been cut across party lines. At a caucus meeting, GOP leaders were advising the members to vote for the increase. Ernaut, showing the irrepressible streak that would become his hallmark, spoke up. He told the politicians he worked for that they were making a huge mistake that would cause retaliation at the polls. He was shouted down. But he was later proved right as the pension increase cost a raft of Democratic and Republican assemblymen their jobs in 1990.

Bergevin called on Ernaut again that year, asking him, along with his new business partner, a pollster named Mike McGuire, to run Jim Gallaway's futile campaign against the anointed Gov. Bob Miller. Ernaut accepted the duty and he and McGuire ran a spirited effort until Gallaway, like so many wealthy candidates, saw the handwriting on the wall and stopped writing checks. But before the race was over, Ernaut met someone who would turn out to have a pervasive influence in his life and career: his counterpart in the Miller campaign, Billy Vassiliadis.

Their relationship developed slowly over the years. Ernaut continued to act as a Republican operative while Vassiliadis remained a member of the Democratic governor's kitchen Cabinet. During a 1991 legislative debate over teacher raises, Ernaut had one of his patented blow-ups with John Cummings, the head of the teachers union and a close friend of Vassiliadis. Cummings subsequently sent Vassiliadis as an emissary to smooth over the rift with the Assembly caucus operative, and later all three men became friends.

At the end of 1991, Ernaut began thinking of running himself for the Assembly, in a primary against a generally disliked incumbent named Joe Elliott. All of his time spent with the likes of Vassiliadis, Cummings and the legendary Jim Joyce paid off when he called for campaign help. They came through and he won by 370 votes.

Ernaut bided his time, learning issues and developing bipartisan relationships. He became known as one of the building's best deal-makers, heeding his mentor Bergevin's admonition to "find out what everyone wants and give part to them." He was named co-floor leader of the Assembly during an unprecedented 21-21 partisan tie in 1995 and developed a close relationship with his counterpart, Democrat Richard Perkins. It was a coming-out party for the exuberant lawmaker. He became a legislative star that session, cultivating relationships with key lobbyists, many of whom had ties to gambling, including Vassiliadis, Harvey Whittemore, and Greg Ferraro, a Vassiliadis lieutenant at R&R Advertising who also happened to be a former fraternity brother of Ernaut's. Ernaut become known as one of the pivotal figures in Carson City and was seen as a future congressman. He ran again in 1996 and won easily, but he was beginning to make some enemies, too, including within his own party. He was a steadfast supporter of the main item on the Establishment agenda that session, an increase in the sales tax to pay for a new water system in Southern Nevada that the gaming industry and development community considered essential for future growth.

The Democrats had clobbered the Republicans in the 1996 election cycle, turning the 21-21 tie into a 27-15 advantage. Ernaut was frustrated and a little bored—the thrill was gone. As the 1997 session waned, Vassiliadis, who had become friendly with Ernaut in a part-avuncular, part brotherly way, had watched Ernaut's hands-on management of the Assembly caucus. He also knew that Ernaut worked for Forsythe Francis, a full-service ad agency that could fill Guinn's needs. He seemed to Vassiliadis, the man who had run the last two successful gubernatorial races, to be a perfect fit.

Ernaut barely knew Kenny Guinn in 1997. He had met him once during the 1995 Legislature in a literally smoke-filled room where Ernaut and some of his cronies were drinking and puffing cigars. A lobbyist, Charlie Sylvestri, had brought Guinn into the inner sanctum to meet Ernaut and a couple of other legislators. Ernaut later partied with Guinn, Ferraro, and a politically connected Republican attorney, Joe Brown, at the 1996 national convention in San Diego. But that was the extent of their relationship.

In fact, when Rogich sent out letters to all the GOP legislators shortly after Guinn announced, asking that they sign up and commit early, Ernaut demurred. He was one of only a few Republican lawmakers who didn't immediately sign on the dotted line and commit their political capital to Guinn. Why? Mostly because Ernaut had promised the secretary of state, Dean Heller, that he would never be involved in a race against him. The agreement reached back to 1991 when Ernaut, then-Assemblyman Heller, and another assemblyman, Bill Gregory, had all agreed to a perpetual non-aggression pact. Guinn, ever one to take things personally, was miffed at Ernaut's refusal at the time, but Ernaut thought nothing of it. Actually, he believed his old college buddy, Ferraro, would be tabbed as the campaign manager. The Guinn organization at the time was essentially Rogich and Vassiliadis, and Ferraro was Vassiliadis' right-hand man. It seemed natural.

But then a strange thing happened. The Guinn campaign called a meeting in Las Vegas and Brian Sandoval, another young Republican assemblyman, attended. When he returned to Carson City, Sandoval told Ernaut, "You must be happy; you're going to be the campaign manager." Ernaut retorted, "That's the first I've heard of it." Ernaut didn't think much of it until a day or so later when Rogich called and asked him if he would consider the job.

By that time, Ernaut had pretty much decided not to seek re-election. He loved being in the Assembly and the relationships he had nurtured. But the legislative role was wearing thin; his big feet and occasional big mouth had landed him in dutch with some members of his caucus, which was in disarray. He had even seriously considered running for Congress the year before. He met with Rogich, Vassiliadis, Ferraro, and Steve Forsythe, Ernaut's private-sector partner in the ad agency. The conclusion was that he would have been the front-runner to fill retiring Rep. Barbara Vucanovich's seat. But he and his wife, Wendy, wanted to start a family. He didn't want the life of a cross-country commuting congressman just as he was about to become a father.

A few days after he talked to Rogich, Ernaut received a call early in the morning from Ferraro, who also lived in Reno. "Why don't you drive down to Carson with me today?" his old friend asked. He didn't know it at the time, but there was a purpose. Shortly after Ferraro picked him up, the car phone rang. It was Vassiliadis calling from Las Vegas. "Do you want this job?" Vassiliadis' voice crackled over the cell phone. "Because it's going to be offered to you." Ernaut said he would have to talk to Wendy about it that night, and he did.

He was concerned about a couple of things. First, there was the perception that he was being repaid for legislative favors by the power lobbyists. He knew he would have to live with the nasty whispers if he took the job. Second, he thought campaigns were like a massage—"they hurt like hell but along the way it's pleasurable." Ernaut was incredibly competitive and hated to lose. And here he was being set up: Asked to manage the campaign that couldn't lose, what if he lost it?

Even then, Ernaut didn't believe Del Papa was really in the race. He knew she had tremendous name identification, was beloved by many women's groups, and thrilled to give speeches. But Ernaut also remembered that as a second-term assemblyman, he'd challenged her during a committee hearing and, as he recalled it, "ate her lunch." He also believed she could never raise enough money and didn't have the stomach for the contest. So he felt confident that there would not be a strong opponent.

Rogich flew up to Carson City a few days later to seal the deal with Ernaut—it was early June, only a few weeks before the 1997 legislative session ended. Ernaut met with Rogich, Ferraro, and Vassiliadis at a restaurant called Bodine's, a few miles from the Capitol. Throughout the evening, during which the party moved over to Adele's, the official legislative watering hole, Ernaut negotiated the financial details and the job description with Rogich. Five bottles of wine were consumed.

By coincidence, Guinn was in Carson City at the time. He strolled through Adele's and stopped at the table. Ernaut talked to him for a about five minutes and, even in his addled state, was struck by the man he was about to work for. "He looks like a governor. He looks like a former athlete, so it's easy to be intimidated," Ernaut said. "But he was a pretty easy guy to talk to. I felt like I was having the King say, 'Come into the chariot and ride down Coronation Street.'"

On the way back to Reno, Ernaut sat in the back of the car as Ferraro drove with Rogich in the passenger seat. Ferraro and Rogich reminisced about their days in the disastrous Jim Santini for U.S. Senate campaign in 1986. All three were feeling no pain as they sang and drove back to Reno. That night was the birth of a family of sorts, the Guinn inner circle: Rogich, Ferraro, Ernaut, and the spirit of Vassiliadis.

The next morning, Ernaut rose early to meet Guinn and Rogich for breakfast at the Eldorado hotel in Reno. He told Guinn his conditions for employment: He made all the decisions, and no one but he could spend campaign funds. Guinn agreed. Ernaut was on board, unofficially because the Legislature was still in session. But even though the official announcement wouldn't come until Aug. 15, nearly two months later, Guinn had his campaign manager. And Frankie Sue Del Papa was about to find out how this family treated those who weren't part of the clan.

As the summer of 1997 waned, Kenny Guinn was moving to neutralize Del Papa's advantage in Northern Nevada. He'd rented an apartment in Reno and was spending his days doing what he does best: talking to people, presenting his down-to-earth mien for the Renoites to experience.

Meanwhile, Del Papa was busy preparing a financial plan to present to Emily's List representatives in September—an outline of how she would use regional fundraisers to garner $2 million, about $1.5 million more than she had collected for any previous race. But there were already signs on the home front that money would be a problem for her. Messages were coursing through the political grapevine that she would not be able to raise as much money as she needed from the state's gaming and business communities. Rogich and Guinn had been asking people not just for their support, but their exclusive backing. "Get on board early and we'll remember," was their message.

Pete Ernaut had just taken over the Guinn campaign, and he sensed Del Papa could be forced out of the race. He set out to achieve that goal no later than the beginning of 1998. He believed she didn't have the stomach for the campaign and he determined to do everything he could to make her dyspepsia so acute that she'd have to retire to her political sickbed. His plan was simple: He would hire all the political talent in Nevada, cut off her money, and strip away key interest-group support, especially labor and the police. An attorney general without the adherence of organized labor and the endorsement of the law-enforcement community, Ernaut knew, would be a mere shell of a candidate.

When Ernaut took over in August, he realized immediately that the Guinn "campaign" was still an illusion. Only two people manned the headquarters. Rogich had retained Wayne Pearson, an old crony who had done polling for years, and Judy Brusa, a Democrat who had worked in numerous campaigns, including Richard Bryan's efforts for governor and U.S. Senate. After a year and a half of being a candidate, Guinn's foundation was still based on Rogich's spin and the perception of inevitability. Ernaut knew, as he later recalled, that it's "not a bad thing when you want people to vote for you to be anointed. But it's also not built on anything. [Guinn] had a million and a half dollars because Kenny Guinn had done everything anyone had ever asked of him in the community, with bond issues, the Lung Association, Shade Tree Foundation. He never said no. But if he were a candidate perceived to be the puppet of the gaming industry, with no individual thoughts of his own and with every consultant known to man, how were we going to keep a semblance of balance? How could we build a foundation to inoculate us against even the biggest screw-ups?"

Ernaut believed in his gut that politics in Nevada had changed. No longer could a Republican candidate simply win with money. Gone were the days when Paul Laxalt knew everyone in the state and that was enough. So his challenge was to construct a grass-roots organization for Guinn in a state with a population of 1.4 million people. Ernaut had a sense, as he would memorably describe it later, that political insiders expected the campaign "to be run in the boardroom of R&R [Advertising] with caviar and sandwiches. There were going to be way too many fingers and not enough doers. [Guinn and company] were going to decorate the campaign with party hacks."

Ernaut persuaded Guinn to allow him—not Rogich, not anyone else—to hire all the campaign staff. He told Guinn that they were about to assemble the most extensive grass-roots campaign in state history. They would do what no Republican had ever done before in Nevada, essentially construct a Democratic campaign—much like the model Vassiliadis had set up for Miller in 1994 and 1998. Ernaut knew that he had to counteract the legion of teachers and workers who were the bedrock of the typical Democrats' grass-roots effort. This was especially true, if, as rumbles had already alerted him, there might be a ballot question in 1998 designed to constrict labor's ability to earmark a portion of membership dues for political action, a so-called paycheck-protection initiative that would energize labor. "Republicans don't start with one hundred twenty-five thousand union guys or seasoned teachers," he remembered thinking. "We start with twenty-five overweight sixty-five-year-old women with bad wigs who spend half their days on the phone."

Ernaut knew he would have to sell the rest of the campaign advisers on this plan, especially Rogich and Vassiliadis, who was now, since the Legislature ended in July, out of the closet as a Guinnite. So in late August, Ernaut convened a meeting at the Alexis Park Hotel near the Strip. He invited Rogich, Vassiliadis, Ferraro, Steve Forsythe, and Mark Brown, a close Guinn family friend and politically astute operative for Howard Hughes Corporation. Ernaut laid out to these men—most older and more seasoned political insiders—his plan. The goal was simple: "We're going to scare the living crap out of Frankie Sue going into this thing. We're going to hire our team now. We'll open a headquarters now. We're going to call her bluff." It would be an expensive strategy, Ernaut later told Guinn, but one that would provide any margin for error later if things went haywire.

No one objected. In fact, they were enthusiastic and helped him come up with staffing ideas. Terry Murphy, who had recently departed Clark County government where she was the director of administrative services, would be perfect to run the Southern Nevada office, Vassiliadis told him. Vassiliadis also suggested Ernaut go after Rob Powers, who had been employed by R&R, done press work for Miller's successful gubernatorial campaigns, and was now working for the Las Vegas Convention and Visitors Authority. Ernaut himself came up with the idea to hire Josh Griffin, son of the Reno mayor, to work Northern Nevada.

But the most important staffing decision the group agreed upon that day was to try to hire someone to oversee this massive grass-roots operation envisioned by Ernaut. They settled on Steve Wark, known for his ability to organize the religious right, which had helped catapult him to the state Republican Party chairmanship in the late '80s and had almost gotten him elected to the Assembly in a Democratic district.

Getting Wark would not be easy, Ernaut knew. In fact, a few months earlier, Wark had given a speech to a campaign school sponsored by the Clark County Republican Party. The theme of his speech: How to beat Kenny Guinn in a Republican primary. It was classic, contrarian Wark— after all, he was the kid with the near-shoulder-length blond hair, Hawaiian shirts, and cutoffs who had been ousted as the executive director of the Republican Party in the mid-1980s, only to resurface as an evangelical Christian who used the power of church groups to organize the rank-and-file and get elected state chairman in 1988. The Establishment helped boot him from that post, too—and Ernaut had been one of the kickers. Wark ran for office himself a couple of times in the early 1990s, narrowly losing to an incumbent in a very Democratic district. By 1996, he was back to his antiestablishmentarian ways, helming the Nevada component of Alan Keyes' hopeless fight for the GOP presidential nomination

Like some other ideologically committed Republicans, Wark was not sure about Guinn. Not only was Guinn pro-choice, but he seemed squishy on most issues. Wark seemed more likely to go with a primary challenger to Guinn, perhaps even a populist ranter such as Aaron Russo. Russo actually attended Wark's speech to the county Republicans

93

and came to the GOP operative's office shortly thereafter. Russo was his usual rambunctious self during the 90-minute chat; Wark remembered Russo raising his voice so often that after he left Wark's receptionist asked, "Who was that man screaming at you?" Replied Wark: "Some guy who wants to be governor. The guy is out of his gourd." But Wark, hoping to find someone, anyone to latch onto in the governor's race, checked out Russo despite the poor first impression. Wark actually went to some lengths to ask around about Russo in Los Angeles; he says his sources told him to stay away. So he did.

Around this time, toward the end of 1997, Wark's friends were beginning to call him to urge him to consider helping Guinn. Ernaut actually had generated some of the calls, including one from Keith Lynam, a friend of Wark's and ex-executive director of the state GOP. Ernaut knew Wark would be reluctant to hitch his star to a frontrunner, having championed underdogs. He told Lynam to feel out Wark about the job and to tell him Ernaut would be calling.

Ernaut was a consummate salesman and he had his pitch ready on that August day. He phoned Wark and turned the screw for 90 minutes. He told Wark that this was his ticket to the mainstream, that he would have the money to do on grand scale what he had only done in small political subdivisions. Wark didn't buy immediately. He told Ernaut he would think about it, that he would have to pray about it. Wark had mixed feelings about Ernaut because of his role in ousting him as state chairman a decade earlier, or as he remembered it, that Ernaut "systematically tried to cut my throat when I was state chairman." There may be no permanent friends or enemies in politics, Wark knew, but there are permanent memories. On the other hand, Ernaut had been there for him when he ran for the Assembly, helping Wark raise money in what many thought was a futile effort. "I was ambivalent about my feelings for Pete but I respected his prowess," Wark said.

Wark called Ernaut back a few days after that call and told him he would become part of the campaign on one condition: He had to sit down with Guinn and gauge whether he was a real Republican. A few days later, Wark and Guinn sat down in a conference room in Sig Rogich's office suite. Wark had talked to his friend and fellow grass-roots expert, Judie Braillsford, about Guinn. Braillsford, known for her expertise in organizing Mormon voters in Southern Nevada, generally for incumbents, was already on Team Guinn. She understood Wark's doubts and was in Rogich's conference room for part of the time he talked to Guinn that day.

Wark was immediately impressed with Guinn, whom he had never met. Guinn seemed to be much like his own father—he had pulled himself up from a hardscrabble upbringing, he had common sense, he was an honorable man. After asking Guinn about his background, Wark pulled out the state Republican Party platform. He asked Guinn to give him yes or no answers on the various planks, expounding only if necessary. Guinn held up well under the grilling as he displayed what Wark believed were the would-be governor's true conservative bona fides. Even on abortion, he found that Guinn wasn't as pro-choice as the candidate thought he was—or as Rogich had told him to sound for the purposes of the campaign. He was for parental consent and opposed to partial-birth abortions. By the end of an hour or so, Wark was convinced. He told Guinn: "I'd like to get you elected as governor."

On Tuesday, Aug. 26, 1997, Frankie Sue Del Papa held her first campaign fundraiser at the Polo Towers, a time-share complex on the Las Vegas Strip. Although almost every Democratic officeholder, including Miller, was listed on the invitation, none of them showed up at the event, which raised her only $30,000. Not one casino executive graced the scene.

And if that weren't depressing and embarrassing enough for Del Papa, that same week news of Guinn's labor of labor love began to surface. First, Guinn had been named the keynote speaker of the annual AFL-CIO convention in Las Vegas the next month. The Guinnites knew what kind of signal that would send, which is why Guinn had been working on his longtime friend, Blackie Evans, the iconic head of the labor organization. Guinn had also informed Evans and others that he might be open to signing a bill giving state employees collective-bargaining rights, which had been anathema for Republican governors (and even some Democratic chief executives) in the past.

Del Papa, more significantly, had a frosty relationship with the Culinary Union, the largest labor organization by far in Nevada, which represents the casino workers and is a potent grass-roots force. Ernaut had already fashioned an intermittent colloquy with D. Taylor, the Culinary's staff director and local leader. Ernaut had been helpful on several union issues during the 1995 Legislature, and he had kept in touch with Taylor ever since. Vassiliadis was also a friend of Taylor's and others in the Culinary hierarchy, including John Wilhelm, Taylor's boss, and Glen Arnodo, the up-and-coming Culinary political director.

Guinn not only knew Evans, but he also had a close friendship with Andy Anderson, the police union chief. Among his myriad extracurricular duties, Guinn had served as chairman of the Las Vegas Metropolitan Police Department's Fiscal Affairs Committee. And the last time the cops were up for a raise, Guinn made the motion. Anderson was there the moment Guinn announced.

Del Papa, by contrast, had never sought to develop relationships with any of the labor folks. Yes, she had a friendship with Danny Thompson, an ex-assemblyman now running the AFL-CIO's political and lobbying arm in Carson City. But the Culinary leaders actually felt she had gone out of her way to be hostile during her term. She had done nothing to help the union in its protracted struggle with the

Frontier Hotel on the Strip, the longest-running strike in America. And when she had to rule on whether sidewalks in front of the anti-union MGM Grand could be used by Culinary pickets, she not only ruled against the labor organizers, but fired a deputy who was sympathetic to their position. Add in building-trade leaders who were enraged about her office's rulings in prevailing wage cases, and she had serious trouble with labor. Although she was a veteran pol, Del Papa seemed clueless about how serious her problems with labor really were. She'd convinced herself that the rank-and-file would admire her for her independence and that she didn't need any coziness with the leadership.

The Guinnites knew that if Del Papa could be denied the AFL-CIO endorsement in September, it would set her campaign reeling. And they were working the inside to ensure that the Democratic candidate, a natural for a labor endorsement, was snubbed. Danny Thompson tried to help her. He had offered her the keynote slot at the convention, which she turned down. Then he called the White House to try to knock Guinn off the speaking list at the AFL-CIO convention. Del Papa chewed out Evans when she learned Guinn had received the plum. "It was stupid," said one Democrat at the time who was sympathetic to her cause and familiar with the machinations. "She called the White House after the fact and had them call the AFL-CIO. She didn't change the outcome, but she did manage to incense the troops on the ground. She yelled at Blackie in her shrill way and their perspective is she has never lifted a finger to help." Worse, she had no organization, not even a campaign manager to help her work the inside.

In fact, as Guinn's organization began to teem with consultants, Del Papa didn't need all the fingers on one hand to tally hers. Her loyal aide in the attorney general's office, Misty Young, and another friend, Robyn Powers, were trying to coordinate the fundraising. Her high-school pal, Bill Prezant, was advising her, as was Scott Craigie of R&R. Del Papa's fund-raising efforts focused on snaring dollops of $10,000 from out-of-state events, including a fundraiser in San Francisco in early September. Las Vegas Mayor Jan Jones also hosted a fundraiser that month for Del Papa at her home for the group, Emily's List, where Jones gave an impassioned, inspiring speech to the gathering of female activists, talking about the importance of electing a woman to the governor's office—the first in Nevada history. Among those who applauded her remarks was Patty Becker, a former chief of staff to Gov. Bob Miller who was well-connected to women's groups in Northern Nevada. Having Becker on board would be a boon to Del Papa. But she was still far behind Guinn in fundraising and organizational strength.

Ernaut was quietly continuing his plan to block every possible avenue of support for her. He was especially eager to corral none other than Patty Becker. Though Becker was a stalwart of the women's movement in Reno, her politics were also influenced by her friendships, and she was extremely close to Bonnie Schreck, whose husband, Frank, was a major cog in the Guinn fundraising machine. In turn, Schreck's close friend, Gaming Control Board Chairman Bill Bible, was dedicated to destroying Del Papa's political career.

In addition, Ernaut, flush with campaign funds, was hiring staffers left and right. Most recently, he'd snared Denice Miller, a well-regarded policy wonk from the legislative staff ranks, to help formulate an issues package.

Del Papa tried to counter the swelling tide before the AFL-CIO convention by putting out the word that she'd met with Steve Wynn in early September. Wynn had pledged to give as much to her as to Guinn and insisted later that the state had "the classiest choice in history." Del Papa gushed that "Steve Wynn treated me like the vice president of the United States. He pulled all of his [property] presidents in [to talk about giving money to her campaign]." Del Papa quickly ensured that word of Wynn's bet-hedging became public, hoping it would cause other casinos to follow suit, but that didn't happen. For example, Del Papa tried to call Gary Primm, the head of Primadonna Resorts. But she was told she'd have to go through Primm's political adviser, who just happened to be Sig Rogich.

About a week before the AFL-CIO convention in Las Vegas, Del Papa met with her longtime political adviser, Kent Oram, who had run all of her statewide contests. Oram was a storied Nevada political figure. In the late '70s and early '80s, he was to local politics what Jim Joyce was to state politics—*the guy* to talk to. Most Las Vegas City Council and Clark County Commission incumbents used him. So did Bob Rose when he ran for lieutenant governor in 1978 and Bob Miller when he ran for lieutenant governor in 1986 and governor in 1990 and 1994. He was a mentor to younger political consultants such as Billy Vassiliadis, before Vassiliadis went to work for Rogich. He often sat in his Las Vegas office, dispensing advice over the phone or in person, like a Buddha with bluster. He had the same Chicago edge as Vassiliadis, but was much more dogmatic. He rarely dealt with the media, unlike Rogich or Joyce or Vassiliadis. His specialty was radio, but his mail pieces were legendary, often flowing on for pages and pages. He was also known as a very valuable consultant to talk to if you needed local law-enforcement endorsements.

Oram's success, however, had faded in the '90s. He'd been lambasted in the media during the early part of the decade when he accepted a contract to promote Nevada as the site for a nuclear-waste dump. The deal with the American Nuclear Energy Council was worth millions of dollars, and Oram oversaw a TV campaign starring a former local sports anchor that was roundly ridiculed for trying to assert the safety of nuclear waste and downplaying the impact of an accident during transport of the waste from around the country to a site 90 miles northwest of Las Vegas. Oram still took political clients, but they were fewer and farther between; because of his new client, he had become a liability.

He absorbed high-profile losses, too—including an attempt by an ex-state senator, Bob Ryan, a conservative Republican turned Democrat, to win a County Commission seat. He did elect Erin Kenny, an ex-assemblywoman, to that seat later in the decade, but his star had fallen in the late '90s.

Oram may have been past his prime, but Del Papa owed a lot to him. His ties to the police union had proven invaluable to her in past races. So she'd kept in touch with him during 1997, even though she had made no decision to use him. He wanted to be involved in the contest, but he also wanted a large payday if Del Papa were going to run—at least $300,000. Oram had strongly advised her to hire his friend, Doug Schoen, a national pollster who had done work for many of his races as well as the nuclear industry. But Del Papa, under pressure from Emily's List, had decided to hire its designated pollster, Celinda Lake, which infuriated Oram. And she was not willing to meet his six-figure price for the race. She was being advised by friends and others that she needed to get someone else, perhaps even an out-of-state consultant, to run her campaign.

Rogich was the first Guinnite to make contact with Oram. Rogich told him that Del Papa couldn't win, that she would never get any money. Then, about the time of the labor convention, Oram called Vassiliadis and asked him to set up a meeting with Ernaut, whom he didn't know.

Ernaut was thrilled. This fit perfectly into his strategy of slicing away every layer of support from Del Papa. If he could get Oram to come over to Team Guinn, it would be a severe blow. So he agreed to have lunch with Oram at Cafe Nicolle, the same spot where a year and a half earlier Guinn had told Rogich he intended to run for governor. Oram claimed that he was going to manage Del Papa's campaign. But Ernaut saw through the bravado—perhaps he recognized the act. He left the luncheon and went to talk to Guinn. Ernaut was convinced his earlier instincts were right. "She's not there," he recalled telling his candidate. "You mark my words: She's out of this race."

Ernaut moved in for the kill. He began a Chinese water torture approach. He and others began whispering to the media about Del Papa's failure to jump on board the states' tobacco lawsuits until it was almost too late. He intermittently leaked word of the team he was assembling, including news that Patty Becker was on board, which he knew would be a psychological blow.

Ernaut was also tracking which casino owners she was calling—it was fairly easy given that the few she contacted called Guinn or Rogich to let them know. Many, though, told the Guinn folks that she had never even made the effort.

And he was still thinking about Oram, hoping to apply the coup de grace. So about two weeks after their first meeting, Ernaut asked Oram to lunch at an eatery on the far western end of Las Vegas called East Side Mario's. By then, it was clear Oram had no faith in Del Papa's candidacy. He realized he wasn't being considered for the top spot and wanted to ensure he was with the winner. "He was trying to get on with us," Ernaut recalled. "It was more about him negotiating to work for Kenny."

September 1997 was a tough month for Del Papa. In the days before the AFL-CIO convention, she still held out hope that the labor guys would come home to the Democratic Party. She couldn't believe they'd sell out to Guinn, no matter their personal feelings toward her. But she didn't know how assiduously Ernaut had been working the inside before the convention. He met with Blackie Evans, the AFL-CIO chief, and John Wilhelm, the overall Culinary boss, on the same day, just shortly before the convention. He didn't think Guinn could walk away with the two-thirds delegate vote necessary to snare the endorsement—a knockout blow. But he was confident that Guinn could block Del Papa from getting the endorsement, which would be yet another significant setback.

The day before the convention began, Democratic U.S. Sen. Richard Bryan, a longtime Del Papa admirer, met with the AFL-CIO board and pleaded with the group to back Del Papa. He invoked the effect on the party up and down the ticket if Del Papa was not strongly embraced. He came away feeling pessimistic, though. Later that day, Del Papa met with the board and was taken aback by the members' coolness.

To accomplish their convention goal, Ernaut & Co. constructed Guinn's keynote speech with one objective in mind: Send a message to the Culinary that Guinn was on their side on the Frontier strike, the shibboleth that would give the union ample reason to snub the attorney general. Forget that Guinn's past included running Southwest Gas as a nonunion company and that earlier that year he'd boasted about it to a conservative contractors group. On Sept. 15, when Guinn delivered his speech at the Tropicana Hotel, he declared that if the strike was "not settled by the time of the election, and if I'm elected, then as your governor my number-one priority for you will be to step in and personally involve myself in settling this strike."

Del Papa spoke later that day. Her speech was replete with platitudes and her new mantra that she was going to have a "conversation with the people of the state." She received barely any applause. When the media later asked what she would do about the strike, she cited attorney-client privilege and said nothing.

When pressed after his speech, Guinn acknowledged that he had accepted early contributions from the Elardi family, the owners of the Frontier Hotel. Under normal circumstances, that would have disqualified someone seeking the Nevada labor endorsement. But the animus toward Del Papa was so strong, and the commitment the Guinnites had secured so airtight, that it was merely a blip.

That same day, Democratic Sen. Harry Reid, who gave a raw meat speech to the convention, didn't even mention Del Papa, the presumed standard-bearer for his party the next year. Why weight himself down with Del Papa's labor baggage—he had enough problems with, his opponent, Congressmen John Ensign.

Del Papa left the AFL-CIO convention downcast. The antagonism, the snubs, had sent her reeling. She had only $250,000 in the bank, a quarter of what Guinn claimed to have. Her chief adviser, Kent Oram, was threatening not to do the race unless she could pay him more than she'd already raised. Del Papa was torn because she still believed Oram could deliver law enforcement. What she didn't know was that Andy Anderson, the police union chief, had already committed his organization to Guinn—not because of Oram, but because of Guinn's performance on the police budget board.

Ten days after the convention, word surfaced that Guinn had chosen three honorary campaign chairmen—well-regarded Clark County Commissioner Bruce Woodbury, Senate Majority Leader Bill Raggio, and, the big coup, Patty Becker. All Del Papa could do now, with all the state talent on the Guinn side, was to run a campaign out of Washington, which would surely prove disastrous.

Del Papa went to Washington shortly after the convention, cautiously hopeful that Emily's List and others would ignite her candidacy. She and her friends, including Gordy Fink and Bill Prezant, had worked day and night preparing a $2 million financial plan. But the Emily's List representative didn't even open her plan, treating Del Papa as if she were a first-time contender. They wanted her to commit to spending $1 million she didn't have and probably couldn't obtain as soon as they wanted her to. Del Papa left Washington despondent.

By early October, Oram was all but a Guinnite and Del Papa's campaign was inert. She received a call from a major mining-company executive who wanted to support her after meeting with Guinn, Rogich, and Ernaut. "It's like doing business in Indonesia," he told her. "They were threatening and promising." But that was hardly encouraging to Del Papa. Quite the contrary. The full realization of what she was up against began to weigh on her. And she didn't have the stomach, the will for it.

She particularly didn't relish being cast as the divorced woman running against family-man Guinn; she'd heard the whispers already and they, along with the setbacks in her campaign, had only made her think more about her lack of a personal life, what she had given up for public service.

She had no real professional worries. Sam Lionel, head of the state's largest law firm, had approached her about heading up a gaming practice. But the proverbial belly fire had been extinguished, partly from Ernaut's water torture and partly because she didn't want to, or couldn't, collect the kindling, the campaign money, that might stoke it.

On paper, ironically, Del Papa had nothing to be down about. Guinn appeared to be a prohibitive underdog in most surveys. She had all the name recognition she needed; Guinn still had none. In fact, all Del Papa's second thoughts occurred as she enjoyed what polls were showing to be a 20- to 25-point lead. She was on the verge of quitting a contest she was winning by a landslide. But the polls couldn't overcome her personal angst, her fundamental aversion to fundraising, and the ruthless efficiency with which Ernaut & Co. had boarded up the doors to every special-interest house.

On Oct. 16, 1997, Pete and Wendy Ernaut were shopping for furniture in Reno when the call came in on his cell phone. Del Papa was through: The news would break on television that night, and in the news paper the next day. Ernaut was hardly shocked—he had been predicting as much. But it was four months earlier than his timetable; he didn't think she'd raise the white flag until February, just after the campaign disclosures were released.

As he thought about Del Papa's departure in the ensuing days, Ernaut began to realize the significance. Evaluating the Democratic field in his mind's eye, he found it to be fallow. He figured that while state Sen. Joe Neal might get in, he was a fringe candidate who would have no impact.

Las Vegas Mayor Jan Jones, the only potentially viable candidate, surely would not get in. She and Rogich were very close, and he had assured everyone in the campaign that she was out. "My mindset was there was nobody left," Ernaut recalled thinking.

Del Papa did not go out with a bang, but she did appear to whimper a little in post-mortem interviews. She told the *Review-Journal's* Jane Ann Morrison that because she was "too independent," she couldn't raise money. She also delivered a screed against anointment, telling the veteran reporter, with an oblique but obvious reference to Guinn, that a million-dollar war chest is "raised in concert with a small group of power brokers and lobbyists, people who are unelected and unimpeachable, but who wield a lot of power in this state. A winning candidate arrives in office laden with the baggage of implied promises and expected access." Perhaps that was something she alone was impervious to when she ran for secretary of state and attorney general with the help of power brokers and lobbyists such as Jim Joyce or Mike Sloan.

Two weeks after she dropped out of the race, Del Papa later asserted, she received a call from the Washington, D.C., office of Emily's List. Just a quick call to let the attorney general know that the group had looked at her financial plan and it was the best the group had ever seen. They would use it as a national model.

5

HER HONOR
TAKES A PASS

Jan Jones had never stopped wanting to be governor. Even after she lost in the 1994 primary by an embarrassing 35 points to Gov. Bob Miller, she coveted the job. Even after she mended fences with the powerful coterie she'd alienated by taking on Miller—Sig Rogich, Billy Vassiliadis, and others—then easily won re-election as mayor in spring 1995, her eyes were still on Carson City. Being the mayor of Las Vegas bored her. It was confining. She had no real power. She wanted a job where she would have authority, where she could advocate for big-picture programs, where she could get things done. There was only one job in the state that fit the description: governor.

Shortly after she won re-election—in an echo of four years past—she was again thinking about seeking the job. After all, it would be an open seat; Miller was term-limited. The only other Democrat who stood in her way was Attorney General Frankie Sue Del Papa, and no one knew whether she was really interested.

When a new appointee to the City Council, a preternaturally bright lawyer named Matthew Callister, quickly formed an alliance with the mayor, she was re-energized. Perhaps they might even persuade legislators to pass a strong-mayor bill, which would give Jones the power and authority she craved and would, perhaps, erase her Guinn-envy. But that measure was a non-starter, and the visions of Carson City were dancing in her head again.

At the annual Andre Agassi Foundation function in Las Vegas during the fall of 1995, she talked to Rogich about her musings. "Change parties and run for governor as a Republican," Rogich told her, "and I'll do anything for you."

"I'm a Democrat," Jones replied.

Still, if she ran, Jones wanted it to be different this time. She had no interest in confronting the power structure—and many of her friends—as she did in 1994. That had been an awful experience. Her campaign had no direction; she lashed out at the media; and she disintegrated during a second debate with Miller. This time, she wanted, as she'd been both times she ran for mayor, to be anointed.

When Kenny Guinn announced his candidacy in the winter of 1996, Jones immediately realized she would not be the anointee. She knew what was happening and it sickened her. All of her preconceptions about a white-male establishment picking one of their own were drummed home. Why not me, she wondered? Jones thought she was more qualified, had better ideas, and would be a better governor. But her visceral reaction was that she didn't have the gumption to do it all over again, to go against the Establishment for the second consecutive cycle.

Jones damaged herself, displaying her fatal lack of patience in all things, in November 1996. That's when she cut to the front of that extraordinarily long Election Day line to vote. A media sensation soon enveloped her—the Queen sashaying past the peasants—and she finally had to release an apology. The author of her statement was none other than Sig Rogich, who was deepening his friendship with the mayor.

During this time, Frankie Sue Del Papa was clearly the favorite gubernatorial choice of Democratic Party insiders, who believed she had more drawing power and did not have the poor track record of Jones in statewide races. When Del Papa decided to run in early 1997, Jones was almost relieved. She'd no longer have to think about the governorship; she might even help Del Papa get elected.

But later that year at a Democratic Party event, she had a searing experience. Maggie Tracy, a Democratic Party activist in the vanguard of the state's abortion-rights movement, approached Jones. As if she'd forgotten how much Jones had coveted the governorship, Tracy told the mayor how gratifying it was that the state would finally have a female governor, that Del Papa would be wonderful in the job. When Tracy walked away, Jones' precocious 13-year-old daughter, Katie, looked at her mother and declared, "That was rude." Yes, Jones thought again. Why not me?

Jones was relaxing at Harvey's resort near Lake Tahoe when Del Papa called her one Friday in late October 1997 to tell her she was quitting the race for governor. She seemed very sad to Jones, wistful about her personal life, saying she was tired of being alone. "I'm not up to this," she told Jones. "But if you decide to run, I'll be with you." In fact, it would be as if Guinn had two opponents, Del Papa told her, because she would do all she could for the Las Vegas mayor, especially in her home base of Northern Nevada.

The entire fate of the Democratic party's chances of defeating Guinn now rested with her, Jones realized. If she didn't announce her candidacy—and quickly—the race for governor would be over a full year before the election.

The timing for Jones could have been better. She had recently become involved with Richard Schuetz, a former executive of the ailing Stratosphere Tower and now a gaming-industry consultant, and the relationship was headed toward the altar. And, as she later remembered, "I was finally in a position where no one was mad at me. Why did I need to go piss off Billy [Vassiliadis] and Sig [Rogich]?" But the flip side was that Del Papa's departure had reignited Jones' passion to be governor. She really wanted it.

Rogich, though, was certain Jones would not run. He assured Vassiliadis, Ernaut, and others that she would not take on Guinn. They were friends; he had talked to her; she was out. Still, Rogich didn't want to leave anything to chance. He met with Jones and a mutual friend, Amy Ayoub, a financial consultant and sometime fundraiser, shortly after Del Papa announced her withdrawal. They sat down at Keuken Dutch, a restaurant not far from Rogich's house in the affluent Spanish Trail development in southwest Las Vegas. Rogich had a pitch to make to the mayor: Jones was so talented that Guinn would want her to be a part of his administration. She could, if she so desired, have the chairmanship of the state Gaming Commission. It was a clear quid pro quo—stay out and we'll take care of you. Rogich was offering Jones what may have been the state's most important appointed position. It was understood that he was speaking for Guinn, although Rogich had not cleared the appointment with the candidate. "I didn't think Kenny would say no," Rogich said later. Jones, though, recalled thinking that Rogich probably couldn't deliver on the promise. "I didn't think I'd ever get it," she said.

Unlike Rogich, Vassiliadis thought Jones might run. He knew how much she salivated at the thought of being governor. And he was concerned, too. He and Jones had worked since 1994 to heal the wounds inflicted by the gubernatorial primary campaign that Vassiliadis had orchestrated against her. They'd collaborated on an eminent-domain bill in Carson City that the city of Las Vegas and the gaming industry were behind. Their personal relationship had progressed to the point where they were friendly again—he had never had much of a relationship with Del Papa. And, in his heart, Vassiliadis was still a Democrat.

After Del Papa got out, Vassiliadis called Jones to see where her head was. She told him that she wasn't really looking at the race. But he knew her well enough that without a statement akin to William Tecumseh Sherman's famous definitive denial—"If nominated I will not run; if elected I will not serve"—the door was still open. So Vassiliadis called Ernaut and told him that if Jones did decide to get into the contest, it would be problematic for him. He'd probably have to step back from the Guinn campaign and be neutral. He was hoping, however, that he wouldn't have to make the choice.

Jones did nothing to tamp down speculation that she would enter the contest. She told Jane Ann Morrison of the *Review-Journal* that she would consider running against Guinn, "because nobody's talking about issues." Jones told Morrison, though, that her decision would be guided by personal considerations, including her three children and her budding relationship with Schuetz. Morrison quickly followed up with an "apres-Jones-le-deluge piece" in which Democrats confided that without the mayor, the race was lost.

Interestingly, though, U.S. Sen. Harry Reid expressed publicly what some of his advisers had been saying privately for weeks. Reid stated that he was not concerned about having a potent Democratic candidate in the top race. "Reid expressed little worry about that possibility," Morrison wrote. "He said Guinn's people told him that if the retired businessman faced token opposition, there wouldn't be the need for [Guinn's] camp to mount a heavy get-out-the-vote effort among Republicans."

"Guinn's people" in that story was code for Rogich, with whom Reid had a tumultuous relationship over the years. Rogich had been with Reid in his congressional bids of 1982 and 1984, then, after promising not to be, against him in his U.S. Senate race in 1986. But both men are the consummate political pragmatists and later operated on the "no permanent friends, no permanent enemies" principle and began talking again in the late 1980s. Rogich, as an adviser to President Bush, actually worked with Reid to help the freshman senator pass a bill designating a pristine section of Nevada as a national wilderness area. Their well-known collegiality gave rise to suspicions that there was a tit-for-tat arrangement between the two for the 1998 cycle: If Reid wouldn't recruit a candidate against Guinn, Rogich would make sure the Guinn campaign didn't help Republican Rep. John Ensign's campaign against Reid. That is, both men thought, if no viable Democrat challenged Guinn, he could coast to victory, without having to gin up Republican turnout, which would help Ensign.

Not all of Reid's advisers agreed with the scenario the senator bought from Rogich. What if Guinn, pressured by Ensign, didn't keep the Faustian bargain his guru had made with Reid? What if Guinn poured all that money he had been stockpiling into a GOP turnout effort? How could that not help Ensign? But at least at that time, Reid and others believed the no-candidate-against-Guinn-is-good-for-us hypothesis. Rogich had no problem making the promise, too. He and Ensign didn't get along. Ensign had never swooned before Rogich as other GOP candidates had, and the congressman's far-right views in some areas didn't jibe with Rogich's more moderate outlook.

Jones remained torn. She canceled a scheduled fundraiser designed to restock her mayoral piggybank, saying she didn't want to mislead donors. That was taken as a sign that she might actually get into the race. One Democratic consultant who met with her in late October 1997 said he thought she really wanted to run, but that the countervailing force was her impending marriage to Schuetz.

Pressure began to rain down on Jones from Democrats in Nevada and from Washington, including a conversation with Vice President Al Gore. Gore and Jones discussed that Gov. Miller was being floated as a possible ambassador to Mexico at that time—a job Miller had always coveted. If Miller received the appointment, mercurial Lt. Gov. Lonnie Hammargren would become acting governor. Jones and others believed that would hurt Guinn because Hammargren, his ample political baggage notwithstanding, would have the advantage of incumbency. She told Gore as much, but he rejoined that she should run whether or not

Miller left. Sure, Hammargren would eventually lose to Guinn, but he could force the GOP favorite to deplete his war chest, making him potentially vulnerable in the general election. Just before Del Papa receded, the *Review-Journal* ran a large spread on Hammargren, portraying him as an oddball and fueling Democratic hopes of a Miller-goes-south, Hammargren-goes-north scenario.

Everyone Jones talked to had an opinion, and many had an agenda, too. But one conversation had a greater impact on her than any other during this time. In late October, she chatted with D. Taylor, the political director for the Culinary Union. Jones figured that while the Culinary leaders would never have supported Del Papa because of their long-held animosity toward the attorney general, she had a decent chance of securing the backing of the state's largest union. She had quietly tried to negotiate an end to the Frontier strike, briefly acting as an intermediary between the union and her friend, Frontier matriarch Margaret Elardi.

Taylor gave it to her straight: "He said, 'Look, if you run, you'll just be the sacrificial lamb,'" Jones later recalled. "'Kenny has set himself up to take the middle ground. You'll end up on the liberal side. A moderate Republican running statewide in a changing Nevada, with registration tilting toward the GOP, will be very difficult to beat.'" He was giving her the unvarnished truth, also knowing that elements of the union movement were already in the Guinn camp. Even though she had never been seen as someone labor would die for, Jones would be a complication. As the mayor of Las Vegas, she couldn't have much effect on the union either way. "If anyone had the most impact on me, made me realize I was going to get skewered, it was D.," Jones said later.

Jones was almost certain by late October that she wouldn't run when Guinn called and asked if she wanted to sit down and talk. Why not? Jones thought. So on the night of Oct. 29, she agreed to meet Guinn at the coffee shop at the Desert Inn Country Club. The locale was convenient, because Jones had to be there later for a fundraiser to help legislative Democrats. They conversed for about an hour, with their later recollections having a Rashomon-like quality. Guinn told people that he thought Jones was angling for an appointment to his administration; the mayor saw Guinn as trying to offer her something to cement her decision to stay out of the race. As Jones and Guinn talked inside the first-floor coffee shop, Democrats on their way to the fundraiser upstairs did double takes as they passed by. Jones, their last hope in the governor's race, was breaking bread with Guinn. It was a signal that she wouldn't run, most of them felt. The shocking sighting was the talk of the fundraiser. There were grumbles, resigned sighs, and chatter about whether the party might avert an implosion if Jones indeed declined to run.

Two days later, on Oct. 31, two weeks and a day after Del Papa withdrew, Jones announced she would not run for governor. She lamented that Guinn would not be challenged on issues, but insisted she was refusing to run for family reasons: She wanted to spend more time with her fiancé and her three children. She told the Associated Press it was "the hardest call I've ever had to make." She was truly in agony.

That same day, Halloween and Nevada Day, the anniversary of the state's entrance into the Union, Guinn rode in a parade in Carson City with his wife, Dema. Gov. Bob Miller was in the procession, too, and the symbolism was unmistakable: The lame duck governor in front, his heir apparent in the back. The last obstacle had been removed to Guinn moving to the front seat in a little more than a year. Or so it seemed.

Jones' decision thrilled Guinn and his kitchen Cabinet. They knew that without Del Papa and Jones, the Democrats had no candidate capable of raising the money or putting on a credible contest. Even better, Jones' exit from the stage seemed to catalyze a cascade of good news for the Guinn folks as 1997 wound down.

First, Aaron Russo, the ex-Hollywood producer and federal-government hater, announced that Pierre Salinger, the one-time-JFK press secretary and current conspiracy theorist, would appear with him during the first week of November at a rally. An alternative health specialist was also on the program. This was pure theater, a joke, a perfect foil for Guinn.

Then, state Sen. Joe Neal, a veteran Democratic maverick, declared he might run for governor, saying the centerpiece of his campaign would be an attack on the casino industry. Sweet music to the Guinnites. They knew that not only could Neal not raise any money, but that most Democrats wouldn't eagerly embrace an anti-casino platform. In fact, some would distance themselves as fast and as far as they could from the state legislator's theme of assailing the state's most powerful special interest. If this is the Democratic candidate for governor, the Guinnites thought, bring him on.

They also calculated, as did many Democrats, that the impact further down the ticket could benefit Republicans, especially in critical legislative races. The only question was whether Harry Reid, who thrived on meddling in other races, would change his neutral stance and actively try to get someone in the race so he wouldn't be hurt by being associated, even if on the same dais, with Neal during the campaign.

Another sign of Democratic desperation came in the second week of November, when Assembly Speaker Joe Dini floated his name as a possible gubernatorial candidate. Dini, then 68, had no chance to win and he knew it. His political base was in the tiny town of Yerington in Northern Nevada and he could never raise the money to be competitive. But he also knew that the Democrats needed at least the appearance of competitiveness in the state's most important contest. As a veteran of three decades in Carson City, Dini was the longest-serving speaker in history, and might be able to gather enough resources to provide a believable facade, although a veneer of credibility is all it would be. With the Democrats controlling the Assembly by a relatively narrow margin of three seats, though, Dini was fretting about the impact of Neal at the top of the party's ticket, too.

The futility of what the Democrats were doing, though, was drummed home on the night of Nov. 14 at the Las Vegas Racquet Club, a sprawling recreation center near Las Vegas. There, Guinn held his first major fundraiser, a $500 per-person affair. The evening had all the trappings, as one Democratic attendee put it, of "a victory party." But it was more than that. Hundreds upon hundreds of people, running the gamut of special interests and Las Vegas' social strata, came to the event, desiring more than anything to be seen by the man they viewed as the presumptive governor.

When Ernaut had first scheduled the party, it was part of his plan to discourage Del Papa from continuing her quest. Such a show of strength and financial muscle would surely induce her to drop out after the financial-disclosure reports were released in February. But she was gone already, as was Jones. The throng that swarmed the grounds and boosted Guinn's coffers by $350,000, putting him close to $2 million, only served as an exclamation point to what appeared to be a victory celebration one year before the election.

With the Democrats in disarray after Del Papa and Jones departed the scene, the only concern among the Guinn advisers was the Republican primary. It was a minor one. Even if Secretary of State Dean Heller, Lt. Gov. Lonnie Hammargren, and gadfly Aaron Russo got into the race, Guinn's money would give him an insurmountable advantage.

As if they needed the help, fate continued to smile on

the Guinnites in December when the news came that Miller would not secure the Mexican ambassadorship. Thus, Hammargren would not be elevated to the governor's seat, which would have had the potential to embarrass the GOP and confer incumbency advantages on the lieutenant governor.

A few days later, Guinn sent out his first mail piece of the campaign, a colorful and expensive offering to voters. Emblazoned on the cover was the slogan, "When a person runs for governor of Nevada, you should know who he is." Yet Guinn's flier offered little about him beyond his resume and a few platitudes such as: "I believe that Nevada can give its people the best of tomorrows. Our ranching, mining, and tourism industries are rising to the challenges of the 21st century. I want to make sure our government and our education system do as well. Our future depends on it."

On. Dec. 10, 1997, Brendan Riley, the Associated Press' bureau chief in Carson City and a veteran of many decades of reporting in the state, essentially declared the race over in a story he put on the wire. "Election Year Hasn't Started, But Gov's Race Seems Certain," the headline read. Riley described how Guinn's "anointment" made his election "all but certain," considering that no major Democrat was going to run. The conventional wisdom from the political class had seeped into the mainstream media. It began to sound like a funereal chorus for the race when the *Las Vegas Sun's* Larry Henry piled on less than a week later with a story quoting Dini as saying the Democrats might not even have a candidate.

Not every dance step in the carefully choreographed waltz to Carson City, however, was quite so deftly executed. As the year ended, Guinn began what his campaign claimed would be a series of events called "Listening to Nevada," wherein he would receive the views of experts on a variety of topics. The first one, held at the Golden Nugget in downtown Las Vegas, focused on crime. Guinn, to the surprise of the impressive assemblage of law-enforcement types, asked few questions. Even after Clark County District Attorney Stew Bell pleaded with him to let the array of experts know what he wanted, the candidate had no questions. The meeting was much palaver and little substance, seemingly an attempt by his campaign to show that he cared about issues. The media wasn't kind, portraying the event as a stunt. And it proved to be the first and last stop in Guinn's abortive listening tour.

But even if the candidate wasn't saying much, the message was loud and clear by the time the actual election year arrived. Kenny of The Thousand Days could see the coronation ahead in November. Jones and Del Papa were gone. Russo would be a gnat, noisy but merely a nuisance. And even if Secretary of State Dean Heller and/or Lt. Gov. Lonnie Hammargren got into the race, time was running out and Guinn had most of the money and organization locked up.

The only hint of trouble on the horizon came from the Republican Party-sponsored initiative to hamstring union political participation, the so-called paycheck-protection proposal. But even that surely couldn't open enough of a rift in the party to cause Guinn any serious problems, could it? After all, there was no viable competitor on the horizon.

Yes, there was always the possibility that the unpredictable Jones could change her mind. But on Jan. 3, 1998, the mayor, shockingly, was diagnosed with breast cancer. She would be undergoing treatments for months. Her mind would be on anything but running for office.

The contest for governor, barring a miracle, was over.

Attorney General Frankie Sue Del Papa was a brief player in the campaign.

Physician Elias Ghanem was rewarded for his fundraising prowess with a seat on the Nevada Athletic Commission.

Lt. Gov. Lonnie Hammar-
gren, though a candidate,
was never a factor in the
1998 governor's race.

Secretary of State Dean
Heller came to the water's
edge, but didn't take a
dip.

Former Gov. Bob Miller (L) chats with his successor, Kenny Guinn, as Guinn's wife, Dema, looks on.

Pete Ernaut (L), Sig Rogich, and Steve Wark celebrate Kenny Guinn's victory.

Democratic gubernatorial candidates Joe Neal and Jan Jones share a light moment.

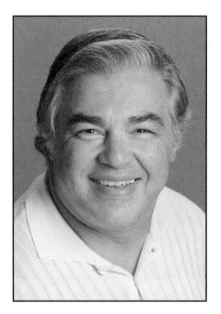

California transplant Aaron Russo was full of sound and fury in the Republican primary.

The gaming lobby strategists in Carson City: (L to R) Richard Bunker, Harvey Whittemore, Billy Vassiliadis, and Greg Ferraro.

Sig Rogich (L) and Billy Vassiliadis were the heart of R&R Advertising during the 1980s.

Attorney Frank Schreck has raised hundreds of thousands of dollars for Nevada candidates.

Gaming executive Mike Sloan is a key member of the industry's brain trust.

6

THE MAKING
OF A RACE

As 1997 came to a close, the Nevada Republican Party was suffused with euphoria. The governor's race had become an oxymoron. The GOP had a decent chance of picking up both congressional seats and was favored in most of the constitutional-officer contests. "Take the State in '98" was not just a slogan; it looked like it could become reality.

In that dizzy atmosphere, a Republican Party operative named Chuck Muth approached state GOP Chairman John Mason with an idea. Muth was Mason's eyes and ears in Southern Nevada. The chairman lived in Zephyr Cove, an enclave right on Lake Tahoe, isolated from the rest of the state. Mason loved the game of politics and reveled in being state chairman. But he paid little attention to the daily operations of the party apparatus and delegated most of the operational and ministerial duties to others. Muth and his friend, George Harris, a longtime Republican activist and the party's finance director, were the de facto party bosses in Las Vegas. Harris was also on retainer to Sheldon Adelson, chairman of Las Vegas Sands, Inc., and the bane of the Democratic Party for his avowed antipathy toward the Culinary Union. He was actively blocking the Culinary from trying to organize his new megaresort, the Venetian.

Muth told Mason late in 1997 that the time was right

for a so-called paycheck-protection initiative. The idea, first generated in Congress by GOP leaders, was to unlevel the partisan playing field by making it more difficult for unions to raise money for political action; its handle, paycheck protection, made it seem as if the beneficent Republicans were interested in shielding union workers' take-home pay from their avaricious leaders. The initiative, similar to those in other states, including neighboring California, would force union leaders to get permission from the rank and file before using dues for political action. Mason, seeing no downside, readily agreed to allow the party to sponsor the initiative.

So Muth penned an eight-page screed, signed by Mason, that was headlined, "Are Today's Big Labor Union Bosses the Mike Tysons of American Politics?" Capitalizing on the notoriety of the pugilist's recent savagery in the ring against Evander Holyfield, Muth's inflammatory epistle accused AFL-CIO boss John Sweeney of "the political equivalent of biting the Republicans' ear" with the millions spent by unions during the 1996 cycle. "The question is," Muth continued, "having been bitten once by labor bosses in 1996, will Republicans be ready for more 'political ear-biting' in the 1998 campaigns—and will we have the money and resolve necessary to defend ourselves?" Muth and Mason knew that Adelson, a billionaire, would be only too happy to help fund the effort to collect signatures and qualify the ballot question. It was almost a sure thing—and the capper to what was shaping up to be a Republican sweep that year in Nevada.

Neither Mason nor Muth saw any reason to inform Kenny Guinn or any of his advisers—not even his top two political confidants, Sig Rogich or Pete Ernaut—of their plan. Nor did it strike them as dissonant with Guinn's quiet attempt to court labor support. After all, Guinn had no Democratic opponent, so how could it hurt him?

❖ ❖ ❖

Guinn, and even more so, his kitchen Cabinet, were incensed when they learned about the state party's plan to put a paycheck-protection initiative on the ballot. Their reasons for being upset were multifarious. For one, though Guinn didn't have an opponent, there was no reason to energize labor during Campaign '98. It could only hurt Republicans and force Guinn to take a stand on an issue that could generate opposition—from the left if he were for it, and from the right if he were against it.

There were personal reasons, too: Guinn's campaign manager, Ernaut, and some of his close advisers, including Billy Vassiliadis, had warm relationships with labor, especially the Culinary Union's hierarchy. What's more, the paycheck-protection efforts surely would be funded by Sheldon Adelson, who was reviled by some of the Guinnites, especially Vassiliadis. Vassiliadis' largest client was the Las Vegas Convention and Visitors Authority, and he had been an Adelson critic since the days when the casino boss was the head of COMDEX, a computer trade show he eventually sold for close to a billion dollars. Adelson's set-tos with the Convention Authority over exhibitor rates were the stuff of legend; a mutual disdain had not abated.

Sig Rogich also felt a sense of betrayal by the paycheck-protection plan. He and Mason, whose campaign for lieutenant governor he had overseen in 1994, were supposedly friends. Why had the state chairman not informed him or Guinn of what he was doing? Not only was Guinn leading the ticket, he was the de facto governor, for crying out loud. Rogich felt he should have been told.

Labor reacted almost immediately to the news of the GOP strategy. Blackie Evans, the longtime head of the AFL-CIO, wrote to Mason in early December, laughably claiming that his group was a "non-partisan organization" and decrying the chairman's fundraising letter. Union leaders put out the word that they were considering a ballot question of their own: to ban corporations from making campaign donations without a vote of their shareholders. It was a bril-

121

liant tactic. The labor folks knew it would remind the only corporations in Nevada that really matter—casinos—of their stake in squelching the GOP initiative.

The unions also reacted out of fear: The leaders knew that the initiative was inherently popular—polls would show the concept of forcing union leaders to ask whether dues could be used for political purposes would have wide voter appeal. The main reason they didn't want it on the ballot was they knew it might pass.

Ernaut remembered having a chat with Guinn about the proposal. "It could be the greatest single lightning rod for Democrats in the history of Nevada politics," Ernaut thought. "I told Kenny, 'If they put this on the ballot, you'll have a huge ground war coming at you.'"

Rogich and Ernaut brought in a couple of moderate state senators, Mark James and Randolph Townsend, to try to talk Mason out of the initiative during a late December conference call. They suggested to the chairman that he let Adelson take up the cause and leave the party out of it. But Mason refused to recede, insisting he had invested the party's credibility.

As New Year's Day of the election year loomed, Guinn released his massive list of campaign contributors. It showed that in the nearly two years he'd been running, Guinn had accumulated $2.5 million in donations. His handlers, as well as Guinn, went to pains to emphasize that the hundreds of contributors on the thick report indicated they were indeed running a broad-based campaign. "If this doesn't signify grass roots, I don't know what does," Guinn told the *Review-Journal's* Jane Ann Morrison. The campaign also went to great lengths to point out to the media that only a third of the contributions came from gaming companies, a relatively small amount for a candidate accused of being anointed, they insisted. But this was a ruse: They had purposely not added in the hundreds of thousands that had been personally contributed by casino executives, their spouses, and others with ties to the industry. The actual percentage was nearly half, or $1.1 million, including the $300,000 in checks from the Circus Circus properties. Guinn and company's obvious skittishness about being tagged as gaming's candidate only served to highlight the issue even more in reports by media members, who tallied the additional contributions and did the math.

A few days later, State Sen. Joe Neal, an advocate of raising the casinos' gross-receipts tax who would surely highlight the anointment, formally announced he would run for governor. His candidacy, while not a direct threat to Guinn, could affect the GOP contender. What if ticket-leading U.S. Sen. Harry Reid now decided to try to find someone to knock off Neal so he wouldn't cause problems for other party candidates lower on the ticket? But who? Del Papa was out. Jones had just announced she had breast cancer. It was a concern, but there was still no one out there.

On the Republican side, though, it was a different story. Aaron Russo, who reported on his disclosure form that he had poured $300,000 of his own money into the contest, was definitely running. Secretary of State Dean Heller was still encouraging rumblings that he might run an insurgent campaign against Guinn. In fact, Heller took on the gaming industry for anointing Guinn in a story in the *Reno Gazette-Journal* on Jan. 3 that was headlined, "Heller Weighs Entering Race Against Guinn." He told the newspaper he was still considering a primary bid, because he didn't think the casinos should be selecting contenders for "pre-marked ballots. I do not believe the public feels they have a choice at this point in time," Heller told the newspaper.

When called for comment, Ernaut, stunned by this broadside from his friend and former colleague, gave an uncharacteristically tepid response, saying Guinn had broad support and was not the beneficiary of a "deep-seated conspiracy."

Ernaut waited a day before deciding how to approach

Heller, whom he didn't want in the race for personal and professional reasons. Before he'd signed on to be Guinn's campaign manager, Ernaut had taken an afternoon with Heller in Carson City to tell him that he still remembered the pact the pair had made in the Assembly never to run campaigns against each other. Heller had told him that he still wasn't sure whether he would run, but that Ernaut was relieved of his obligation.

A few days after the story ran, Ernaut called Heller. He asked his old friend why he had attacked Guinn, telling him he had accepted poor advice in doing so. Heller became angry. He told Ernaut that he didn't have to answer to him or anybody else and that it did indeed look like the industry was being heavy-handed. Ernaut, his fuse lit, exploded, accusing Heller of self-righteous hypocrisy, saying he knew him when he was eager to accept casino money, especially after Ernaut sold him on the idea of running for office years ago on the way to an event at Harvey's Tahoe. Heller concluded the tense conversation by advising Ernaut that it might be better if the two didn't talk during the rest of the campaign.

Ernaut hung up thinking the war was on, and that something had to be done. He wasn't sure that Heller's wealthy in-laws would mortgage the family's future by funding Heller's campaign, but he didn't want to take any chances. And though he believed that with Heller and Russo and Hammargren in the race, Guinn would still be the heavy favorite, the simpler strategy was to ensure as few candidates as possible. It was the same course Ernaut and others had adopted with Del Papa— shove the potential opposition off the field.

Ernaut telephoned Guinn's Southern Nevada campaign chief, Terry Murphy, and the grass-roots maven, Steve Wark, and asked them to oversee a letter-writing campaign from Guinn supporters based on the *Gazette-Journal* article. He wanted the letters to commend Guinn for fully disclosing his contributions and chastise Heller for his criticism.

As Murphy and Wark saw to their task, their office

suitemate, Bill Gregory, the former assemblyman turned lobbyist, asked them what they were doing. They told him. Gregory, party to that long-ago pact with Ernaut and Heller never to run against each other, decided to call the secretary of state to try to tamp down the hostilities. Instead, Heller was furious when he learned from Gregory about the letter-writing campaign. He called Ernaut at home and laid him out.

Then Heller informed the media about what was happening, expressing outrage about the letter-writing tactic. Heller followed up on Jan. 5, 1998, with a speech to an activist group, the Republican Men's Club of Las Vegas, in which he stressed the importance of issues. But he added: "Nobody gives a five-thousand-dollar contribution and says they don't care how someone stands on issues. Nobody gives a three-hundred-thousand-dollar contribution without a feeling on where someone stands on issues." Despite the obvious reference to the Circus Circus donation to Guinn and the implication that Guinn would be a rollover for the casino industry, Heller risibly told the audience, "I'm not up here to bash any particular candidate." By virtue of his willingness to publicly take on Guinn and contrast himself with him, Heller seemed closer than ever, thanks to the incident with Ernaut, to entering the contest.

As Guinn's team fretted about paycheck protection creating a rift with labor and the possibility of a nettlesome Heller candidacy, problems on the left were developing, too. U.S. Sen. Harry Reid indeed had come to the conclusion that even if Rogich could keep his promise about not ginning up the GOP grass-roots organization, he had to make sure that Joe Neal was not the Democratic nominee. Reid knew how difficult a candidate Rep. John Ensign would be against him and he couldn't afford to take a chance with a weak and polarizing candidate such as Neal.

Reid and his campaign advisers believed that, with Frankie Sue Del Papa and Jan Jones out of the picture, no one could defeat Guinn. But that wasn't the point. The point was that Neal could damage the image of the Democratic Party by leading the ticket. Reid would constantly have to distance himself from the state senator, so he needed to get a much less controversial candidate into the contest to knock off Neal. Reid had a history of persuading and dissuading contenders in other campaigns. But this was his political life, not someone else's. And he was deadly serious.

"How he [Neal] hurts us is that he frames the issues so that every Democratic candidate can be asked where you stand on his positions," one prominent Democrat said in early January. "They will say, 'He's your candidate for governor.' And he won't bring in any money. We're better off defeating him in a primary."

So in early January, Reid settled on a former state senator and ex-chairman of the state Ethics Commission, Spike Wilson. Wilson had challenged Rep. Jim Gibbons in 1996 and been destroyed by a landslide. His campaign manager, Larry Werner, was a Reid legislative aide who took a leave to oversee that race and was now, in 1998, running Reid's campaign. Wilson was just what Reid was looking for. He was respected by the political elite, adored by the media and, best of all, he was milquetoast. Wilson wouldn't make waves. Reid knew he couldn't defeat Guinn, but Wilson would be able to get enough money and votes to beat Neal and ensure Reid didn't have to run with the state senator in the fall. There was one slight problem: Even after Reid floated the idea, Wilson had no interest in running. But it signaled what was to come—an all-out effort to ensure Neal would not be on the ballot in November.

Neal was already garnering a higher profile. After Guinn gave what his campaign touted as his first major policy speech in late January—to the Greater Reno-Sparks Chamber of Commerce about educational accountability—the media called Neal for the Democratic response.

❖ ❖ ❖

Less than a month into the election year and the euphoria of late '97 had dissipated inside the Guinn campaign. The paycheck-protection initiative was causing a split within the Republican Party and inviting a primary campaign against Guinn. It also was giving Democrats hope and forcing Guinn to do what he hadn't done previously: take a position on a controversial issue. The fact that his campaign had insulated him in a cocoon of money and campaign consultants had served him well in his first two years, erasing potential opponents and leaving little to chance. But now, with Heller thinking of making a bid and Neal's candidacy encouraging Reid to find a better Democrat, it was no longer so simple.

By late January, Lt. Gov. Lonnie Hammargren was telling people he was all but certain to run. But what really worried the Guinnites was that the party structure had been hijacked by supporters of paycheck protection, including the Venetian's Sheldon Adelson, who was profoundly skeptical of Guinn's courtship of labor. Adelson, along with his right-hand man, Bill Weidner, attended a Republican meeting in Southern California in mid-January with state Chairman John Mason. And with Mason's Southern Nevada surrogates, Chuck Muth and George Harris, pushing for paycheck protection and aligned with Hammargren, the Guinn folks believed they had to act.

First, Guinn moved to shore up his base in advance of the upcoming Clark County and state party conventions. On Jan. 23, he mailed a letter to all members of the Clark County Central Committee, the dozens of activists who were party regulars. Guinn was attempting to declare, despite any rumbles emanating from Russo or elsewhere, that he was indeed a real Republican. In fact, the letter obliquely referred to Russo: "Please beware of candidates for any office that tell you what you want to hear without going through the rigors of informing you how they intend to get there.

The last thing the GOP needs in this campaign season is noisy rhetoric." Guinn, the numbers man who had studied the state budget, was incensed that Russo was promising to reduce high motor-vehicle-registration fees to $35 without telling voters where he would find the savings. In the missive, Guinn also called the party platform the "unifying symbol of what we are as Republicans," and he alerted the faithful that he would even inform them about issues that weren't within his purview as governor. That is, he was sending a signal that he was a Republican, through and through.

Attached were two sheets with classic conservative positions, designed to blunt any impression that he was a Democrat in Republican garb. Despite his dalliance with labor, he "supported Nevada's right-to-work laws." He backed the Second Amendment, he told the regulars. Message: I'm pro-gun. And despite his initial claims to being pro-choice, he came out in the letter against late-term abortion and said he supported "parental notification for minor children and informed consent on the part of physician and mother."

Then, on Jan. 26, Guinn released a statement on paycheck protection. He was against it. The statement read: "As a Republican, I was disappointed and angered by the blanket anti-Republican attacks by the national AFL-CIO in 1996. However, two wrongs don't make a right, and I do not want to see the divisiveness and gridlock created in Washington, D.C., come to Nevada.

"This initiative would limit participation in the political process and inject more governmental intrusion into our lives. I refuse to waste time on factional bickering when Nevadans have important issues to discuss—issues like education reform, taxation, traffic congestion, domestic violence, senior citizen needs, and government accountability." Issues, however, that Guinn hadn't discussed yet in any depth.

In response, Lt. Gov. Lonnie Hammargren quickly announced his support for paycheck protection. Clark County Republican Party Chairman Milton Schwartz declared, "I think [Guinn] stands alone on the issue." It was an astonishing turn of events: The man leading the Republican ticket was being isolated by those who theoretically were his core supporters, because he was taking a position that was antithetical to their wishes.

The Guinn folks, trying to stanch the hemorrhaging, called a summit on Jan. 28 at the Airport Plaza Hotel in Reno. The party, apparently undaunted by Guinn's opposition, was going ahead with an announcement that week of what it was now calling, for public-relations purposes, the "Workers' Rights Initiative." State Chairman John Mason, several elected officials, and the Guinn folks attended the gathering.

Rogich, according to one insider, "blasted Mason. He tried to explain to the chairman that the Republican Party should be there for the presumptive nominee for governor, not for one guy to screw labor, no matter how much money he gave to Mason." That was a reference to Adelson, who many elected officials thought should take up the initiative on his own, not with the party's blessing. Rogich even went so far as to invoke Frank Fahrenkopf, the former Renoite and erstwhile general chairman of the national GOP and now a gaming-industry lobbyist in Washington, as being opposed to the party embracing the initiative. Mason retorted that Fahrenkopf had told him just the opposite. The disagreement led to a conference call among Mason, Ernaut, and Fahrenkopf. Fahrenkopf later denied having told Mason that he thought the party should be the vehicle, but he was clearly mortified that his conversation with the chairman had become public.

Guinn's growing intimacy with labor was also a topic of discussion at the meeting, and one of concern to state Senate Majority Leader Bill Raggio, perhaps the most influential Northern Nevadan. Raggio had been hearing rumblings that Guinn's attempt to cozy up to labor included promises to sign a bill allowing collective bargaining for state employees—legislation Raggio had scuttled for years. After the meeting, Guinn released a statement saying he believed state employees should be paid more, but that collective bargaining was not the answer. That contradicted what labor leaders whispered Guinn had assured them in advance of the AFL-CIO convention the previous fall.

If the Guinn folks wondered whether they'd made an impact on Mason at the Airport Plaza meeting, they didn't have to wait long for the answer. The chairman was torn—torn between his beliefs in the initiative, his gratitude toward Adelson for his donations, and his loyalty to Guinn and Ernaut. He also had his ego at stake—he had started paycheck protection, and he didn't want to look as if he had given in.

Gratitude and ego won out over loyalty. Two days later, the party began airing radio spots touting the initiative. And the following week, the state GOP filed the petition with the secretary of state's office, cryptically acknowledging only "rookie mistakes" in the early going and announcing the hiring of a professional signature-gathering firm. Ernaut & Co. were furious at what they saw as Mason's duplicity, but they weren't worried. Sure, the California interloper, Russo, was fulminating in the media about Guinn being a "Democrat at heart" who was trying to "cuddle up" to unions. But still no Democrat was available who could exploit the situation.

During the next few weeks, Russo and Lt. Gov. Lonnie Hammargren snared news coverage. Russo touted a contradictory education plan that promised savings, teacher salary increases, and lower taxes, all at the same time. Hammargren, meanwhile, was being courted to run for Congress. It was a phony romance—the suitors were Guinn surrogates. Guinn didn't fear Hammargren in the governor's race, but he and his advisers preferred not to have him in the contest. If they could woo him into the congressional race, it would be a perfect marriage of convenience. No one thought he could defeat the Democratic front-runner, Shelley Berkley. But that wasn't the point. The point was about clearing the field so as to leave nothing to chance.

The utility of "no opponent is a good opponent" strategy was highlighted on Feb. 24, when the first poll of the governor's race was released by the *Las Vegas Review-Journal*. It showed Guinn ahead of presumptive Democratic nominee Joe Neal by only 11 points, with 41 percent of voters undecided. The numbers were not the sign of a juggernaut.

Good news came, though, in early March, as word reached the Guinn camp that Secretary of State Heller would not enter the race. Despite his saber-rattling and fury with Ernaut a few months earlier, Heller had decided to take the path of least resistance to re-election. Heller and his guru, Don Carlson, had enjoyed needling the powers that be. But he would be risking too much; he would have had to give up his job as secretary of state to run in what would probably be a futile challenge to Guinn.

Around that time, the Guinn inner circle gathered in the Las Vegas conference room at Forsythe-Francis, where Ernaut had worked and whose principal, Steve Forsythe, was doing the media buying. At the meeting, Vassiliadis told the group that he had been approached by one of Heller's friends, a Carson City businessman named Kurt Brown, about making a deal. Heller was willing to get out of the race, Vassiliadis said Brown had told him, but wondered what he could get in return. Perhaps a clear shot at being lieutenant governor? Guinn slowly sat back in his chair and contemplated the proposal for a moment or two. Then he gave a non-verbal answer: He pointed his middle finger toward the ceiling.

A few days later, Heller called and asked me to meet him at the Gold Coast Hotel off the Las Vegas Strip. I ordered a beer and he a Coke at a casino bar and he asked if we could go somewhere more private. We rode the elevator to his room, and as we sipped our drinks, he told me he wanted me to be one of the first to know: He was not going to run for governor; he was seeking re-election as secretary of state. At only 37, with several young children and the prospect of taking on the state's entire political Establishment, he'd decided not to jeopardize his career. In a Sunday column about Heller's decision, which ran in the *Review-Journal* on the Ides of March, I once again declared that Guinn had nothing to beware, that the governor's race was over. No viable Democrats or Republicans were left.

Two months remained before the two-week candidate filing period opened. The Guinn folks simply needed to run out the clock. Heller was gone. Neal was a perfect foil on the Democratic side. Their only worries, if they could be so named, were Russo and Hammargren. Despite all the noise over paycheck protection, Guinn's path to Carson City seemed relatively unobstructed. Even that tempest seemed to be ebbing. Repeated pounding on Mason had resulted in plans to set up outside committees to oversee the union-dues initiative—at least to give the appearance of distance from the party. The Guinn folks were also moving to control the Clark County and state conventions, both of which would occur before the filing period ended. They began putting out the word that their organizational strength had assured they would dominate the delegates at the Clark County meeting, slated for late March.

The Guinn team also had some concern about the portrayal of their man as an issueless front for the power elite. They had hoped Guinn's late January speech about education would help dispel that notion, but it had proved to be a one-day non-event. They needed more to show that there was substance behind all the money and consultants. On March 16, the campaign issued a news release announcing a "major policy speech by Republican gubernatorial candidate Kenny Guinn addressing the needs of Nevada's senior citizens" two days hence. The proposal, though, turned out to be anything but major. Guinn, speaking to a seniors group in Las Vegas, suggested expanding a 25-year-old program

that allows certain senior citizens with low incomes to receive property tax rebates. This undertaking would cost
about $3 million, insignificant compared to the general-
fund budget of $1.6 billion. Even so, Guinn couldn't tell
reporters where he would find the .002% of the state budget and he ludicrously referred to the bite-sized plan as "priority one."

On the eve of the county convention, Guinn took time
to help organize a fundraiser for Rep. Jim Gibbons, who
was likely to have minimal opposition in his re-election bid
for the House. It was a testament to Rogich's influence in
the campaign and the state. He organized the event, which
was to feature his former boss, ex-President George Bush.
And it would be held at the home of Gary Primm, the chief
of Primadonna Resorts, which employed Rogich as a consultant and where he served on the board of directors. The
fundraiser also showed how ephemeral political disputes can
be, as it cemented a relationship between Gibbons and
Rogich, who had overseen Cheryl Lau's unsuccessful 1994
gubernatorial campaign against Gibbons.

As the convention neared, the Guinn forces continued
to feel confident about their delegate count. For one, they
had Steve Wark, their grass-roots coordinator and an expert
in organizing party conventions. A decade earlier, Wark had
used the power of the Christian right to take over a Republican convention and get himself elected state chairman.

Guinn's forces had another reason for optimism, too:
They were buying delegates. On March 24, Guinn sent a
letter to all the delegates to the Clark County Republican
convention and made them an offer: "I know that this weekend may be an inconvenience in time as well as finances. I
would like to make it easier financially for you to participate in the convention by having the Guinn campaign take
care of your ($25) registration fee. This is just a small token
of our gratitude for the selfless giving of your time."

Russo was apoplectic—it seemed like a constant condition for the California carpetbagger—about what he saw as

Guinn trying to buy the convention. But as the Clark County faithful convened the weekend of March 27, the Guinnites weren't worried. They had left little to chance. Sure, a few party crazies, a few Russo rabble-rousers, would attend. But they would get their people elected as delegates to the state convention, so they could control that gathering, too. Everything was under control. Or so they thought.

On Friday night, the convention erupted into bedlam as Russo and his backers complained about a vote on a key parliamentary measure involving the seating of delegates. Guinn backers accused Russo's adherents of pushing and shoving, even spitting.

When Guinn's top advisers heard about the scene late that night, they were mortified. They were supposed to have had the convention wired. "When you've got the presumptive nominee for governor not having control of his convention, that's pretty bad," Vassiliadis remembered.

At about 6:30 on Saturday morning, Vassiliadis' phone rang. It was Guinn, telling him that he'd wanted to punch Russo in the mouth, he was so incensed. Vassiliadis advised Guinn not to return to the convention and forgo his speech. Guinn fretted that he would appear to be timorous, intimidated by Russo. Vassiliadis said that he would rather see news stories about Guinn not showing up than about a physical set-to between the governor-to-be and Russo or his supporters. Fifteen minutes later, Rogich had joined the conversation. He immediately agreed with Vassiliadis' assessment. Vassiliadis advised Rogich to attend in Guinn's place to keep an eye on the proceedings.

The scene Saturday was even worse than the previous evening. Russo gave a 15-minute speech lambasting Guinn as a "counterfeit Republican" and intoned his rhyming campaign mantra: The choice was between "the status quo or Russo."

Guinn campaign operatives marched around the convention floor, wearing Team Guinn T-shirts and hats, along with headphones. They looked like an army trying to quell a popular uprising. The Guinn delegates sat passively in rows in the back of the banquet room, waiting for orders from the floor generals. Eventually, Clark County Chairman Milton Schwartz threatened to evict Russo. After his acolytes surrounded Russo, making a human wall, Schwartz called for security.

Beyond the chaos that enveloped the affair, though, was more evidence for the Guinn team that the enemy was within: not just Russo and his followers, nor Mason and paycheck protection, but Adelson, the casino mogul and Republican Party donor. Adelson had made his mark in Nevada politics two years earlier by funneling hundreds of thousands of dollars to a Clark County Commission candidate through the party to evade campaign finance laws. His plan had been facilitated by then-party finance boss George Harris, still a GOP activist, but now also on Adelson's payroll. Since then, Adelson's influence in the party had become pervasive. At the convention, one of his lawyers had filed a brief questioning the seating of Guinn delegates. In addition, Milton Schwartz made sure that Adelson's right-hand man, Bill Weidner, was kept abreast of all convention-related developments. Adelson was furious that Guinn was against paycheck protection because he was determined— his critics would say obsessed—with restricting the power of the Culinary Union. He and his minions, though, while flirting with Lt. Gov. Hammargren, a friend of Harris, didn't seem to have a clear plan. But they obviously wanted to hurt Guinn at the convention and beyond.

Kenny Guinn was always fundamentally against paycheck protection, those close to him insisted later. But he was caught between Republicans committed to the concept, including the Legislature's two highest GOP leaders, Bill Raggio and Lynn Hettrick, and his desire to placate his new labor friends. "He was seeking some safe water and in doing so, he stumbled and bungled several times," one of his advisers remembered.

Indeed, the day the Clark County Republican Convention ended, Guinn told a TV interviewer, "I'm not for either side at this point." That, of course, flew in the face of the press release he'd issued earlier in the year announcing his opposition to the plan. But as much as he and his team hoped that the issue would not be a defining point of Campaign '98, the AFL-CIO was moving to make it a litmus test for candidates. On March 30, AFL-CIO Secretary-Treasurer Blackie Evans sent a letter to Republican candidates asking for their "written position on the anti-worker petition that has been promoted by some anti-union individuals ..." Evans also asked for a position on collective bargaining and the state's right-to-work laws.

Guinn appeared lost on the issue. Worse, the media continued to focus on the convention and his refusal to appear after the Friday-night debacle. Veteran reporter Cy Ryan penned a piece comparing what he implied was Guinn's abhorrence for confrontation to former Gov. Mike O'Callaghan's decision not to "shy away from the state Democratic Convention when there was a threat of violence." Ryan followed up a few days later with a piece hinting that Lt. Gov. Hammargren, emboldened by the Russo-Guinn farce, was considering a bid for governor more seriously than ever. The *Review-Journal's* Jane Ann Morrison also did a story about the fallout from the convention, quoting some Guinn supporters as worried about their man's refusal to confront Russo. And Russo was highlighting Guinn's problems by going to court to ask for a reduction in fees for the state convention, slated for mid-April.

If Guinn had had a serious opponent, the atmospherics would have been ominous. But polls showed Guinn destroying Russo by 20 points. The Democrats were still looking for an alternative to Neal. In fact, two prominent Democrats, Gov. Bob Miller and Sen. Richard Bryan, announced in mid-April that they would not support the prospective party standard-bearer because Neal favored the proposed nuclear-waste dump at Yucca Mountain, that most incendiary of Nevada issues. Reid, who was desperately reaching for an alternative to Neal, commented, "I can't say I won't support Joe." But as Neal spoke to the Democrats' Clark County gathering on April 19 and attacked the gaming industry, Reid knew he had to redouble his efforts to find a blander candidate who would not cost the party—and especially him—votes in November. The filing period was less than a month away.

The state Republican convention in late April proved to be boring compared to the county carnival. Russo actually extended an olive branch to Guinn, the speeches were uneventful, and the Establishment forces rebuffed Russo's attempt to oust Mason as party chairman. The main speaker, though, was a reminder of the disharmony just below the surface. J. Patrick Rooney, the prime mover behind the California ballot proposition on paycheck protection, showed where the party insiders still stood. They cared about the issue, believed in it, wanted it passed.

But a general spirit of unity prevailed. Guinn gave one of his better speeches of the campaign. Russo and his followers didn't create a scene. The biggest news of the convention instead revolved around Hammargren, who all but announced his gubernatorial candidacy during a speech to the faithful. But that was of little concern to the Guinn folks and received scant coverage from the media.

Filing for office opened a few days after the convention climaxed. On May 7, Neal filed for governor, insisting the gaming industry had too much power over politics and government and should pay more into the state treasury. In his report of Neal's filing, *Review-Journal* reporter Sean Whaley mentioned that a variety of Democratic Party officials, including Reid, had announced they would not support his campaign." Reid, who had been unsuccessful in finding an alternative, later asked for a retraction, saying he had "not taken an official position on Neal's candidacy." Unofficially, though, he was at the end of his rope, settling on a last resort, state Sen. Mike Schneider, an ambitious legislator who had no chance to defeat Guinn, but who probably could knock off Neal and be a placeholder for the Democrats in November.

On May 13, 1998, Kenny Guinn filed for governor, stating he had raised $3 million and would spend a maximum of $3.5 million. He reaffirmed his opposition to paycheck protection, saying it represented government intrusion into private business, and invoked education as his main priority. He was still relatively unknown and had not defined himself through an early TV campaign, as had once been contemplated by his advisers.

But they had abandoned that strategy once Del Papa dropped out and Jones decided not to run. Why waste money defining Guinn for a non-race? If Guinn couldn't defeat Aaron Russo, Lonnie Hammargren, or Joe Neal, then he didn't deserve to be governor, they felt. In only five days filing would be over, and with Guinn's war chest, his grass-roots and institutional support, and the major Democratic candidates cleared out of the race, the rest of the campaign should be a breeze.

7

THE FLY IN
THE ANOINTMENT

In late 1997, after she had agonizingly decided not to run for governor, Las Vegas Mayor Jan Jones had to face a much more personal crisis. After a routine mammogram, her doctor, Joe Quagliana, thought he felt something, perhaps a lump in her breast. Neither he nor Jones thought it was anything, but he removed the mass and performed a biopsy nevertheless. On Jan. 3, the biopsy results revealed the awful reality: breast cancer.

Jones released the information to the media a few days later, saying she was having more tests to determine a course of treatment. Her fiancé, Richard Schuetz, a former gaming executive, was incredibly supportive. Jones discovered she had to have surgery, which was scheduled for Jan. 20. For Schuetz to be kept totally in the loop, to get all the information from her doctors, they had to be married. So Jones and Schuetz accelerated their timetable for their nuptials and 10 days before she was scheduled to have the operation, they were married in a small private ceremony.

Despite her pending surgery, Jones pushed ahead with plans to deliver her first State of the City speech at the Jan. 26 City Council meeting. (It was later postponed.) She wanted to project a business-as-usual veneer, saying she was looking ahead to the millennium. The lumpectomy, performed at the Joyce Eisenberg Keefer Breast Center in Los Angeles, went off without a hitch. No signs of cancer were found in Jones' lymph nodes. The chemotherapy and radiation were sure to be debilitating—they would last for several months—and were scheduled to start in a few weeks. A few days later, she returned to City Hall and declared that despite the treatments in her future, she was eager to take the time to educate people about the disease.

Before she started her treatment, though, Jones had a couple of pieces of business to finish. First, she hastily pushed through a newly created six-figure job for one of her husband's former employees, a woman named Ann Holland. Jones engineered Holland's hiring as a deputy city manager, throwing away political caution, because of her rush to leave town to get treated. A few days later, a government gadfly named Robert Rose filed a complaint against Jones with the state Ethics Commission, alleging cronyism.

Jones delivered her State of the City address on Feb. 9. She spoke about her general ideas for how Las Vegas should look in the new millennium. She emphasized restricting neighborhood gaming and doing more regional planning—not exactly bite-sized or bland ideas. As if to send a message along with her bold pronouncements, Jones implied she planned on seeking another term in 1999. "I want to *bring* this city into the new millennium," she said.

Jones clearly wanted to project an image of energy and commitment to dispel any fears about her health. She put on a brave face, but most observers believed they were witnessing the end of her political career.

For a woman suffering from breast cancer, Jones was amazingly active. Her State of the City call for a ban on slots in neighborhoods received tremendous attention and commentary. It was typical Jan Jones—provocative yet not well-thought-out. She was proposing the ban despite having applied only two years earlier for a license to operate a tavern with slots not far from a neighborhood and a park. This revelation, coming a week after her speech, was embarrassing, but as usual, it didn't slow her down. She was soon garnering national attention for her slot-restriction proposal, including a major story in the *Los Angeles Times* on March 16, then an appearance on "The Today Show" on April 1. As Kenny Guinn was slogging through the paycheck-protection nightmare and navigating through internal party warfare, Jones was garnering a national profile on an issue with inherent appeal. Among those helping her on the issue was Sig Rogich, who crafted statements and messages for the public. And why not? Jones was no threat to Guinn now.

Jones was feeling well, too. She was having chemotherapy treatments every three weeks and by the end of April, she was talking about the disease in the past tense. "I don't have cancer, I had cancer," Jones said at a news conference with Dr. Quagliana. He marveled that Jones had not had a sick day during the chemotherapy sessions.

Jones was doing so well, in fact, that her friend, Matthew Callister, started whispering to her that she should reconsider running for governor. Callister was a brilliant state assemblyman who had left Carson City for a Las Vegas City Council appointment. During his short stint on the council, from 1995 to 1997, he and Jones were inseparable. They liked each other politically and personally. Then, in the spring 1997 election, political disaster struck: Callister was ousted by 63 votes. But he and Jones remained close. And part of Callister's motivation, surely, was that if Jones were elected governor, she could punch his ticket back into the political arena.

Jones scoffed at Callister's suggestions. Granted, she was disgusted with Guinn's campaign, telling people it was vapid and arrogant as it proceeded toward a fait accompli. She felt Guinn's handlers had made a joke of the electoral process—or at least that the joke should be played with her instead of him. But what could she do about it?

At least take a poll, Callister implored her repeatedly. Then she could really make up her mind.

Finally, she agreed to let a survey be done, as she recalled, "just to shut Matt up." She hardly gave it another thought as the candidate filing period opened.

On May 7, the day Joe Neal filed for governor, Jones taped a radio show on the Las Vegas news station, KNEWS-970, and let her feelings about the Guinn campaign show. "What happened to the whole idea of democracy?" Jones asked interviewer Fred Lewis, lamenting that the public didn't have a choice. "Well, why not run yourself?" Lewis asked. "It's not too late."

"I know it's not too late," Jones retorted. "I've got two weeks." The remarks caused a bit of a stir that was quickly dispelled by Jones' spokeswoman Cathy Hanson, who dismissed the comment as flippant. Jones would not be running for governor, Hanson told the *Las Vegas Sun*.

By this time, Guinn & Co. had picked up on the renewed whispers of a Jones candidacy. But they dismissed them immediately. "By then it was the woman who cried wolf," Billy Vassiliadis remembered thinking. Rogich thought the rumors were a joke; he was very close to Jones, he felt, and he would know. In fact, on May 5, Jones and Rogich were the co-hosts at Jones' home of a fundraiser for a Justice of the Peace candidate named Jennifer Togliatti. Jones simply was not running for governor, Rogich reassured Guinn and others.

Guinn needed no such reassurance. About 10 days before filing closed, Guinn and his wife, Dema, attended a dinner party at the home of Steve Wynn. It was a fairly large gathering, and Jan Jones was there. Jones sought out Guinn to tell him that if there was anything she could do to help, he should let her know. Guinn told his wife what Jones had said, but Dema Guinn shook her head. She was not yet convinced Jones wouldn't enter the race.

Harry Reid, on the other hand, was firmly convinced Jones was out. After the breast cancer diagnosis, she wasn't even on Reid's radar screen. It would have been perfect if Jones were in the contest—she'd attract female voters and energize the party. But that was not in the cards, so Reid was looking for anyone but Neal. The senator had cycled through several other possibilities and by early May was wooing that state senator, Mike Schneider, known to be ambitious and who was at mid-term. As the filing deadline approached, Reid and his aides told Schneider that he'd be in line for bigger and better things if he'd be the party's political gun to shoot Neal. Reid knew Schneider could not beat Guinn. But with Neal out of the picture, Reid's chances against a very tough opponent, John Ensign, would be greatly enhanced.

On Wednesday, May 13, five days before filing closed, Jones and her husband, Richard Schuetz, went out to dinner at Fellini's, a western Las Vegas eatery. Their companions were Billy Vassiliadis and his wife, Rosemary. This dinner was the culmination of many months of work by Jones and Vassiliadis to re-establish their relationship, having finally cleared away the emotional rubble of the 1994 gubernatorial primary. The couples spent four hours together, discussing many in-depth personal topics. The Vassiliadis' told Jones and Schuetz they were thinking of buying a house near where they lived in an opulent northwest community called Eagle Hills. The governor's race came up briefly; they all talked about Jones running in the future. But she never mentioned that she was still thinking about taking on Guinn, nor that she had commissioned a poll.

Jones had hired Celinda Lake, a national Democratic pollster known for her work with female candidates, to conduct the survey. She had worked with Lake during her 1994 gubernatorial bid. Lake conducted the poll starting on Tuesday, May 12, less than one week before filing closed the following Monday. Her firm interviewed 400 registered voters during the next two days to gauge Jones' chances.

On Thursday, May 14, Lake disclosed the results of the poll on a conference call with Jones and Matthew Callister. Jones' numbers were impressive, especially compared to the other candidates, Lake told her. Fifty-five percent of voters viewed her favorably and only 15 percent unfavorably. As for Kenny Guinn, nearly half the voters either didn't know him or had no opinion of him. His favorable-unfavorable ratio among those who did have an opinion was 34-20. Hardly daunting. The survey also showed that possible Guinn opponents Aaron Russo and Lonnie Hammargren were not well-known, and those who knew them didn't like them all that much. In addition, three-quarters of voters had never heard of Joe Neal, the prospective Democratic nominee.

Then, Lake unfurled the results of the horse-race question: "If the election for governor were held today, would you vote for Jones or Guinn?" Jones had a six-point lead— 39 percent to 33 percent.

Lake then tried to flesh out those numbers by asking respondents how they felt after hearing the following description of each candidate:

Jones: "Jan Laverty Jones is the mayor of Las Vegas. Known as a dynamic leader who has guided Las Vegas through a time of change, Jones combines strong business experience with a record of effectiveness. In this time of change in Nevada, Jones will be a governor with the energy and with the vision to lead Nevada into the 21st century. As governor, Jones will work to control growth, to protect seniors, to fight crime, and to strengthen Nevada's commitment to the best public schools for our children."

Guinn: "Kenny Guinn is one of Nevada's most successful businessmen and is known for his success in turning around the University of Nevada. Guinn's success in both business and public service gives him the maturity and the know-how to lead Nevada into the 21st century. As governor, Guinn will make sure government and taxes are under control, and he will work to improve the state's schools and colleges so that Nevada's economy remains strong for years to come."

Both descriptions were glowing, designed to give the candidates the best of it. Lake then asked this question, "Sometimes in surveys like this people change their minds. If the election were held today …"

Jones' support grew—it was now 44-35 in her favor, a decisive nine-point advantage after both candidates had been presented to voters in the most favorable light.

Jones hung up the phone, stunned. She actually had a great chance to defeat Guinn. He'd not defined himself. His lack of a TV campaign had ensured voters still didn't know much about him. She immediately showed the survey to her husband. "What do you think?" she asked him. Schuetz told her that the sample was statistically small. But even with the variables built in, he told her, "You'd be nuts if you didn't do it."

Jones' eldest daughter, Maura, wanted her mother to run, too, but she knew that Schuetz couldn't imagine what it would be like. Maura remembered 1994 and going up against a favored opponent. "You don't understand," she told Schuetz. "It's not fun."

The next morning, Jones called Reid, who was campaigning in Northern Nevada. The mayor told the senator that she had a poll showing that she could win the governor's race and was planning to file on Monday, the last day to do so. Reid was thrilled. "I would love it if you would do this," he told her. "I can help you with the Democratic party's coordinated campaign and I don't think you'd have to raise much more than seven hundred and fifty thousand dollars." But, Reid told her, she'd better be sure, because he was trying to get Schneider into the race.

"Don't worry," Jones told him. "I'm sure." She was leaving that day for Arizona to attend her stepson's graduation, but would return Sunday and file Monday, the last day candidates could put their names on the ballot.

Reid was not the kind of man, though, who liked to

leave anything to chance. He immediately called Washington and tracked down his friend, Al Gore, the vice president. He wanted Gore to call Jones to close the deal. Hearing from the vice president would ensure that she'd follow through, Reid figured. Gore agreed to call, but in typical Jones fashion, she'd made a big splash, then vanished. No one, even the vice president of the United States, could find her.

The senator broke the news to the state party chairman, Paul Henry, a Reid surrogate. Henry's unpleasant duty, Reid told him, was to inform Schneider that his role as Neal-slayer had been written out of the script. Before she left town, Jones had faxed the poll to a few Democratic leaders. The circle of those who knew was widening.

It got too wide, as it turned out. I was tipped to Jones' incipient candidacy when the poll was faxed to me by an excited Democrat late that afternoon. I broke the news on the CBS affiliate that evening, and the *Las Vegas Review-Journal* had the story the following day.

State Senate Minority Leader Dina Titus stoked the fire, too. "I think the mayor's going to run for governor," she said on Friday. But, she added, "She [Jones] hasn't said it's definite; she wants to think about it over the weekend."

Reid was upset that the story was out. He worried that all the attention might cause Jones to change her mind. He and others immediately began trying to find the mayor. But she was in Arizona and not returning phone calls.

Jones had heard the story was out, though, which had concerned her as well. She feared that word that she was running might dissuade Lonnie Hammargren from entering the contest, too, on Monday. Jones wanted Hammargren in the race to batter Guinn in the primary, so he had some bruises before the general election campaign.

The Guinn folks were ready for a blood-pressure check. Rogich refused to believe that she was really thinking about filing on Monday. It just couldn't be happening. If it was, he told others in the campaign, she had lied to him. Some believed Jones ultimately wouldn't go through with it—the "cry-wolf" syndrome Vassiliadis had talked about. But there also was a palpable sense of fear in the Guinn camp. "There was an emotional roller coaster kind of ride," said one Guinn insider. "We were three days out and we thought we'd be facing Hammargren, Russo, and Neal. All of a sudden we were dealing with the Democrats' strongest candidate for governor. There was a lot of anxiety."

Jones returned from Arizona on Sunday night, still fairly sure of her commitment, though not all the way there. The phone rang at her home that evening and on the other end of the line was Steve Wynn. Jones was stunned by his attitude. "He said, 'It's not right not to have a race,'" Jones recalled Wynn telling her. "'This guy [Guinn] is unproven.'" Wynn was actually calling to encourage her to get into the contest, Jones thought. "'You know we've been on opposite sides before,'" Jones said that Wynn reminded her. "'But Bob Miller was proven, he was in office. Kenny is not proven. Jan, you are. If you run, I'll give you the same amount of money, and I think you should do it.'"

Jones and Schuetz discussed how to leak the news about what time she would file the next morning. Schuetz wanted to give the story to George Knapp, the high-profile reporter for the CBS affiliate. Jones thought giving anyone a heads-up might cause her a problem later in the campaign; the media were funny that way and some held campaign-long grudges. She and Schuetz had a row about the plan, but he eventually called Knapp and tipped him off.

That Monday morning, some of the Guinn team gathered at Rogich's office to plot strategy. They still weren't sure Jones would file, but they had to be prepared, as Ernaut put it, to "run a real campaign now." Rogich was furious, feeling a sense of personal betrayal. He kept muttering that he had just talked to her the previous week about meeting with

Guinn about a role in his administration. And he had not heard a word from her. He convinced himself that her husband was pushing her into the race, wanting to be close to power.

As the inner circle chatted, Vassiliadis' cell phone rang. He answered and Jones was on the line. He quickly excused himself and went into the bathroom to take the call. Her first words were, "'Do you still love me,'" he remembered.

"You're making it a lot harder, mayor" he retorted.

Jones then said she was not sure why she was running, that she must be crazy to have changed her mind. And then she pleaded with Vassiliadis not to let their friendship be affected, the way it had in 1994.

Jones arrived at the Grant Sawyer Building near downtown Las Vegas about 11 a.m., with a full media entourage (14 reporters and photographers) in tow. Though George Knapp was supposed to get the exclusive, the lid was off. Virtually every news organization was there. Jones strolled into the offices with Schuetz on her arm. How impulsive had she been? When asked for the $300 filing fee, Jones asked if she could write a check. No, she was told; the law mandates cash. So Schuetz had to run out to an automated teller machine to withdraw the money so she could make it official.

Jones implied to the media that her breast-cancer experience had given her a sense of *carpe diem*, which was partly responsible for her sudden entry. "I know the importance of life and the time you have," she told the media. "And I can't let the democratic process go ignored." She was peppered with questions about her health, so she repeated her mantra of a month earlier: "I don't have breast cancer. I had breast cancer."

As shocking as her decision was, Jones had to share the media spotlight. Lonnie Hammargren, after months of oscillating between running for governor or running for Congress or not running at all, officially became a gubernatorial candidate. Even more surprising than Hammargren's candidacy was his rhetoric, which was a blistering screed against Guinn. He called Guinn a "Republican in name only, a RINO," words that had been whispered earlier about Guinn and an acronym coined by his friend, George Harris, the GOP finance director and Sheldon Adelson's paid lieutenant. Hammargren also told the media he would spend a half-million of his own money, which could force Guinn to unload some of his war chest. He even went so far as to froth, "Kenny Guinn is controlled by the gaming industry and union bosses."

Hammargren was as peculiar as any Nevada elected official in many, many years. But now that he and the equally mercurial Russo were willing to expend hundreds of thousands of dollars attacking Guinn in the primary, the entire calculus of the race had changed. Guinn would have to spend money defending himself. His negatives inevitably would rise. And Jones could stand by and watch. She wouldn't have to do much to erase Neal from the landscape. She could concentrate on raising money and be ready for a strong general-election challenge after the September primary. It was a dream scenario for the Democrats, especially Harry Reid, who now had the lightning rod to attract female Democratic voters to the polls in his race against John Ensign.

For weeks, months, even years afterward, people speculated that Jones had been coaxed into the race by Reid, who merely wanted to use her as that proverbial stone to kill two very big birds: She would obliterate Neal and get women to the polls who might otherwise be turned off by Reid's prolife stance. But as much as Reid wanted her in the race, that wasn't why Jones filed. She certainly hadn't thought it through. She reacted impulsively to the poll results and didn't require much to push her the final step. She later reflected that given another week to ponder the decision, she probably wouldn't have gotten in.

Jones' breast cancer also played a role, and not just because it could prove, ironically and perhaps sickeningly, to be an asset: The brave woman who had fought a deadly disease returning to fight yet another daunting battle. "It sort of put it in perspective," Jones mused later. "It's a game. The worst thing that was going to happen was I was going to lose."

One other astute political observer and longtime Jones-watcher put it this way: "She had just gone through her terrible fight with cancer. People were talking about the distant future, that she might run for governor again in four or eight years. And I think her attitude might have been as a result of the cancer, 'If not now, when? I may not get tomorrow to try it.'"

The Guinn campaign, though, had unwittingly provided the opening for Jones to get in. If Rogich, Ernaut, & Co. had followed the original plan to begin running positive ads early in 1998, rather than being consumed with Russo and internal GOP warfare, that window of opportunity would have slammed shut for Jones. Ernaut later remembered that he was almost left alone during the first few months of 1998, the rest of the consultants having checked out because it seemed Guinn had a clear path. Opined another Guinn insider: "I think we allowed for a candidate like Jan Jones to read the tea leaves favorably. We hadn't done much, hadn't said much. A poll would say it's a close race."

Indeed, Jones said she was convinced by Celinda Lake on that Thursday before filing ended that she could win. "I never would have gotten in just for Harry," the mayor said. "I absolutely got in that race because I thought I could beat [Guinn]."

As it turned out, though, even if Jones was leading Guinn thanks to her superior name recognition, the poll devised by Lake was badly flawed. Statewide voter registration was very close at the time—the Republicans had about a 1,000-voter edge. Yet Lake's sample had more Democrats than

Republicans—about five percent more, in fact. Surely, Jones' numbers were inflated.

So Jones decided to run based on a false premise gleaned from a faulty survey. But she saw in the poll what she wanted to see. And she was running for governor again, challenging the elite's favored candidate for the second gubernatorial cycle in a row. This time, though, she wasn't running in a contested primary. Her opponent, in fact, had to weather his own three-way primary. And she believed that other gaming figures would follow Wynn's lead and give her what they were giving to Guinn.

In the space of a few days, an assured anointment had turned into a potentially competitive race for the state's highest office.

8

A FISHY BEGINNING

Two months before Jan Jones filed for governor, her husband paid a visit to his friend, Clyde Turner, who had only recently resigned as chairman of Circus Circus Enterprises. Turner and Richard Schuetz had worked together for Steve Wynn at the Mirage and had stayed close as their careers diverged. In fact, Schuetz once said he believed Turner to be the "finest person on the entire planet" and the two were good friends. Ironically, a few months earlier, Turner had eagerly rounded up the $300,000 in Circus Circus money for Republican Kenny Guinn, having no clue that his pal's wife would soon be in the race. That day in March, though, the subject was not politics, but land.

Schuetz's interest was piqued after Turner described a land deal he was about to enter into with Dick Etter, another friend and a former Circus Circus board member. The transaction was for a piece of property in northwest Las Vegas owned by a consortium that included executives of the Boyd Gaming Corp. In another irony—and a testament to the small-world nature of Las Vegas politics and economics—Guinn was once a Boyd Gaming board member.

Turner told Schuetz he was welcome to get in on the deal. So Schuetz went home to his wife and asked if it were proper, with her as mayor, for him to buy land within the city limits. Her Honor told Schuetz that it was no problem, as long as it was disclosed. Thus Schuetz went ahead and entered into the transaction, forming an acronymic company with Turner and Etter called TES, Ltd. Once the papers were filed, TES owed $4 million to Boyd Gaming founder Bill Boyd and other partners.

On May 26, eight days after Jones filed for governor, the City Council met to consider what at the time seemed like an unrelated matter. The landlord of a building that housed a locally owned bank—BankWest of Nevada—was trying to get zoning for a restaurant called Nick's Fishmarket. BankWest was founded by Bill Boyd; one of its directors was Perry Whitt, like Boyd one of Schuetz's creditors in the land deal. The project was opposed by BankWest because of access and view concerns. Jones had been lobbied by others on the bank's well-connected board, including Todd Marshall, a local businessman, and his father, Art Marshall, a state gaming regulator and a bank board member. Finally, the bank had hired Paul Henry, who also happened to be the state Democratic Party chairman, as its lobbyist.

In this game of insiders versus the landlord, a man named Marc Gordon, the fight was not fair. The zoning change to allow the restaurant Gordon desired was unanimously denied. Jones, who'd led the fight against the project, appeared to have been swayed by an intense lobbying effort by friends, community luminaries, and the boss of the party whose gubernatorial nomination she was seeking. It was unseemly, sure. But it was also standard fare for Las Vegas politics.

Two days after the council hearing, Jones signed her financial disclosure form as required by the secretary of state for gubernatorial candidates. Under debtors, Jones listed TES, whose creditors, listed on the form, included Whitt and Boyd. The connection was there—Schuetz, and by extension, Jones, was in business with the same men whom she had just assisted in her elective position.

Jones didn't know it, yet, but her husband's meeting in

March with Turner had planted a land mine that she would have to try to tiptoe around just as her bid for governor was getting underway. So Turner not only had been part of the single most important campaign contribution to Jones' opponent, but he'd also unwittingly initiated a land deal with her husband that would threaten to destroy Jones' candidacy.

If John Donne had changed the gender of his famous observation about the interconnectedness of all human beings in *Mediations 17*, he could have been referring to Jan Jones after she filed for governor on May 18, 1998. Jones truly was an island in the sea of Nevada politics. She'd commenced a gubernatorial race with no organization and no plan. She'd informed few of her friends, many of whom would later say they were shocked to get the news from the media. And she was about to leave town for breast-cancer radiation treatments in San Francisco. It was an absurdity—a woman recovering from a life-threatening disease filing impulsively against a candidate who had the entire political Establishment and millions of dollars at his disposal.

Jones didn't even have the sitting Democratic governor to call upon for help. Bob Miller had defeated her in the 1994 primary, which had been quite vitriolic for a time before the mayor realized she couldn't win and surrendered about a month before the election. Miller and Jones had repaired their personal animosity in the intervening years, but First Lady Sandy Miller was not so magnanimous. What's more, Miller was a good friend of Guinn's. He was not likely to do much. If Jones expected anything, Miller sent a signal to the contrary in his first post-filing quote: "In my opinion, we have two very good candidates. I'll support Jan, but the state is well-served in either capacity. ... A legitimate race between two qualified candidates is better for the state." Not exactly a ringing endorsement for the mayor.

And as she began to consider who to hire for her campaign team, Jones knew the pickings were lean. "Kenny Guinn has hired everyone in the state," Senate Minority Leader Dina Titus lamented shortly after Jones filed.

Jones, though, had her husband. Schuetz knew little about politics, but he had marketing and management expertise. He also was at the apex of influence over his wife. He had been a mensch during her breast-cancer ordeal, writing a beautiful piece that appeared in the *Las Vegas Sun* and seeing her through the initial treatments. He'd also urged her to get into the race after hearing Celinda Lake's poll results. And he was a businessman who had once run a gaming property, albeit a failed one—the Stratosphere near downtown Las Vegas. So Schuetz told Jones he would take over the task of assembling a team while she concentrated on getting her health more robust for the marathon to come. He would be responsible for hiring a campaign manager and the rest of the team.

Jones recalled, "What Richard said was, 'Jan, you do a lot of things well. But hiring people isn't particularly one [of them]. You confuse loyalty too much with ability.'" (The irony was that Jones' main hire at the city that year was one of Schuetz's ex-employees, which had caused her trouble with the state ethics panel.)

After she filed, Jones left town for her radiation treatment. Schuetz immediately got to work. That weekend, he interviewed Jim Mulhall, one of the state's most skillful campaign operatives. Mulhall had been a congressional staffer for years, including a stint as Richard Bryan's press secretary. He'd been involved in many Nevada campaigns, including several cycles for a Nevada congressman named Jim Bilbray, and he'd never lost one. Mulhall was now Miller's chief of staff and was considered one of the best campaign minds in the state. He was a natural first choice for Jones. In fact, Jones' friend, Matthew Callister, met with Mulhall a couple of days after the mayor filed and tried to coax him into the contest.

But the situation was difficult for Mulhall, who was very close to Billy Vassiliadis, a key cog in the Guinn machine. Mulhall also had a friendly relationship with Pete Ernaut; the chief of staff and opposition-party floor leader frequently had interacted in Carson City. On the other hand, Mulhall was a fiercely partisan Democrat and badly wanted to see Guinn have a race. But at what cost personally and perhaps professionally? Only a few days after he met with Schuetz, Mulhall was seen by a Jones supporter as he dined at Cafe Nicolle with Vassiliadis. He was suspect already.

Schuetz was also trying to balance the role of overprotective husband with campaign administrator. The same weekend he interviewed Mulhall, Schuetz saw quotes in the *Review-Journal* from both Ernaut and Aaron Russo about Jones' breast cancer. Ernaut declared: "If any staff person makes her health a political thing, they'll be out the door the next day." Schuetz, and others, saw that as a classic way to raise an issue by saying you weren't going to raise it. Russo was more blunt: "People are going to question whether she's going to be able to finish her term out. They're going to question why she's come into the race when she's not physically fit."

Schuetz, who much later would take out full-page ads defending his stepdaughter after newspaper coverage of a fender-bender, was apoplectic. He wanted to start a letter-writing campaign against Ernaut and Russo. He also called the CBS affiliate in Las Vegas, demanding that a semiweekly commentary segment called "Reality Check," featuring Guinnites Vassiliadis and Rogich, be taken off the air. Those close to Jones, and those who wanted her to succeed, wondered about the utility of having someone so emotionally close to the candidate be in charge.

A historical precedent existed in Jones' career. Dan Hart, a Boston native, moved to Nevada to run Jones' first successful mayoral campaign in 1991. Hart later became romantically involved with Jones and his estimable talents were diluted in the 1994 gubernatorial campaign by his personal relationship with the candidate. He suffered the next few years by being isolated because of his overt challenging of friends in the power structure he had made in 1991, but he had succeeded in smoothing over most of the damage. Jones and Hart were still close, and he was her chief political confidant. He wondered, though, about her ability to pull off a campaign with her husband, who was not a pol, assembling the team. Hart tried to help Jones, but inevitably came into conflict with Schuetz, including at least one screaming encounter. The omens were not good.

Team Guinn briefly wallowed in anger and disappointment before revving up its machine to combat Jones. Rogich was still fuming—at Jones for misleading him and at Harry Reid for breaking what he thought was an implicit quid pro quo not to recruit an opponent. But the rest were ready, as Ernaut had put it, to run a real campaign.

Several in the inner circle, especially Vassiliadis, were familiar with their opponent's vulnerabilities. The research to flesh them out began in earnest. Dick Cooper, a former journalist and information-gatherer nonpareil for that 1994 campaign against Jones, was retained to look into her mayoral record. Cooper, a short, bespectacled man nicknamed "the Mole," was told to focus especially on Jones' attendance at meetings, which had been the subject of sporadic news reports over the years. Some in the campaign felt her absences could be a silver bullet once the entire record was compiled. They knew they had to be careful, because she could use the breast cancer as a potent defense. So they decided to focus solely on her pre-1998, pre-breast cancer attendance.

Ethics, too, could be a potent issue, Guinn insiders believed. Jones had been before the state ethics panel many times. Rogich, his fury fueling his creativity, immediately began crafting in his mind's eye a spot that would describe

Jones as having appeared before the commission more than anyone in state history. About a week after she filed, the campaign received a transcript of Jones' most recent appearance before the panel just a few days before she decided to run. That was the case involving her hiring of Schuetz's former employee, Ann Holland. She was exonerated, but the chairman of the panel scolded her for being "high-handed as hell." Now that had potential.

Guinn had raised about $3 million by the time Jones got into the race. Jones didn't get a penny until June 1, but she did surprisingly well that month, thanks mostly to Steve Wynn making good on his promise to help her. His multiple corporations seeded Jones' campaign with $40,000. Downtown casinos—Binion's Horseshoe and the Lady Luck—also gave to the woman under whose jurisdiction they operated. Jones also had a couple of other reasons to be optimistic—Newmont Gold, a major player in state politics, and Coast Resorts, a large gaming company, also contributed. Even so, by the end of June, Jones still had raised only $112,000, about $2.9 million behind Guinn.

Guinn also had acquired something Jones could never buy in time—an unprecedented, statewide grass-roots operation. Steve Wark, armed with the money to do what he had done only in local races, had been executing a fully integrated plan. It included direct mail, personal letters from Guinn and his wife, Dema, phone banks, and walkers. Wark also set up what he called people-to-people postcards, urging various community leaders and regular folks who wandered into the office to write post cards to their Christmas card lists. With Wark's well-oiled machine, and with Russo and Hammargren still more likely to self-destruct than force Guinn to spend any of his war chest, he and his team felt only mild discomfort.

They had the best campaign team money could buy. They still had most of the money. And Jones had shown in 1994 that she was vulnerable, that she was not ready for prime time. Even though Guinn was not the most articulate candidate, and surely would not match up well in debates, they could still use their resources to protect him and destroy her. It was no longer a sure thing. But Guinn was still the favorite.

Normally when a candidate announces for office—especially an important office—the person has huddled with trusted advisers and friends to make the momentous decision. Evaluations have been conducted: where the money will come from, who will run the campaign, what the chances are of success. But Jan Jones had gone though no such process. She had leaped into a pool without testing the water's temperature or depth.

Harry Reid knew it—and he wanted to help. Jones, with her ability to be a female-voter magnet, was Reid's ticket to victory over John Ensign. No one in Nevada politics played all the angles the way Reid did. He was also a control freak, enmeshed in nearly every aspect of state and local politics, especially campaigns. Reid was the self-appointed anointer of the Democratic Party. But often his dabbling in other races proved disastrous, including a 1990 Clark County Commission race where his favored contender was crushed and a 1994 state Senate contest where he actually signed on as chairman of a challenger's campaign that never got off the ground.

But this time the effect on Reid was not so distant. So when serendipity smiled with her filing, Reid swung into action. His chief of staff and alter ego, Rey Martinez, had already brought in the nationally known firm of Greer, Margolis, Mitchell, Burns and Associates to run ads for the state Democratic Party attacking Ensign. It would be a perfect synergy, Martinez and Reid believed, to have the same company do commercials for Jones. And that would give the Reid campaign an inside view of what was happening in the Jones organization. So a few days after Jones got into the race, with a little prodding from Martinez, two partners in the ad firm, Frank Greer and Roy Behr, came to Las Vegas to meet with Jones. They sat down with the mayor and her husband, and it went well. A contract was discussed. The firm was on board.

On Wednesday, May 27, nine days after filing, Jones put out the first press release of her campaign, announcing the hiring of a "prominent media consultant." Greer, in turn, gushed about the woman he hardly knew: "Jan Jones is one of the most impressive public servants I have ever met."

The public geyser of optimism belied what Greer, Behr, and others privately saw as a haphazard beginning to a difficult endeavor. The campaign had no media plan, no budget for commercials, not even a ballpark figure of what Jones was willing to spend. Jones said she would try to raise $2 million, but even she was privately skeptical that she could get much more than half that number. She also didn't want to put in any of her own money, as she had done against Miller in 1994. That was a red flag for Behr and Greer; but they and others felt that if polls showed Jones close to Guinn when the time came for a cash infusion, she would write the check.

The ad men also knew that Jones had to get on the air right away, and not just because it was a benefit to them financially. She also had to hire a campaign manager. Schuetz hadn't liked anyone he interviewed, and Jones knew that she had to find someone quickly.

So she reluctantly called on her old confidant Hart in early June. Hart resented that Jones had allowed him to be excluded by Schuetz and others, who saw him as tainted by the 1994 debacle. But when she left a voice mail for him in early June asking if any of his friends in Philadelphia or Boston could run the campaign, Hart relented. He called an old associate named Denise Rawles, an intense grass-roots specialist who had worked with Hart for various Democratic causes on the East Coast. Rawles was interested, and by late June she was hired.

Jones still needed to fill two critical functions: press secretary and polling. A couple of people were floated as possible media mouthpieces—Gary Thompson, a veteran and respected reporter for the *Las Vegas Sun* who was a friend of Schuetz; and Rob Powers, publicist for the Las Vegas Convention and Visitors Authority, who had done a fine job for Gov. Bob Miller's campaigns. But Reid, seeing another chance for control and influence, had a different idea. His former press secretary, Susan McCue, had just started working as a spokesman for Housing and Urban Development Secretary Andrew Cuomo. It would be dicey with Cuomo, but Reid knew how much McCue enjoyed the game and would want back in. He told Jones he could get it on. And he did just that—McCue, too, was part of the Jones campaign before long.

Jones was torn on the pollster, though. Women's groups were applying tremendous pressure to hire Lake, whose survey had induced Jones to file. But on the other side were those advising her to hire another Democratic pollster, Peter Hart, who had conducted surveys for casinos and had tremendous credibility on the Strip. In the end, the capital pressure outweighed the local pressure and she retained Lake. The final piece of the early team fell into place when she hired Hal Malchow, a capital specialist, to do her direct-mail campaign.

It was early June, only two weeks after she had filed, and Jones was doing well. She was assembling a team, she was garnering plenty of free media attention, including publicity over appearing with Vice President Al Gore in a breast-cancer charity event in Washington on June 6. The story of a woman overcoming breast cancer to run for governor was the stuff that campaigns are made of—and Jones & Co. knew it.

Guinn, knowing that Jones was retaining a staff and

trying to raise money, reacted accordingly. His team began checking TV-time availability, with an eye toward going up with image-defining spots. There were two reasons. One, Guinn needed the definition—he was still relatively unknown. Two, the Guinnites wanted Jones, who claimed to have $500,000 in commitments, to start spending, too.

The well-connected team also began contacting various major donors, trying to maintain the exclusive commitments they had received. The Guinn folks believed that some of the Strip companies would shut out Jones—Circus Circus, Hilton, Caesars Palace. She would get money from the downtown casinos because she was mayor. But the rest of the gambling corporations might be persuaded to stick with the money they had invested in Guinn.

The Guinn strategists also believed they could dispel any talk of anointment by pointing to both candidates' tax returns so voters could see this was a race between two millionaires.

Tensions, though, were running high. This was the race that was not supposed to be a race. Tempers began to flare; personality conflicts started to percolate. By early June, Ernaut and Rogich were squabbling over the content of the first Guinn ads, which would show the candidate being questioned by a faux journalist to try to defuse any concerns that he was not substantive. Vassiliadis had to mediate the disputes, which were more about hierarchical muscle-flexing than anything else—Ernaut wanted to show he was boss.

Then, on June 10, a deus ex machina rescued the Guinn campaign from its doldrums. The *Las Vegas Review-Journal* reported that Marc Gordon, the landlord for the bank building who had lost that zoning item before the city, was considering an Ethics Commission complaint against Jones because her husband was in business with the project's opponents. It was a complex story, but its prominence in the newspaper, and the linking of Jones to the Ethics Commission, were enough for Team Guinn. "We thought the campaign was over," Vassiliadis recalled. "It looked pretty bad [for Jones]."

The Guinn campaign once again settled into a comfort zone, much like the one they slipped into after Jones announced at the end of 1997 that she wouldn't run. She was badly damaged by the *R-J* article and the Guinnites knew the paper would bird-dog the story. Even if she were exonerated again, it would still bog down her campaign before it even got started. And it would at the very least create a resonating issue—Jones before the Ethics Commission again—that could scuttle her campaign ship before it had a chance to leave the harbor. All Guinn had to do was dodge the torpedoes on that pesky paycheck-protection ballot initiative, which was still in play, and he could probably sail home.

9

MANAGING THE
LABOR VOTE

In June 1994, Las Vegas Mayor Jan Jones was optimistic she could secure the AFL-CIO's endorsement for her gubernatorial bid. Granted, she was running against an incumbent governor, Bob Miller. But labor was disenchanted with Miller, who had pushed that worker-unfriendly reform of the state's insurance system through the 1993 Legislature. Miller had also vetoed a collective-bargaining bill proposed during the session, saying in his veto message that the "lengthy process of preparing a budget ... should be free of the collective-bargaining process." Jones had plenty of fodder.

In a Democratic primary, labor support, especially from the populous Culinary Union, was important, if not essential. And when Jones sought the endorsement at the AFL-CIO convention, she had every reason to believe that she would receive labor's blessing in her insurgent bid.

She didn't even come close. Miller not only had locked up the inside game—he and his team had all the relationships with labor leaders. The governor had appointed AFL-CIO chief Blackie Evans' brother, Danny Evans, to a prime state job, director of the Division of Enforcement of Industrial Safety and Health. Jones derided the appointment as an example of "power traded among the few," but the move couldn't have hurt Miller's labor convention cause. Miller and his friends had also used their connections to President Clinton to get the White House involved: political-affairs director Joe Velasquez helped make phone calls. And, on the convention floor, D. Taylor, the Culinary's skillful organizer, rounded up the votes for Miller.

Jones, on the other hand, didn't have the same connections; her main nexus to the unions, Jeanne Maust, a women's-rights activist, could not match Vassiliadis & Co. for political firepower. It was like a Beetle racing a Porsche.

By the time it was over, Jones garnered only 75 votes out of 367 cast, easily giving the incumbent the two-thirds he needed. Afterwards, commenting on the vote being held in a closed delegate caucus, Jones' campaign manager, Dan Hart, lamented, "Any time you have a smoke-filled room with Bob Miller supporters in it, you know Bob Miller will win."

It was the shape of things to come in that governor's race: Jones lost in a landslide.

Before Jones jolted Kenny Guinn's anointment by entering the 1998 gubernatorial race, his campaign had every reason to believe that labor would endorse the frontrunning Republican candidate. His team's attempt to scuttle the paycheck-protection initiative, his whispers at the end of 1997 that he would sign a collective-bargaining bill, his longtime friendship with Blackie Evans all indicated that he would get the endorsement. And Joe Neal was the Democratic standard-bearer at that time: Neal was a labor stalwart, but no one gave him any chance of becoming governor, and the union leaders wanted to be with the winner.

Jones' candidacy, however, changed the odds—all bets were off. The labor community was convulsed by the turn of events. Evans floated the idea of endorsing Guinn, Neal, and Jones. Others suggested endorsing no one.

Jones was not known for being especially close to labor. She was, however, a Democrat and perceived, unlike Neal, as a potential threat to Guinn's election. Now the question for the Guinnites was whether, through their relationships and Guinn's paycheck-protection posture, they could prevent Jones from getting to two-thirds and securing the endorsement.

If the Guinn insiders could prevent Jones from getting the endorsement, that would be seen as a victory. And they had the connections to do it. Vassiliadis still had ties to the Culinary leadership. Guinn had his own relationships with Evans and Culinary leader Jim Arnold. Guinn's top two advisers, Sig Rogich and Pete Ernaut, had cultivated Wilhelm and Taylor, as well as Glen Arnodo, the union's up-and-coming political operative. If the Culinary delegates sat on their hands, representing nearly a third of the delegates to the AFL-CIO convention, Jones almost surely could not get the nod.

Jones, however, was popular within the construction trades, likely to sweep through their ranks. She also had another asset: Guinn was not as solid on collective bargaining as he had appeared to labor leaders at the end of 1997. For most of his career, Guinn actually seemed to support collective bargaining. He had wondered as far back as the 1970s when he was schools superintendent why certain classes of local-government employees should have the benefit, while state workers did not. He repeated those sentiments during the 1998 contest, winking and nodding to labor leaders that he might sign a collective-bargaining bill during the heat of his courtship of the unions while Attorney General Frankie Sue Del Papa was still in the contest. But a few weeks later, under pressure from Republican leaders, Guinn had publicly declared his position against collective bargaining. Some in the labor contingent felt betrayed. Jones had a hook she could use.

When Jones addressed the AFL-CIO convention in Reno on June 1, 1998—less than two weeks after she had filed—she had a focused message. She immediately went after Guinn, albeit obliquely, for not being a tried-and-true friend of labor. "My public record is one that has always supported labor—not just when convenient, or if I needed something. And with threats facing labor today, it is increasingly important that the AFL-CIO remembers who are and who are not their friends," Jones told the delegates.

Then she seized on Guinn's difficulty in articulating a consistent position on paycheck protection. "And speaking of friends, the Republican Party has launched its so-called workers rights or paycheck-protection initiative, which I adamantly oppose. I didn't say I wanted to think about it. I didn't say I was kind of against it. I said that I am unequivocally against those efforts."

Finally, she hit the collective-bargaining high note: "I am also for the right of state employees to use collective bargaining."

So in the first two minutes of her speech, Jones had reminded labor of its Democratic roots and expressed her purity on paycheck protection and collective bargaining, the two most important issues to the delegates. How could she not get the endorsement?

In her peroration, Jones urged the delegates not to "compromise your principles. ... This is not the time for you to sit on the fence." And her last statement was powerful: "There is only one choice for this group to make today. It is a simple choice and no matter how you try and rationalize it, no matter how hard you try and wish it went away, it is still a simple choice—support the Democratic Party in this election. It is the honorable thing to do. It is the fair thing to do. It is the right thing to do."

Guinn was scheduled to speak the next day, the same day the delegates would vote on their endorsements. If Jones' speech was pandering in its purest form, Guinn's address was the same kind of mushy rhetoric he had used throughout the campaign. "We have worked closely for the common good of our communities and our state and to be sure, we have agreed and disagreed from time to time," he told the delegates. He talked about general issues that "unite us as Nevadans. They motivate all of us to make this state a better place for ordinary citizens." Guinn then detailed the "rich history of cooperation between labor and management in Nevada. Employers make their profit and shareholders receive their returns and workers are rewarded with good wages, good benefits, and respect."

Guinn also reminded the labor delegates of the workers-compensation reforms—which remained a painful memory for many of them because of lost benefits—and extolled the virtues of putting the system back in the black. And then he addressed collective bargaining from the dais. He sounded like an echo of Bob Miller in his veto message four years earlier, using the budget process as his explanation for opposition. "Although I believe state employees are not being compensated like they should and I support collective bargaining in general, I do not support collective bargaining for state workers. Because of the way the Legislature and governor work during the budget process, collective bargaining does not work well in state government. I prefer to work as a partner with state employees to remove the unfair disparity among public employees in Nevada."

So Guinn was saying, with another wink and nod, I'll give you a raise, don't worry.

Although the beginning and middle might not have thrilled the assembled laborites, Guinn closed his speech with a statement that could not have been more potent. And it sent a message to the Culinary that he was still with them, so the union should be with him. "I share your opposition to the so-called paycheck-protection measure," Guinn said. "It is big government that should not be memorialized in a constitutional amendment. My opposition to this initiative has cost me support within my own political party. But I know what's right and what isn't. This isn't."

Even with Guinn's stirring finale, the delegates were faced with what seemed like a clear-cut choice: A Democrat who supported them on their two major issues and a Republican who was only batting .500.

After his speech, Guinn dramatically signed the labor unions' own petition designed to nullify paycheck protection. That petition, which was supported by a group called Nevadans For Fairness, created by union-aligned forces to fight the initiative, was likely to qualify for the ballot, too. The Culinary was much more concerned with paycheck protection, which would eviscerate its political clout, than collective bargaining, which had no effect on its membership. So the state's most powerful labor group would keep its commitment to Guinn and his team. Remember, back in 1997, Taylor had advised Jones not to run, saying that a middle-of-the-road Republican such as Guinn would destroy her. The Culinary, quite simply, believed Guinn was going to win the election.

When the vote was taken, none of the candidates could muster close to the two-thirds needed. Neal received the most votes, but it wasn't even a majority. And in this case, a non-endorsement was a win for Guinn, because he blocked Jones from getting labor's imprimatur. The Culinary, paying off its debt to Guinn for his stand on paycheck protection and desirous of sitting with him in the winner's circle come November, ensured Jones did not get the early boost she could have used.

Less than a week after blocking Jones from being able to wear the union label, Guinn had to confront yet another labor-related challenge. The paycheck-protection initiative, begun by the state GOP despite his objections, was thrown off the ballot for constitutional reasons by Clark County District Judge Myron Leavitt on June 10. A similar proposition had been defeated by voters in California a week earlier. Still, labor leaders in Nevada remained concerned that polls showed it had overwhelming support. Although some

Democrats were wistful that a tremendous reason for labor to turn out in November was now gone, the unions were thrilled. But the question about whether the state Republican Party would appeal the ruling lingered, especially with the unions pressing forward with their own initiative designed to retain their sovereignty over how they used dues taken from their members.

The GOP, after much prodding from Guinn and others, had backed off the petition drive. Paycheck protection was proceeding under the GOP aegis, but much of the signature-collection had been taken over by Sheldon Adelson's troops. The chairman of the Las Vegas Sands, who hoped to open his new megaresort, the Venetian, non-union, had been an early proponent of the concept and had helped fund the effort. But Adelson & Co. were moving against the wishes of the top two Republican candidates, Guinn and senatorial hopeful John Ensign. Ensign was an ardent backer of paycheck protection, but he knew what Guinn knew: Putting it on the ballot would ensure a high get-out-the-vote operation by labor in November. He would have little chance against incumbent Harry Reid if paycheck protection were on the ballot.

The day after Judge Leavitt's ruling, Chuck Muth, the man who wrote the first letter John Mason signed in 1997 promoting paycheck protection, faxed a clarion call to the GOP network. "The Judge May Have Ruled ... But the Fat Lady Didn't Sing," Muth declared in pleading for signature collectors, who would be paid up to $34 an hour, to make a weekend push to get enough signatures should an appeal be filed and Leavitt overruled.

But the next day, the fat lady began to clear her throat. Mason, acceding to pressure from the Guinn and Ensign campaigns, drew up a legal document that would form the guts of an agreement with the unions for a mutual cessation of signature-gathering. What was about to occur during the next few days showed the true power and reach of the team Rogich and Guinn had put together.

About 4 p.m. on June 12, two days after Judge Leavitt's ruling, Mason dialed Vassiliadis, who, as he would later write in a memo to GOP officials, "is the common element between Nevadans For Fairness (the union-aligned petition group), Governor Miller, the Nevada Resort Association, and the unions." Vassiliadis informed Mason he would see what he could do to get Mason's treaty signed. Vassiliadis contacted labor leaders, who initially were skeptical. Why should they pull the plug on their initiative? Leavitt's decision would stand up on appeal, they figured. The GOP petition drive was in trouble, anyway. Why not push forward with theirs to prevent paycheck protection in the future?

That weekend, Mason tried to rally support for his plan to kill his own initiative in exchange for the unions killing theirs. On Saturday, he met with 10 county chairmen and took an advisory canvass—six voted to pursue an appeal of Leavitt's decision. But later, three of those six chairmen—George Peek, Beverly Willard, and Don Dallas—told Mason that in their capacities as members of the state party executive board, they would support the pact. Rich Strickland, representing Clark County Chairman Milton Schwartz, told Mason he would not relent. Mason called Schwartz, who was in Israel, and confirmed his opposition to capitulating to the unions. By Sunday, Mason had talked to 10 of the state executive board members and only two—George Harris, who was helping Hammargren and Russo and worked for Adelson, and Strickland—opposed his compromise.

The deal was finally made during a Sunday conference call involving Mason, Ernaut, Vassiliadis, AFL-CIO attorney Richard McCracken, and labor's point man on the issue, Culinary staff director D. Taylor. That evening, McCracken assured Mason by phone that the agreement would be ratified the next day by the unions at an AFL-CIO executive board meeting in Las Vegas. Mason informed him that if he didn't hear from McCracken by 3 p.m. Monday, he would have no choice but to begin the filing process to ensure all the petitions were submitted by the Tuesday deadline.

On Monday morning, Leavitt's office put out the word that the judge would be signing an agreement that the GOP was waiving its appeal rights late that afternoon.

The AFL-CIO executive board meeting, however, turned out to be more than a formality. In fact, it was a donny-brook. Although the Culinary folks saw the utility in taking their petition off the table so labor could devote its resources to candidates and hotel contracts, other union leaders, who had worked so tenaciously for their own petition, were re-luctant. Those included AFL-CIO leaders Blackie Evans and Danny Thompson, the teachers association, and Northern Nevada building-trade unions. But by now, the national AFL-CIO, realizing all was lost in Nevada, wanted to pull the plug, so it could concentrate time and money in Colo-rado and Oregon, where paycheck initiatives were still alive.

The meeting went on until about 2:30 p.m. when the executive board took a vote. It was 7-6 to abandon the Ne-vadans For Fairness initiative and negotiate with the Re-publicans. One vote. One vote that might have changed the course of an election.

But more than a few bumps remained on the road to settling the issue. Shortly after the vote, McCracken called Dan Burdish, the GOP's executive director and Mason's loyal aide, to tell him of the result. However, he added that the unions would not agree unless Secretary of State Dean Heller signed onto it. Besides the GOP, only Heller had standing to appeal Leavitt's decision. The request was absurd. A con-stitutional officer could not be a signatory on such a docu-ment between two private groups. But the unions were, to some extent, understandably paranoid.

Mason, who was in his Los Angeles law office and had been notified by Burdish of the union request, called Heller, who told him he couldn't sign. As he prepared to leave to catch a plane to Reno, Mason believed the deal was dead and called his Nevada operatives to green light the filing process. Mason called Adelson, who also was in Israel, and told him he thought the accord was aborted. The chairman also informed Harris, who was euphoric.

Just before he got on the plane, Mason tipped off Ernaut, who became incensed. After all the commitments and promises Ernaut believed Mason had made and broken, this was the final straw. He hung up the phone and decided he had only a few hours to salvage the accord. When Mason alighted in Reno after 5 p.m., Ernaut was waiting for him at the gate. They spent several hours together imbibing beers at the airport bar and making phone calls to key Republicans, including Ensign. Even so, when he began the drive to his Lake Tahoe home, Mason was still planning to appeal the decision.

Down in Las Vegas, Judge Leavitt waited until about 6 p.m. for labor and the Republicans to arrive to sign the mutual surrender. But when it became clear no one was coming, he left.

Ernaut was a busy man that evening. He contacted dozens of GOP officials who also wanted the initiative off the ballot and urged them to call Mason. Guinn himself called Mason several times, reminding him in blistering terms that he had saved Mason's chairmanship at the state convention by guiding his delegates to vote for the incumbent instead of Russo's candidate. Ernaut also tried to activate Ensign, reminding the congressman that he had the most to lose if labor was energized to turn out in November.

At 5:30 a.m. on Tuesday, June 16, Mason's phone rang at his Zephyr Cove residence. Adelson was on the line, calling from Israel. Mason assured Adelson that the proposed mutual non-aggression pact was on hold. In fact, Mason had instructed party officials in rural Nevada to submit their petitions to the secretary of state's office. Harris was exultantly winging his way to Elko to personally help gather them up. The labor folks, too, were poised to file their initiative as the deadline loomed at 5 p.m. that day.

Only minutes after he hung up from Adelson, Mason

talked to Ernaut, telling him that he was still committed to the appeal. Ernaut went ballistic, and hung up. Guinn's campaign manager knew he had very little time. It was like the end of the legislative session—sine die was coming, and he had to close the deal before the gavel came down.

Ernaut again dialed as many Republicans as he could urging them to call Mason. Shortly thereafter, Mason left the house for a breakfast meeting with former Gov. Bob List at an eatery called the Coffee Grinder in Reno. He called Ernaut and invited him along. List, echoing Ernaut's words, urged Mason to sign the agreement. But Mason was far from finished hearing about the issue, thanks to Ernaut. He was deluged with phone calls from prominent Republicans, including Senate Majority Leader Bill Raggio, state Sen. Randolph Townsend, and Assembly Minority Leader Lynn Hettrick. Ensign, too, weighed in, urging Mason not to jeopardize his chances against Reid.

As Mason was being lobbied, a frenzy of activity was occurring in the rural counties. Petition organizers on both sides were preparing to file with the secretary of state. Time was short, and Mason had yet to give in. The Culinary's Taylor was doing all he could to hold back his colleagues, some of whom were itching to file their petitions, too. By 9:30 p.m., after being pounded for hours by Republicans, Mason realized he had little choice. Even Muth, worried that the entire operation had been botched, advised Mason to ink the pact with the archenemy. Mason then had the unpleasant task of bearing the bad tidings to Adelson in Israel. The Venetian developer was dejected and angry. He told Mason, then later Ensign, that he was the only one willing to stand up to a union he believed was harassing him and threatening his business.

In addition to talking to the apoplectic Adelson, Ensign made a propitious call to Culinary International boss John Wilhelm, just to let him know that he had played a role in killing paycheck protection.

Mason called Burdish and instructed him to call the

petition-gatherers to ensure the documents were not filed. Burdish also called the 17 county clerks to instruct them not to accept any petitions that might slip through. Harris, now in Elko, was furious when he learned the news. After making the calls, Burdish headed down to Leavitt's office for a scheduled 11:15 a.m. meeting to consummate the elusive pact. When he arrived, Taylor was there, along with McCracken, GOP lawyer George Chanos, and David Frederick, a Lionel, Sawyer & Collins attorney who also represented the party. After a brief presentation to Leavitt, the mutual non-aggression pact was signed about noon.

One month after the shock of Jan Jones' re-emergence, Guinn once again looked like the presumptive governor. Labor, the critical interest group for any Democratic candidate, had been neutralized. His campaign had stopped Jones from getting the AFL-CIO endorsement and paycheck protection was off the ballot, thus preventing a major union turnout effort in November. And the polls showed him running strongly in the primary and general elections.

In fact, a mid-June *Review-Journal* survey, the first comprehensive one released, showed Guinn with a 14-point lead over Jones, a 41-point lead over Russo, and a 47-point advantage over Hammargren. Russo fulminated that the numbers were cooked because of the close connection between the newspaper and Guinn's campaign team. But that was merely noise. The primary was essentially over, and Guinn had a sizable lead over his inevitable general-election opponent, who still faced another Ethics Commission inquiry.

It was only June—three months until the primary and five months until the general. But Guinn & Co. had made paycheck protection disappear and labor had taken on a Swiss stance. Team Guinn felt very, very confident.

10

ANOINTMENT LOST

It was the last thing Jan Jones and Kenny Guinn agreed on before November. And when the news broke on June 20, 1998, it seemed to have no relevance to the governor's race specifically, or Nevada politics in general. Two months after the state's two largest power companies—Sierra Pacific Resources and Nevada Power—had announced a merger, Guinn and Jones were among a slew of elected officials who signed letters of endorsement for the proposal. The letters were cited in full-page ads in the *Las Vegas Review-Journal* and the *Reno Gazette-Journal*, proudly trumpeted by the proposed merged entity.

In her letter, Jones gushed how the utilities had "earned the trust and respect of Nevadans by fulfilling their commitment to provide reliable, quality, electric service at reasonable prices." Guinn similarly fawned, saying in his endorsement that the merged companies "will eventually serve as a model for all electric utilities." Other power brokers endorsed the merger, including the state's U.S. senators, congressmen, Assembly Speaker Joe Dini, and Senate Majority Leader Bill Raggio. Not one regulatory hurdle had been cleared. Not one detail had been released regarding the potential impact on ratepayers or shareholders.

So what spawned these gushing endorsements of a deal

with no detail? It was simple: The most powerful political consultants in the state had requested them. Billy Vassiliadis and Greg Ferraro, both of R&R Advertising, represented the two power companies. Both, of course, were in Guinn's kitchen Cabinet. Both were advisers to Raggio and other prominent pols. The utilities were also major campaign contributors.

Rabble-rousing underdogs Aaron Russo, Joe Neal, and Lonnie Hammargren criticized the letters and the ads. But that was a one-day story. No one found it questionable that Jones and Guinn, one of whom would soon be responsible for making appointments to the state Public Utilities Commission that would have to approve the merger, would take so early a position on such a complicated transaction. Weren't they giving an a priori signal to state regulators to sanction the deal? Wasn't that kind of strange?

Apparently, no one thought so. At least not publicly.

After Guinn's team had ensured that the AFL-CIO convention had not given Jones any buoyancy, and after paycheck protection had been erased, the time came to make a statement. A statement about what he had—and, more importantly, what Jones did not: money.

Guinn commenced a mammoth television buy, beginning with a spot outlining his resume, then following up with the series of ads featuring an actor posing as a journalist "interviewing" the candidate—the latter clearly a reaction to criticisms of Guinn's vapid campaign. Next, he began to air spots about his plan for ethics reform and his commitment to education. Standard fare. But the statement was in the amount of the buy, one that his campaign team said would continue unabated until November. And Guinn had the resources to do it—about $3.5 million—and he was raising more. Even Hilton Hotels' chief Arthur Goldberg, a well-known contributor to Democratic Party causes, was considering an event for Guinn in New York.

All the atmospherics were coming together for Guinn. Jones wasn't even in town for most of the late spring and early summer, as she was absorbing radiation treatments in San Francisco. When she returned, she released a statement from her medical team on June 17, trying to reassure voters about her recovery from breast cancer. Her oncologist, Joe Quagliana, said in the release, "There is no doubt that Jones is capable of running for, and serving as, governor of Nevada." But she was playing defense.

Then, one day later, a story broke that seemed at first to be recurring static from a lawsuit from an old Jones nemesis, former City Councilman Steve Miller. Miller had unsuccessfully challenged Jones for the mayoralty in 1991, then sued her for libel after she crushed him in the primary. Partly responsible for the trouncing was a last-minute flier that implied, outrageously, that he was a drug dealer. The June 18 story reported that a Supreme Court justice, Charles Springer, had said during a hearing on the case that the flier "looks like libel per se to me." Miller, who made a career in the '90s of losing elections, then pursuing his conquerors with an Ahab-like zeal, blast-faxed a release to the media and others. In addition to Springer's quote, Miller included an old quote from Gov. Bob Miller (no relation), who defeated the mayor in a brutal 1994 gubernatorial primary. "It's apparent she's willing to run a negative gutter campaign," Miller had said at the time in response to a Jones attack. "The important thing here is the fact that the mayor is willing to besmirch the reputation of anybody for her own political gain." The story was just a distraction, but no one knew then what a harbinger the Steve Miller release would be for the fall campaign.

By the end of June, Jones had raised about $500,000, ordinarily a fairly impressive pace for a candidate who had been in the race for only 45 days. She had one major fundraiser before July, a June 29 event at her home. She made a point of telling people that she had received money from prominent donors—the Howard Hughes Corp. and Station Casinos, for instance. But Guinn had raised seven times as much at that point.

And Guinn was on a roll. He was very visible, scooping up money at a historic pace and dominating the airwaves. The campaign wasn't resting on its laurels, by any means. Team Guinn was looking for a way to make an even more forceful statement to elevate their man and diminish Jones— and Greg Ferraro, the R&R executive from Reno, had an idea how to do it.

The idea was beautiful in its simplicity and in the message it would send: Get as many mayors as possible to endorse the candidate for governor who was running against the mayor of Las Vegas. Not only were these men influential in their communities, the symbolism would not be lost on the media: Why can't Jan Jones get her own colleagues in the mayoral fraternity to support her? What does that say about her ability to be a leader? The truth was, as Kenny Guinn's campaign knew, that Jones was one of the most unpopular politicians ever among her fellow elected officials. Her colleagues were jealous of her media attention, disgusted by her occasionally blithe statements, and offended by her lone-wolf attitude.

The Guinnites were convinced the melange of mayors would have a crunching psychological effect on Jones, while sending a strong message to the public and the major donor community. So they lined them up, these mayors, at Guinn's headquarters in Las Vegas on June 25. Many of them barely knew the candidate, but they surely knew his campaign advisers. Reno Mayor Jeff Griffin's son, Josh Griffin, was working as Guinn's northern coordinator. Greg Ferraro's father, Bob, was the mayor of Boulder City. Mike Montandon, the North Las Vegas chief executive, counted Steve Wark, Guinn's grass-roots overseer, as his top political adviser.

Most of the mayors were Republicans. However, Jim Gibson, mayor of fast-growing Henderson, was considered

one of the Democratic Party's future statewide officehold-
ers. Yet he'd committed to Guinn long before Jones got into
the race, and he never saw her as a team player. Gibson's
endorsement was a harsh setback. Not only was he a Democrat, but as a Mormon, he also sent a message to a key voting bloc. And his words were hardly temperate: "[Guinn]
has an ability to grasp the big picture, and at the same time,
deal with details," Gibson said. "This is a man of vision
who has the knowledge and the insight to work with local
leaders in guiding Nevada's future."

Guinn was extravagant when he called the endorsements
from all the mayors "an unparalleled, unprecedented, defining moment in Nevada politics." But the embrace of the
municipal establishment gave further definition to the coa-
lescing of the political elite behind the candidate who had
been anointed 1,000 days before the election.

The campaign followed up on July 10 with a news conference celebrating the endorsement of three dozen Republican Party leaders, including the state's highest elected officials. This, too, was symbolic—no one thought Russo or
Hammargren, who was, although no one seemed to care,
the state's highest-ranking GOP elected official, could garner any Establishment support. It would have been news
had any of those elected officials *not* endorsed Guinn, the
man they saw as lifting up the entire GOP ticket that year.

But even state GOP Chairman John Mason, who had
caused the Guinnites so much consternation with his encouragement of paycheck protection and coddling of Donor
Numero Uno Sheldon Adelson, signed on with the anointment. Poor Mason—he just couldn't win. Soon afterward, a
move began to censure the chairman for his endorsement of
Guinn, which was highly unusual, coming as it did before
the primary. The censure effort was catalyzed by Russo and
activists he had on the party's central committees.

The Guinn campaign conducted a survey the second
week in July to gauge where he was vis a vis his opponents,
especially Jones. In the poll, Guinn had a 14-point lead—

49-35—over Jones, which confirmed the *Review-Journal* poll results of a few weeks earlier. Guinn was now known by 80 percent of Nevada voters, thanks to his TV campaign, and he had only a 14 percent unfavorable rating only two months before the primary and four months until the general. Both Hammargren (23-27) and Russo (23-36) had upside-down totals, meaning more voters saw them unfavorably than favorably. They were political corpses, with little hope of resuscitation.

The subtext of Jan Jones' campaign—that she was running to prevent a perversion of the democratic process—would wait for the general election. During the primary against Joe Neal, the underfunded state senator whose populist anti-gaming rants had marginalized him, Jones happily accepted the embrace of party leaders. The Democrats saw Jones as their savior. Harry Reid and others, of course, didn't think she could win—nor did they care all that much—but they knew she would bolster the top of the ticket.

So when she finally and formally kicked off her campaign on July 10, Jan Jones was the Anointed One, joined even by the man, Gov. Bob Miller, whose roots in the power structure had been impossible for her to pull up during her 1994 bid. Reid, not known for meticulousness in his political speeches, could barely contain himself at a rally outside Jones' headquarters. The senator called Jones "the perfect candidate." For him, at least.

Reid alluded to the Guinn anointment, insisting "There's going to be a queen's coronation, not a king's." And Jones, the center of an event designed to show that the Democrats were unified behind her and that Neal was irrelevant, called herself "the fly in the anointment." She oscillated from issue to issue, though she did stress education. She talked about knowing, from her political experience as mayor, how to build consensus—belied by her record—and also dropped into her remarks that unlike anyone else in the race, "I'm a mother." Reid was beaming.

But the euphoria of that summer evening dissolved quickly into the reality that Jones was trailing Guinn by double digits, and millions of dollars, and needed to do something to show that she was viable and vibrant. She couldn't compete with Guinn's endorsements, although she made a token effort. The Las Vegas Chamber of Commerce was a case in point. Guinn had gone through the interview process weeks earlier, knowing that the endorsement was assured. On the morning of July 14, Jones breezed into the organization's offices for her interview. She displayed her signature tardiness—she was 45 minutes late—but that wasn't why she never had a chance. The chamber, after giving her the courtesy of an interview, wasted no time in "deciding." The organization voted the next day to endorse Guinn. The vote was unanimous.

Jones tried to answer that failure with an announcement that the State of Nevada Employees Association had endorsed her candidacy, but almost no media attended the news conference. She also trumpeted the fact that House Minority Leader Dick Gephardt would be coming to town to help her raise money. But no one paid much attention. The state employee group had little political cachet, and Gephardt was coming to Las Vegas to meet with labor leaders more than he was to help Jones.

Meanwhile, Jones tried to mine the fundraising lode in Washington, with the help of her friends, Eric and Heidi Hanson. These two lobbyists had assisted in her mayoral campaign and she had reciprocated by securing city lobbying contracts for them. The D.C. trip helped secure a favorable review from national pundit Stu Rothenberg, who rated the Nevada governor's race a dead heat in a round-up of gubernatorial contests.

Jones then returned to Las Vegas and tried to inject life into her campaign by airing her first TV commercials, two months after she had entered the contest. The ads, which ran for 10 days and cost her campaign $200,000, were classic image spots, with some of the political resume airbrushed. She took credit for creating 200,000 new jobs, a wildly exaggerated claim, and for working with Gov. Bob Miller to improve education, also a stretch because of their frosty relationship.

If Jones already thought she was running on an oil-slicked track, greased with Guinn's money and organization, the ground completely went out from underneath her on July 23. That day, the state Ethics Commission met in Reno and found enough evidence to hold a full-blown hearing on the mayor's involvement in the City Council's denial of Nick's Fishmarket. Richard Schuetz shoved a reporter away from Jones after the hearing and Jones refused to comment. They seemed shocked that the panel had decided to move forward, even though the questions appeared legitimate: Should she have talked to Bill Boyd, who lobbied against the project, about a campaign contribution? And should she have disclosed her husband's financial relationship with Boyd and others? Whatever the answers, the hearing was set for Aug. 14, two weeks before the primary. Erasing Joe Neal would be no problem, even if an adverse finding occurred. But if she were found guilty of an ethics violation 75 days before the general election, the race was over. And the Guinn campaign knew it.

"On our part, there was pretty much an assumption of guilt," said one Guinn insider. "We kind of thought she had pretty much shot herself in the face, not even in the foot." To the Guinn team, it felt like Frankie Sue Del Papa dropping out all over again—part complacency, part arrogance. "At that point, for the second time in the campaign, we made a mistake and settled into a comfort zone," one campaign adviser remembered. And why not? Jones had an ethics cloud that at the very least darkened her prospects and might even rain out her chances. And what else did Guinn have to worry about? A carpetbagger named Aaron Russo and an oddball lieutenant governor name Lonnie

Hammargren? Not likely. The campaign's internal polling in late July showed Guinn 35 points ahead of Russo and 46 points ahead of Hammargren.

The skies brightened even more for Guinn on July 30 when a transcript of the ethics hearing revealed Commission Chairwoman Mary Boetsch scolding Jones and Schuetz for behaving as if they had "a bank merger, not a marriage." Boetsch and other commissioners expressed disbelief that the pair had not discussed any of Schuetz's dealings with Boyd and others who were involved with the bank that opposed the restaurant zoning. It wasn't pretty.

The only good news for Jones in July came during the last week when an alternative weekly, *CityLife*, published an interview with both candidates conducted by reporter Steve Sebelius. Whether it was his rambling performance during the interview, which was published in what Sebelius indicated was an edited version of 12,300 words, or the way it was distilled, Guinn came off badly. For instance, here's the exchange on a question about gay marriage:

Do you think there should be a state sanction of gay marriages?

Guinn: Well, I think that's an issue that should go through again, our open process of government, which we have where people who have that interest and they want to introduce a bill, then it goes through the regular process like hundreds or thousands of other bills for us.

What about just your gut instinct on the issue? Do you support it?

Guinn: Well, I think consenting adults have the right to participate in a variety of areas, as long as it's not adversely affecting other people. I think when you come down to some of those issues, and I'm assuming that you're kind of driving at the one now where if you have two consenting adults, do they have the same rights as a man and woman, male and female, who would end up being married in terms of their hospitalization, medical benefit packages and that kind of thing. And I think before that can happen on an individual company-by-company or city-by-city basis, that has to come through the process of legislation for the state of Nevada.

Luckily for Guinn, not too many voters read *CityLife*.

As for Jones, she needed a press secretary, especially after her nightmarish week of coverage in the mainstream media on her ethics-panel appearance. This was when the ever-controlling Harry Reid helped bring his ex-press secretary, Susan McCue, into Jones' orbit. McCue's job was to energize Jones' seemingly faltering effort enough to make the mayor competitive, at least, so Reid could reap the benefits in his Senate re-election.

In the prelude to her date with the Ethics Commission, Jones, with McCue's help, tried to generate favorable media. She put out a release on the state teachers union endorsing her. A dud. Almost no coverage. She issued another release declaring she would veto paycheck protection, trying to send a signal to the unions who had declined to endorse her that she, not the inconsistent Guinn, was their real friend. No one bit.

In fact, Jones' only news coverage in those days was coming from out of state, where viewers from afar were captivated by the story of a woman overcoming breast cancer to run for the state's highest office. A wonderful storyline, and one that if used properly in-state had the potential to topple a better-funded opponent.

"Las Vegas Mayor Runs for Governor, Undaunted by Cancer," blared the headline in the Aug. 4 edition of *The New York Times*. Jones had always done better on the national stage than at home and this was no exception. The piece emphasized Jones' openness about her breast cancer as indicative of a trend in politics where those in the spotlight have to reveal more of their private lives. And the *Times*, apparently unaware that her campaign was struggling, described her thusly: "Ms. Jones' volubility about her breast cancer is only the latest surprising chapter in a political career that has pegged her as one of the most interesting up-and-comers in the Democratic Party."

But Jones' star was far from rising at that time in Nevada. In fact, Guinn was getting ready to apply what the campaign hoped would be the coup de grace. One week before her ethics hearing, Guinn began airing a new TV ad that, not coincidentally, played up his commitment to ethics in government. In the ad, Guinn declared that "strong ethical laws are essential to building public trust."

The campaign also announced a fundraising extravaganza in Reno that was meant to drive home the point that the tsunami was coming. The mid-August event would be co-hosted by Don Carano, Larry Ruvo, and Harvey Whittemore. Carano was one of northern Nevada's most influential gaming figures, owner of The Eldorado and known in some circles as the godfather of Reno. Ruvo, who was the head of Southern Nevada Wine and Spirits, was a socially well-connected and immensely successful businessman. And Whittemore was the gaming lobbyist and Ruvo business associate who once mused about getting his law partner, Brian McKay, the former attorney general, into the race. But, ever the pragmatist and expert tea-leave reader, Whittemore had clambered on board the Guinn bandwagon. Guinn was approaching the $4 million mark and this event would help. But the money was not nearly so important as what it symbolized: invincibility.

Then, on Aug. 7, it happened—one of the defining moments of the race. It showed the power of the media to influence campaigns, as well as the enduring proposition that politics is the most mercurial business of all. That day, the *Las Vegas Review-Journal*, which conducted regular polling, published its latest survey. The results were nothing short of shocking: Guinn's 41-point lead over Russo had dissolved into a fragile seven-point margin. His lead over Jones had slipped from 14 points to five.

Guinn and his aides were flabbergasted. The campaign's internal numbers still showed the candidate with gargantuan margins over Russo and Hammargren and a substantial lead over Jones. As Guinn pointed out in the *R-J* story, "I don't know of anything that has happened in the last 60 days to change these poll numbers. It seems an aberration to me."

But Guinn & Co. couldn't be sure what had transpired. Most doubted the *R-J's* polling firm. Mason-Dixon/Political Media Research had hit some Nevada results dead-on in the past. But the firm had also missed the mark occasionally and didn't have the national reputation enjoyed by the pollsters used by the gaming industry—and the Guinn campaign for that matter. As Sig Rogich put it later, "We found it hard to believe. It contradicted what we were showing, but we couldn't take any chances."

Vassiliadis said that most people close to Guinn thought the results were "bullshit. But the campaign was very susceptible to outside pressure, and if you're not paranoid, you ought not to be in this business. The other thing," he added, "is you react in a certain way to soothe the fears of your supporters. And at that point, the troops were pretty shaken." And some of the troops actually were afraid the numbers could be right. Wark and his field soldiers had picked up tremors that what he called Russo's "populist yakking" was cutting Guinn, who had not responded to the challenger's televised attacks and who, in Wark's opinion, was being overhandled.

The fear of the unknown, the unmeasurable, also came into play. Was the anti-Establishment, anti-anointment feeling stronger than any of the savvy veteran campaign operatives had imagined? Could all the money, all the institutional support, be crushed under the weight of a popular uprising led by a carpetbagging demagogue whom no one had taken seriously? Guinn et al. had to find out.

The Guinn campaign immediately commissioned a poll that went into the field the same day as the *R-J* story appeared. The results invigorated the Guinnites. Guinn still led Russo by 22 points, 47-25. Rogich, Vassiliadis, and Ernaut were more convinced than ever that the *R-J* poll was simply wrong. But did that mean they didn't have to act?

I made light of the Guinn campaign's predicament in a column that Sunday headlined, "The Power of Polls." The results of the survey showed, I wrote, "the Anointed One hemorrhaging and the California Crackpot almost within the margin of error."

And then, I wondered, "Can this be so? Can the conventional wisdom—Guinn coasts to victory—be wrong? ... Can it be that the ex-Hollywood movie producer, now using Jack Nicholson to boost his candidacy, could be elected, thus transforming the Silver State into ... The Loon Star State? Say it ain't so, Kenny. Your 'better safe than sorry' campaign seemed so compelling. What could have gone awry?

"Excuse me for being a little facetious in the midst of the terrifying thought that Russo actually has a chance. Hubris humbled is always entertaining, and the Guinnites having to rush into the field with a poll Thursday night just to assure themselves that the *Review-Journal* poll couldn't be right is quite humorous."

An interview with pollster Del Ali, the head of the *R-J's* polling firm, revealed that his own internal numbers didn't jibe. He wasn't even sure of regional breakdowns—that is, how many people he polled lived in populous and Democratic Clark County versus the rest of the state. But the fact that the survey had appeared on the front page of the state's most important and widely read news outlet was enough to shake up the race's dynamic. The poll couldn't really be true, could it? I concluded, "Then again, maybe the mighty Ali has forecast the future once again, Guinnville is shrinking and Carson City is about to become Kook City. I don't believe it. But just in case, I'm packing a bag."

That Sunday morning, my phone rang. I picked up the

receiver and there was no salutation, just this: "Pack your fucking bags." It was Russo in all his profane glory, gleeful, thrilled, downright manic about the column. He assured me that Hammargren would endorse him and get out of the race to clear the way for his challenge to Guinn. And there was more to come that following week.

Russo was now spending $50,000 or so a week on TV, lambasting Guinn as a Democrat in Republican garb. He planned a radio spot with his Hollywood pal, Jack Nicholson, which previously would have been laughed off by everyone, but now was taken seriously. Indeed, the Guinn folks began crafting a response with the theme, "Nevada doesn't know Jack."

The Guinnites had been tracking Russo's TV buy and decided they had to make a decisive move, whether or not their polling numbers were right and Ali's were wrong. Even though turnout in the September primary was expected to be low and the campaign had a high degree of confidence in Steve Wark's grass-roots machine, nothing could be left to the vagaries of Election Day. They began to think about what approach to use. Vassiliadis had always told Rogich and Ernaut that Russo was a one-week campaign—that he could be dispatched with the right negative spots in seven days or thereabouts. Now they were going to find out.

Jones, awaiting a possible campaign death sentence from the ethics jury, was thrilled with the *R-J* poll results. And, in one of those non-coincidences that occur frequently in politics, her extensive opposition research on Guinn, prepared by Dan Carol & Associates, found its way into Russo's hands. Suddenly, there was Russo on TV, with a new ad that mirrored the document Jones had commissioned from Carol. It turned every one of Guinn's strengths—his education background as schools superintendent, his business acumen—on its head:

"Kenny Guinn is consistent, consistently failing. During his term as boss of Southwest Gas, dividends fell in half. To pay for his failure, he raised your gas rates twenty percent. The request for rate increases included the purchase of two corporate jets and a Jaguar. PriMerit Bank assets shrank seven hundred million dollars in two years under his leadership. As superintendent of schools, he denied teachers maternity leave as the school ranking plunged. Kenny, please tell us where you've been successful."

Russo, keeping to his pattern, had used a blunderbuss instead of a laser, disgorging virtually every point of Jones' opposition research in one commercial. Guinn was incensed. A man he had considered a troublesome gnat had suddenly become a mutant-sized fly causing a buzz that actually threatened his path to Carson City. His team leapt into action; the Guinnites' TV response to Russo became the most memorable ad of the campaign.

It was all Russo. And, ironically, it was what had prompted Russo to run in the first place, the video he had produced a few years earlier called "Mad as Hell" that he claimed sold so well in Nevada. It featured Russo, then with long scraggly hair, prancing around on stage, fulminating against the federal government and screaming at one point into the camera: "It's insanity!" He looked crazy and the Guinn camp knew it. They lifted snippets from the video and used that close-up of Russo, then edited it into a 30-second spot. As the video played in the background, a narrator intoned, "Who is Aaron Russo?" The spot then detailed his brief residency in Nevada, his spotty voting record, and tax liens filed against him in two others states. Finally, the memorable kicker: "Aaron Russo. Embarrassing to Nevada. Dangerous as governor."

The spot was brilliant, a Sig Rogich special. Rogich was the one who'd produced the devastating ad for George Bush in 1988 that featured Michael Dukakis looking goofy as he rode around in a tank. The ad was widely credited for helping to undercut the Democratic presidential nominee's credibility. With Russo, as Vassiliadis remembered, "There was a discussion of the various ways you could go at [him]. He was a carpetbagger, had no driver's license, had the tax delinquency in California. The notion was, and this was Sig's, let's make the guy out to be a nut. Let's reinforce people's worst fears about him."

Ernaut, actually, had been the first to see the video of "Mad as Hell" months earlier and knew it could be wielded to destroy Russo if the time ever came. He never thought it would. But when it did, Rogich quickly assembled the ominous music, set off by a perfectly soothing female voice, and let the video clips speak for themselves.

The ad so infuriated Russo—he claimed he was acting on that "Mad as Hell" stage, although he stood by what he said—that he responded with a series of nuclear broadcast attacks on Guinn. He questioned Guinn's record as a businessman—more fodder from Jones' opposition research document. He also wondered about $50,000 Guinn had accepted (and then returned) from controversial gambler/developer Billy Walters. And he again referred to Guinn as a RINO—"Republican In Name Only." Finally, in a burst of creativity, Russo used an old quote from Republican Establishment icon Tom Wiesner, the party's national committeeman, smashing Guinn as a Democrat-lover.

Meanwhile, Russo was negotiating Hammargren's exit from the contest in order to consolidate the protest votes for a shot at defeating Guinn in the primary. Hammargren knew his campaign was going nowhere, but his wife didn't want him to withdraw. By the week of Aug. 11, however, Hammargren was set to bow out. Ultimately, though, he couldn't bring himself to make a formal announcement. Ironically, the media, hot on the trail of the story of his demise, began to give Hammargren attention he had not previously been able to garner. In a couple of speeches that week, Hammargren, appropriating Russo's words, said voters were "mad as hell" at "immense corruption" at the local and state levels. Hammargren also praised Russo, saying he had struck a chord with voters. In a further irony, Hammargren was serving as governor when he spoke the words, acting in Bob Miller's stead while the latter was on a tourism trip to Latin America.

By the end of the week, Hammargren was saying in a speech that he couldn't win, but he wouldn't withdraw. A line in his prepared remarks called for an official exit—but he couldn't bring himself to read it. It didn't matter much; it was too late to take his name off the ballot. All he could do was carry around a mail piece that was creative and colorful, but one which he couldn't afford to send to voters. He held out hope that Russo would "shake the good old boys to their foundation."

Jan Jones was vying with Hammargren for the temporary chairmanship of the Aaron Russo Fan Club. She was gleeful that both Russo and Hammargren had awakened from their somnolence and were finally pounding Guinn. If the pair, especially Russo, could tarnish the frontrunner, after she skated by Neal she might have a real chance. All she had to do was surmount what she knew was the turning point in her campaign—that Aug. 14 date with the Ethics Commission.

The hearing that Friday in the Las Vegas City Council Chambers had the power to end Jones' campaign. After extensive testimony, in which Jones and Schuetz asserted they did not discuss his business dealings, the panel voted unanimously to exonerate her. Chairwoman Mary Boetsch admonished Jones for her ignorance, as she claimed, of her husband's business transactions, telling the mayor, "It is your obligation to find out what they are so that when [potentially conflicting issues] come before you, you will know." But the verdict and the headlines that followed were what mattered: "Jones Absolved in Eatery Vote." Her hopes of becoming governor had been revived, incredibly, by the same panel that she and the Guinnites had viewed as the Grim Reaper.

Two weeks loomed before the Sept. 1 primary, and Jones and her campaign sensed the momentum turning. Despite his money and organization, Guinn was being attacked by two challengers from his own party, while Jones essentially had a free ride. The mayor and her aides figured all she had to do was keep her name in the media virtually every day and hope that Russo and Hammargren could do major damage to Guinn before they were inevitably vanquished on Primary Day.

And so she did. One day it was a discussion of women's-health issues, playing up her breast cancer recovery—the target audience was obvious. Next it was a couple of ads touting her education bona fides. She didn't really have any—the mayoralty has little to do with education policy—but commercials about safe schools and computers in classrooms had poll-tested resonance. (Just ask Kenny Guinn.) Her underfunded primary opponent, Joe Neal, also made a minuscule TV buy, playing up his populist credentials. But it was too small to have an impact.

Jones was closing on Guinn, too. Even before she'd been cleared by the ethics panel, a Mirage Resorts' poll showed her pulling to within six points of the GOP contender. And on Aug. 21, even better news surfaced for Jones. Guinn was about to report raising nearly $4 million. However, thanks to Russo, a consultant-laden staff, and an expensive organization, he had spent more than three-quarters of his war chest, and was down to about $840,000. Jones had only about a fourth of that on hand, but the gap had dwindled.

Privately, a few of the Guinnites were rattled by Russo. They didn't believe the *R-J* poll, but they couldn't be sure until Primary Day. Sensing weakness, Russo was clamoring for a debate. And instead of ignoring him, as he might have done a month earlier, Ernaut responded with a letter on Aug. 21. He informed Russo that Guinn "welcomes the opportunity to debate," but insisted on having Hammargren on the dais, too, which he hoped would be a deal-killer. It was.

The media, though, was salivating over the storyline. The AP's Brendan Riley wrote on Aug. 27: "With strong backing from the casino industry, Kenny Guinn seemed a safe bet to win next week's Republican primary for governor—until a longshot from California changed the odds."

And Jones kept purring along, emboldened by her apparent momentum and issuing almost a release a day to get attention during the final fortnight before the primary. It didn't matter how insipid—in one spot she congratulated a 104-year-old voter for being … a 104-year-old voter—as long as she got the sound bite or the photo. Jones was also shoring up her support in Northern Nevada, where Las Vegas is anathema and Las Vegas mayors have horns. She ran a crime spot and spent the penultimate weekend before the primary campaigning in the north. A few days before the primary she was endorsed by the Service Employees International Union, which represents government and health care workers.

Jones' high hopes for the Republican primary, though, were deflated on Aug. 28 when the last *R-J* poll before the balloting showed Guinn had turned back Russo's challenge and was pulling away. Guinn posted an 18-point lead in the survey. The good news for the mayor, though, was that she remained a mere five points behind Guinn, so the perception was that the race was on. And it was.

As the returns began to trickle in on Sept. 1, they unmasked Russo as a media-created bump in the road for Guinn. Thanks to the "Mad as Hell" ad, Russo's own shortcomings, and Guinn's grass-roots organization, the Anointed One won by 33 points, 59-26. Jones defeated Neal by an even larger margin, 43 points (59-16).

Quietly, the Guinn team had been hoping for a sign that Jones' support was superficial, with Neal perhaps garnering a third of the Democratic Party vote. Now they had to confront the reality that the primary had affirmed: Nine

hundred days after he had announced his candidacy for governor and then assiduously built an organization, Hoovered
up money, and tried to make a race unnecessary, Kenny
Guinn was in a real contest with Jan Jones.

11

ANOINTMENT
FOUND

In mid-1991, when Jan Jones became mayor of Las Vegas, she was the toast of the town. No one had ever brought that much dynamism, that much charisma, to the mayoralty in a city where glitter and glitz were prized. The Southern Nevada social elite was thrilled. One of their own had been elected, not some grubby pol they would have to schmooze. No, they could call Jan at home and chat up city business. She was glamorous, she was getting national attention, she was a media darling.

But she wasn't going to meetings. Oh, she attended the City Council every fortnight—there she got to preside, the queen on a media stage. But she missed two of the first three meetings of the Las Vegas Convention and Visitors Authority board, a high-profile panel Jones wanted to be on because of its impact on tourism. She had also fought to get on two of the more important boards in the valley—the Regional Transportation Commission and the Flood Control District. Yet, after taking office on June 19, she skipped the first two monthly meetings of each board. Just hadn't shown up. Why not? During one set of meetings, she was sunning herself with her husband at their Newport Beach, Calif., getaway. During the other, she was sojourning in Mexico with her kids to watch a solar eclipse.

Although it was relatively early, the question arose: Was she planning to be the dilettante that her critics had feared during the campaign, the jet-set mayor who dropped in just in time for the press conference?

Jones defended her absences by saying that she badly needed time with her husband after the campaign and that the next eclipse wouldn't be for 78 years. "I work twelve hours a day," she told me when I confronted her about the missed meetings. "No one has taken this job as seriously as I have."

Jones handled the first spate of adverse attention in a manner that became typical—a flash of anger followed by her trademark wit. When I ran into her the same day my column about her absences appeared, she saw me across the room, glared in my direction, and offered me her middle finger. A short time later, I received in the mail a button she had picked up in Mexico while viewing the eclipse. "I blacked out in Baja," it said.

The question remained, though: Were these missed meetings an aberration or the shape of things to come, a potentially devastating issue that could destroy what initially appeared to be the beginning of a special political career?

Despite Kenny Guinn's smashing primary victory, Jan Jones was happy with the 1998 primary-election results. And she wasn't alone. The entire Democratic Party was euphoric. Kenny Guinn, the man everyone thought would give the entire GOP ticket buoyancy, had tumbled back to Earth. If Jones could just keep up the momentum until November, it would help all Democratic aspirants, especially Harry Reid. And now, for the first time, insiders were actually contemplating a prospect they'd never considered before: Jones could win.

Reid could barely contain himself. He couldn't have planned it better. He gushed on primary night about "the five women who will be joining me on the ticket." Jones, congressional candidate Shelley Berkley, lieutenant governor hopeful Rose McKinney-James, Attorney General Frankie Sue Del Papa, and state-controller candidate Mary Sanada were being called the Estrogen Ticket. For Reid, a pro-life Democrat running against handsome, energetic John Ensign, it was perfect. What better way to close the gender gap? Now Reid just had to make sure that the anchor of the ticket, Jones, stayed competitive with Guinn for the next two months, ensuring that enough voters would turn out to vote for her—and, of course, him.

Reid's ex-press secretary, Susan McCue, had already asserted herself in the Jones campaign, eclipsing campaign manager Denise Rawles, the Philadelphia transplant who never got comfortable in Nevada. Jones was listening to McCue, media consultant Roy Behr, and Lindsey Lewis, an ex-Dick Gephardt fundraiser she had hired to ensure she attracted enough money to stay in the game. Jones knew she would have to help out with her own check, but she hoped not to go into debt by as much as she had in 1994— $250,000.

Jones was disappointed that Russo hadn't been more competitive on Primary Day. But she figured that because the polls put her so close with Guinn, her fundraising would pick up. She was wrong—at least about the in-state money. "After the primary, it didn't get any easier to raise money," she later recalled. "These guys [the Guinnites] effectively cut off major donors who could write big checks."

Jones' campaign passed around a cover sheet from Fairbank, Maslin, Maullin & Associates, a Southern California polling firm, that showed Guinn and Jones in a statistical dead heat right before the primary. The firm was doing surveys for the state Democratic Party, but the numbers didn't seem skewed. The memo, disseminated by Jones to help her fundraising, began by declaring, "According to our recent survey, the race for governor has changed dramatically in the last two months."

The poll didn't help much with the casinos, however. Jones had lunch with the number-two man at a prominent casino corporation and was seen on the property by the chairman, who had committed to Guinn. After the lunch, the executive was called on the carpet by his boss for eating with her. "Don't you know that woman is going to raise taxes on the gaming industry?" the chairman said to his subordinate, even though Jones had never advocated a gaming tax increase.

"These guys stood by their guns," Jones said later. "[Harrah's boss] Phil Satre is a good friend of mine and I had to fight to get fifteen thousand out of Harrah's." Jones had to coax other industry executives, too, with the exception of Mirage Resorts Chairman Steve Wynn, who openly said he would give $25,000 [aggregated from different properties to comply with a $10,000 cap] to both candidates after the primary.

If Jones hadn't hired Lindsey Lewis, she would have been even worse off. Lewis' Rolodex reached across the country, all the way to the White House. He'd even managed to finagle a presidential fund-raiser for Jones. But Lewis called Jones from Washington and told her she didn't have to come for any event, that he'd made a deal to get the money without her being there. "Lindsey would just pick up the phone and start dialing numbers," Jones remembered later. "He would say, 'Mayor, it's Marvin Davis.' I'd say, 'What do I say?' And he'd say, 'Just tell him Gephardt told you to call him.'"

Team Guinn knew Jones would have trouble raising money—they had stanched the flow, after all—so they adopted a strategy after Primary Day designed to send a message. Guinn unloaded $1 million from his newly pumped-up campaign coffers for a television buy that would both undercut Jones' presumed strength and force her to spend whatever money she had to combat him. The ads focused on an education plan to lessen violence in schools with boot camps, expulsions, and parental-accountability provisions. Jones had tried to establish her education credentials—traditionally Democratic territory—and now Guinn, the ex-schools superintendent, was trying to reclaim his turf.

And then the Guinnites, their superior funds now a decisive advantage, planned to land the fatal blow with an ad about her spotty attendance record at meetings. Research maven Dick Cooper had found that Jones had missed thousands of votes and dozens of meetings during her seven-plus years as mayor. Rogich & Co. believed that the attendance issue would seal the race.

The only question was timing. They had to determine the most propitious moment for handing over the research to the state's pre-eminent political reporter, Jane Ann Morrison. They knew Morrison well enough to know to understand that she would check their research, which would take some time. So they planned to give the voting records to her by mid-September, hoping to see a story before October. Her article would then be the trigger for the TV ads they were preparing.

Jones knew the attack was coming. She'd already tried to defuse it on Primary Night, saying she had never missed an "important vote." But the phrasing seemed destined to haunt her.

The wild card, as the general-election season opened, was a planned series of debates. Jones clearly was quicker on her feet and spoke in sound bites. Guinn's serpentine speaking style and his mania for detail could prove a problem—and his campaign knew it. Both sides believed Jones would destroy Guinn in the debates, which is why the mayor's campaign wanted many televised confrontations and the Guinnites would agree to only a few, maybe only two or three. By the time the negotiations with the public TV stations had climaxed, the Guinn folks were ecstatic—only three TV debates were scheduled, the last of which would be on the Friday before Election Day when no one would be paying attention and the election would be unaffected. The other two would be on Oct. 9 and Oct. 11, so any damage could be tended to before the balloting.

Jones' campaign, led by Behr, McCue, and Lewis, knew they had to attack Guinn on two fronts. They had to demonstrate, first, that Jones was driven by issues, that she was laden with substance. That way, they'd spotlight a virtually issueless Guinn campaign. Yes, he had put on a few ads about education and ethics, but the perception was that the Guinn campaign verged on vapid.

Second, and this dovetailed with the first prong, they planned to show that Guinn—and by extension his team—was in the race for power and money. They'd use the research document compiled by Dan Carol about Guinn's tenure at Southwest Gas and PriMerit Bank to make their case. It was Behr, the media man, who coined the phrase that would become a signature on Jones' commercials later in the campaign: "Out For Himself. Not For Us."

It would also—if successful—undermine the central tenet of Guinn's campaign for the state's top job. As one Jonesite put it, "The guy was running as a businessman and able administrator. His record was fair game. It wasn't true just because they had this giant circle jerk that [said] Kenny Guinn was the ablest administrator of all. Kenny Guinn was put in jobs for the same reason he was put up as governor—because he was safe and he looks good." That encapsulated the opinion of the Jones camp—that they were the voice of the common folk, rebelling against the lord of the manor and his vassals, all of whom were with Guinn to share in the spoils should he move into the Carson City mansion.

Eight days after the primary, Jones began executing her plan by unveiling an environmental initiative at a news conference. The approach was emblematic of what she would do on virtually every issue that fall, later dubbed "Vision Lite." In her 1994 race, Jones had hired research personnel

202

and her city aide, Cathy Hanson, to assemble thick binders on various issues. They did extensive research, culling information from other states, and handed the binders to the media. They were generally ignored, but they gave the impression of substance.

This time, though, the approach was different. There wasn't time for full-blown briefing binders. Besides, whatever they came up with, Jones figured, was better than anything Guinn or anyone else would say that year. Her environmental plan was a mishmash of ideas, almost all of them already in state law. Jones said the difference was she would enforce the laws, though she offered no idea in what ways or how much it would cost. She just wanted the perception that she was all about issues.

Also, she began to cite her mantra in her press releases: "Jones is running for governor to improve the quality of life for Nevada's workers and make Nevada a great place to live, work, and raise families." It didn't say much, but it sounded good.

By the second week of September, Jones was again courting the AFL-CIO endorsement that Guinn had succeeded in blocking a few months earlier. The labor umbrella group routinely re-evaluated its endorsements after the primary. The go-round was different this time, though. Guinn benefited before the primary from having two Democratic candidates in the race, which gave the unions the convenient out of not having to offer up any endorsement. Now, though, there was only one Democratic contender and she had come out against paycheck protection and for collective bargaining for state workers.

Guinn had been part of the effort to get paycheck protection off the ballot, which earned the gratitude of the Culinary Union and a promise to stay out of the endorsement process. But his opposition to collective bargaining now placed his chances of stopping a Jones endorsement in jeopardy. The Culinary, which made up about 30 percent of the AFL-CIO delegates, could help Guinn if its operatives worked the convention floor. The Guinnites urged them to do so, but tensions were high with the other labor organizations. So D. Taylor and Glen Arnodo decided to sit on their hands—not a comfortable position.

Team Guinn kept pushing up until the day of the vote, Sept. 14, and the outcome was unclear as the delegates assembled at the New Frontier Hotel on the Las Vegas Strip. Guinn had the firefighters and police unions in his corner, too, but they, like the Culinary delegates, were planning to abstain. Jones had everyone else, it seemed, including the teachers, the state employees, the service employees, and most of the building-trade unions.

Jones gave her speech on the first day of the two-day convention. She reiterated her pledge to veto paycheck protection and stated that ensuring it did not become law would be her number-one priority. She was greeted enthusiastically by the crowd, which gave her a standing ovation even before she spoke.

Guinn spoke the next day and tried to emphasize his role in erasing paycheck protection from the ballot: "Many of you know that at great political risk, I was the first statewide candidate to oppose paycheck protection. Simply, I believed it was not fair and wrongly attacked the working men and women of this state. And even though I knew it would cost me the support of many in my own party, and of many Republican voters, I stood up publicly and fought against the petition." Guinn added that he and his staff "worked day and night to kill it."

Moments after his speech, in an interview with myself and Jane Ann Morrison, Guinn did a stunning turnabout when pressed on his positions. He told us that if a paycheck-protection bill passed both houses of the Legislature, who was he to veto it? He would "absolutely" sign it. "If it turns out to be a legitimate bill without those cracks in it for constitutionality or wasn't against federal law," Guinn said he would surely ink it. Using similar logic, he said that if a collective-bargaining bill made it to his desk, he would sign it, too. In general, he could not tell us any criteria he might have for vetoing any bill, since if it was vetted by lawmakers, it must be worthy of his signature. In a scathing column after the convention, I described him as a "waffling mushball."

Shortly thereafter, in what was described by those behind the closed-door voice vote as nearly unanimous, with the Culinary, cops, and firefighters silent, Jones won the endorsement of the AFL-CIO. Her campaign was ebullient. The Guinnites spun the tale they had to: that Jones had to fight for what should have automatically gone to the Democratic nominee. Privately, though, they were deeply disappointed. And now they had to count on the Culinary rank and file, with a nod from their leaders, not to turn out for Jones in November.

It was a bad moment for the GOP nominee's campaign. The next day the headline to my column was "Guinn Comes Down to Earth." The same day that Jones got the endorsement, word leaked of a new poll conducted by the casinos that showed Guinn and the mayor in a virtual tie.

The Guinn campaign was fracturing. At a strategy meeting in mid-September shortly after the AFL-CIO convention, the consultant cluster was lobbying for Guinn's attention. Sig Rogich, Kent Oram, and campaign pollster Fred Steeper were strongly advising Guinn that he had to attack Jones. They had delivered the same message privately to campaign manager Ernaut, who was not nearly so sure of that particular course of action. Instead, Ernaut believed that the safe-schools and ethics ads were giving Guinn definition. After meeting with the consultants, Ernaut knew he had to assert himself. Yes, he was in the campaign because of powerful men such as Rogich and Vassiliadis. But he had to let Guinn know that his instincts must be trusted.

Guinn was leaving the next day to fly to Ely in rural Nevada for a horse-racing event. Ernaut informed the staff that he, and no one else, would fly up with Guinn on the chartered plane. Ernaut remembered the day vividly. The plane took off at 6 a.m., one of those "beautiful and pristine days in Nevada you live for." Soon after takeoff, Ernaut made his pitch: "Kenny, every once in a while you have to make a decision in ten minutes. I hope that I've built up a respect in you because what I'm about to tell you may be the most important discussion you have in your life, because your life revolves around this governor's race. You should think very long and hard about the day you attack her. Our philosophy and our strategy are to counterpunch. Let her land a blow, and we will win the day, and you will destroy her. But if you initiate the attack, it's a point of no return. You will either make this race a close race, or make a desperate catastrophic mistake if you attack her. This is ten days into September, and you have to listen to people who know how you can win this race, not listen to people whose advice is tempered by their own agenda. You've got to promise me … you have to side with me."

In that moment, Ernaut believed, his relationship with Guinn was on the line, his position in the campaign was at risk. And Guinn responded in the way he hoped he would: "You've proved to me beyond a shadow of a doubt that you are the one guy who cares. You work the hours. You've earned my trust and my wife's trust. We believe in you."

Yet, even after all the drama and emotion packed into the conversation on the plane, Ernaut was unable to hold fast to his instincts. Shortly thereafter, the campaign conducted a poll that tested two issues: Jones' attendance record and critical audits that had been buried by city staffers. The survey showed that if those issues were unleashed on Jones, Guinn couldn't lose. The numbers were compelling—70 percent said they wouldn't vote for Jones once they'd been told about the audit and attendance problems. Ernaut couldn't discount those results and, he acknowledged later, he "got romanced by polling numbers." Ernaut recalled that his field workers, led by Steve Wark, were reporting that on the street, Guinn still was leading Jones by a significant margin. But the poll numbers told Ernaut that if the campaign went on TV with the ads the other consultants wanted to run, they could put the race out of reach by early October. So he changed his mind.

The Jones campaign, however, picked up the rumblings about an attendance spot and prepared to respond. They began to tell the media that Guinn was about to go negative, and began to play the victim. They put up one of the more vacuous spots of the campaign, called "Vision," which was all platitudes. But as Susan McCue scrawled wryly on a fax of the script she sent to me, "All positive. All the time."

The Guinn folks knew Jones & Co. had heard about their plans, so they concocted what they thought at the time was a brilliant tactic. They would go up first with a spot on the hidden audits, then come back with the attendance ad, which Jones was expecting first.

Before the ad campaign began, though, Guinn tried to highlight a Jones negative, while at the same time buffing his image as a man of integrity. The state Ethics Commission met September 17 to consider more charges against Jones, this time filed by her nemesis, ex-City Councilman Steve Miller, that she had behaved unethically by touting gaming in Detroit, while owning stock in two of the casino companies that had applied for licenses there. It was the ninth time Jones had appeared before the panel. And although she was once again exonerated, only three days later Guinn unveiled a three-point plan on ethics. The idea was not dramatic—he wanted to increase fines and have elected officials sign a code of conduct. Jones, who was releasing a women's-issue "Vision Lite" paper at the same time, played into Guinn's hands by leaving a controversial business dealing off her ethics disclosure form required for gubernatorial candidates—which was later reported in the newspapers. Guinn then, naturally, began airing a spot highlighting his ethics package.

Jones was focusing on two issues to emphasize her heft and appeal to women's groups. She was one of the earlier candidates to capitalize on the resonance of the HMO issue that would become a national cause celebre soon. She combined an attack on the large companies denying health benefits with her fight against breast cancer in one late-September ad. She also issued a white paper on growth issues, which were top-of-mind in burgeoning Southern Nevada.

In response, on Sept. 25, Guinn foreshadowed his attendance attack in a campaign release where he pointed out that her attendance at regional planning meetings was poor "and that fact calls into question her fundamental commitment to effective growth planning."

The stage was set for the last month, and it was bound to be a barnburner as polls continued to show a dead heat. The only question was which campaign would fire the first shot.

On Sunday, Sept. 27, on the front page of the local section in the *Review-Journal*, Jane Ann Morrison's story on Jones' attendance record appeared. It was brutal. The numbers spoke for themselves: From 1995 through 1997, Jones had missed 2,096 out of 8,336 votes cast at the City Council. She'd been absent 31 of 73 Convention Authority meetings, from 15 of 36 Regional Transportation Commission meetings, and from 31 of 36 Flood Control Board meetings. Jones' defense was ill-advised. "I don't think I ever missed a vote that was important to me," she told Morrison.

Guinn was ready with his rhetorical volley, saying he'd probably fired people with attendance records as awful as Jones'. "To make a contribution, you have to be there," he told Morrison. "Nevada needs a full-time governor, not an absentee governor. Looking at these figures here, it doesn't seem to me she has [the] commitment she needs to serve in this role."

Jones tried to mitigate the impact of the story by deflecting attention to Guinn's record as superintendent of schools, reading from her opposition research packet. But Morrison, after her usual detailed recitation of all the facts about the attendance record, along with Guinn's attack quotes and Jones' defense, rightly relegated the mayor's critical comments to the last paragraph of a 1,655-word piece.

The next day, Guinn struck with his audit spot, thinking it would catch a reeling Jones campaign off guard. The spot implied that Jones was responsible for the suppression of 14 audits critical of city practices during the preceding two and a half years. "Jan Jones says she's for open government," the ad concluded. "Fourteen hidden audits say she isn't."

The *R-J* had broken the story the previous spring about the audits, which found the city had spent hundreds of thousands of dollars illegally, and had cost overruns and exorbitant expenses. They had not been shown to the City Council, which had prompted Jones to call for reforms whereby the city auditor would report directly to the elected officials and not the appointive managers. And unbeknownst to the Guinn campaign, the city had actually released the audits to various media outlets after the original story in April. The ad, it turned out, was a total stretch, even for a political campaign.

Jones replied, as expected, by wailing about "negative campaigning." Then, the ex-city auditor who had disclosed the buried reports, Susan Toohey, demanded Guinn pull the ads, saying Jones had helped implement the recommendations to fix the problems detailed in the audits. Toohey, not coincidentally, had been fired from her job after disclosing the audits. She was embroiled in a lawsuit against the city and was being represented by none other than ex-Councilman Matthew Callister, Jones' friend and adviser.

Guinn stood by the ad—at least initially—and said Jones had to take responsibility for her staff.

But the Guinn campaign realized soon that the audit spot had been, as one campaign insider put it, "a terrible mistake." Guinn insisted it be taken off the air, which he revealed on a Las Vegas television station during an interview: "We took that off because they said it was a lie [that Jones had anything to do with hiding the audits] and we agreed."

By her very nature, Jones abhorred confrontation and was reluctant to go negative on TV. Roy Behr, a veteran of many campaigns, including a recent gubernatorial race in California, had some simple advice for her. "If there was one piece of empirical data that staying positive can win an election, I'd tell you to," he said to Jones. "But you can't find it." Behr told her that Jane Harman's refusal to respond to Gray Davis' attacks in the California governor's race cost her dearly in a primary earlier in 1998.

And so she was persuaded. Behr produced an ad that quoted Toohey as saying Guinn's audit claims were "false and misleading." And it charged Guinn with doing "anything to get ahead." Then Behr uncorked the opposition research on television for the first time, trying to deface the picture of Guinn that had gotten him embraced by the power structure. "As CEO of Southwest Gas, he raised rates seven times, but gave himself a million dollars in bonuses. He even opposed rate reductions for low-income seniors, while he made four hundred thousand dollars." Finally, he unveiled the nasty slogan: "Kenny Guinn. Out For Himself. Not For Us." As opposed to Guinn's theme: "For Governor. For Nevada."

The Guinn campaign put out a mountain of paper disputing the assertions in Jones' ad, some of which had validity, while some were hair-splitting. But it didn't matter. The spot clearly had incensed Guinn and his handlers and, Jones and her cadre hoped, would have some effect.

It had to, or she was in trouble. Senate candidate John Ensign's impeccable pollster, Glen Bolger, completed a survey just before Jones' ad went on the air, showing Guinn with a 12-point lead. It also showed Ensign in a dead heat with Harry Reid. The Democrats protested that the poll was skewed toward the GOP contenders, but their fear was palpable. And a few days later, a media poll showed Guinn with a 15-point lead, a devastating blow to Jones. With her negatives soaring, pollster Del Ali had a matter-of-fact analysis: "It's a very simple formula. Unless Jones has a bombshell, they'll just slowly raise each other's negatives until the election, and he'll come out on top."

Guinn was keeping up the pummeling, too. He unfurled three radio ads targeted toward different geographic areas. Each one was highlighted with an old quote of Jones' that declared, "Nevada has an unrealistically low property tax." No matter that many analysts agreed with her, and that Guinn probably did, too. The public wouldn't like it.

The only good news for Jones as the calendar turned to October was an appearance by Vice President Al Gore at the Stardust Hotel on her behalf—an event that raised $600,000. She would need every penny to respond to what she knew would soon be an ad from Guinn lambasting her attendance record. Her campaign staffers—Behr, Lewis, and McCue—were also pounding on her after the second poll, which they knew would undermine her fundraising, to write a large check. Jones didn't believe the survey, but she also didn't want to invest hundreds of thousands of dollars with no way to get it back.

As she pondered whether to raise her personal investment in the campaign to close to $300,000, Reid called. Jones was at home, having just left her campaign team after yet another spirited discussion of her unwillingness to put in any more of her own money. Clearly, they had called Reid to help with the persuasion. The senator couldn't have her stop now—not with the race, his race, so close. "Win, lose, or draw," Reid told her, "I'll help you raise it back." So Jones wrote the check, but told her advisers that it was the end of her money.

The first two debates were slated for the first weekend in October. Jones had to do well in those encounters and win the air war, otherwise Guinn's strategy of putting her on the mat one month before the election would prove successful.

The attendance ad went up in the first week of October, recounting Jones' missed meetings and votes and ending with, "All of us have to show up for work. Why doesn't Jan Jones?" The Guinn campaign was on a high, but their collective sense of humor failed them. Guinn was so incensed by Jones' criticism of his tenure at Southwest Gas that Ernaut sent a letter to Jones' titular campaign manager, Denise Rawles, on Oct. 1 threatening legal action. The Jones campaign immediately provided documentation, official filings with public agencies, that backed up the charges in the ad. And the next day, Rawles sent back a letter, scoffing at Guinn's threat and declaring, "You see, the law does not offer remedies to candidates whose feelings have been hurt by the truth." State Democratic Party Chairman Paul Henry piled on, sending Guinn a mock draft of a legal complaint to fill out and file against Jones.

The Jones campaign, relying on Carol's research, continued to run ads through October, harping on Guinn's record as a utility executive and banker, sparking a furious and swift rebuttal from the Guinn folks. The ads at least tweaked the Guinnites and were so well done they were having an effect.

But the ad that changed the general election went on the air Oct. 6. Jones' response to the Guinn attendance spot was spectacular in both its effectiveness and disingenuousness. "City Council records show Jan Jones has a 94 percent attendance record," the spot said. And then the killer line: "Even during her cancer treatment, she phoned in votes." It then went on to reiterate charges about Guinn's tenure at Southwest Gas.

The claims Jones made about herself in the ad were thoroughly misleading. Yes, she had attended most of the council meetings—or at least part of them. But she had not been sitting on the dais for those 2,000 votes because she had either left the meeting early or dawdled in the back room or in her office. But using the breast cancer as cover was a brilliant and cynical ploy. Those treatments occurred in 1998 while the Guinn ad specifically said it covered 1995 to 1997.

"What we were doing," a Jones insider later explained, "was saying, 'What a rat you are for making attendance an issue when [Jones] was sick.' They let it go. We boxed them. We knew that [the breast cancer] had nothing to do with the missed votes. We also knew that the average person watching the spot wasn't going to understand the time frame." But, the Jonesite added, the campaign felt justified because "they were really playing games with the numbers on the missed meetings." The spot was not only beautifully conceived, it was almost impossible to assail without talking about Jones' breast cancer.

He didn't know it yet, but Guinn was about to start hemorrhaging in the polls as the first two debates of the campaign loomed the weekend of Oct. 9. His campaign cadre already was worried about the debates. For some of them, who had been through this before, Guinn was a brand new animal. He was not only relatively inarticulate, but, as one put it, he didn't seem to have "any core convictions. He didn't have any opinions. He didn't want to offend people." During one session of debate preparation, the consultants urged Guinn to tell them where he stood on various issues. "You have to decide," Vassiliadis implored, echoed by others. A frustrated Guinn responded: "I'm paying all of you to tell me what I have to say to win. You guys tell me what to say." The team was flabbergasted, but they obliged. And then crossed their fingers.

The first debate was a tame affair, televised in Las Vegas by public television station, KLVX-TV, Channel 10. The Guinn campaign knew that expectations were so low for their candidate and so high for Jones that all he had to do was not commit a major blunder and his performance would be perceived as a victory. Jones was her usual glib self, while Guinn was nervous at times and seemed genuinely flummoxed when the mayor asked him his position on raising the minimum wage (he was against it), which had nothing to do with a governor's race. The only issue highlights involved Jones' support for a statewide impact fee on developers and her advocacy for a repeal of the state's right-to-work law. The media played the contest as a polite draw.

The Guinn campaign was split on their man's performance. Rogich thought he had done fine. But he and Vassiliadis argued about the debate at Cafe Nicolle late that evening. Vassiliadis thought Guinn was awful, and he later told the candidate so. The state Democratic Party, though, sent out an over-the-top release on the event, headlined, "Jones Trounces a Rattled Guinn in First Debate." It was rhetorically ludicrous, even for a partisan screed.

A couple of nights later, in a debate that was not televised, Jones and Guinn squared off in front of a crowd of rambunctious Sun City seniors. Again, there were no flashpoints: the crowd got engaged only when Guinn tried to link Jones to President Clinton, then in the throes of the Monica Lewinsky mess and threatening to depress Democratic turnout. Guinn thought he could exploit some of Jones' statements in both debates, including her right-to-work comments and her impact-fee proposal, as well as her assertion Sunday in Sun City that she had not raised property taxes five times (technically the City Council had voted to do so). He also seized on a serendipitous newspaper quote from ex-consumer advocate Fred Schmidt, who defended Guinn's contention that he had not raised rates at Southwest Gas, as Jones claimed. (Rates had been raised—not at Guinn's request, but rather at the behest of state regulators.)

But the debates had proved a bust—at least for Jones. They hadn't given her any advantage. Guinn had held his own.

The polls, however, were a different story. Ernaut received tracking poll numbers on his home computer early every morning. Ever since the Jones breast cancer ad had gone up, Ernaut had seen a slow decline in Guinn's numbers. One morning in mid-October, he called Vassiliadis and Rogich and told them bluntly, "We have a problem. The momentum is in Jones' corner. Her media is killing us."

Other surveys bore out what Ernaut was seeing. A state Democratic Party survey, gleefully released by Jones on Oct. 14, showed her in a dead heat with Guinn. Any partisan criticism of that poll was muted by a survey taken for the gaming industry and released that same day. It was a statewide measure with a gigantic sample of 1,600 voters, which arrived at the identical result. Guinn was bleeding badly, mostly in Reno. And the momentum was all on Jones' side, thanks to the breast cancer ad. "Two-and-a-half years and $4 million after he announced his candidacy for governor, Kenny Guinn now must confront the real possibility that he will lose," I wrote on Oct. 14.

Wark knew Guinn was slipping, too. He had picked up the reports from the field. He had talked to Ernaut and knew how worried, almost to the point of paralysis, the campaign manager was. He urged Ernaut to just "work the plan, work the plan," a reference to the comprehensive grass-roots strategy he had outlined months ago. Wark knew Ernaut was scared, too—he had a lot riding on what had once seemed like a sure thing. One day in the campaign headquarters Wark told a shaken Ernaut, "I will win this for you. I'm not going to let us lose this."

The next day as Wark drove to the headquarters, Ernaut called him and asked him to come to a meeting in Rogich's office. Wark wasn't often invited to the kitchen Cabinet get-togethers, and he had felt slighted. He also believed that the consultants had not paid close enough attention to what was happening in the campaign, that they were too focused on muzzling Guinn and spending money on TV.

When Wark arrived, the campaign's entire inner circle was there—Ernaut, Greg Ferraro, Vassiliadis, Steve Forsythe and Kent Oram. The first order of business was to stop the slippage in northern Nevada, where Jones' attendance problems were not well-known and where the assault on Guinn's administrative abilities was soaking in. Guinn recruited northern icon Mills Lane, a popular judge and boxing referee who later got his own TV show, to do an endorsement ad. And in Las Vegas, Guinn put out a quote from his old friend, former governor and *Las Vegas Sun* executive Mike O'Callaghan, that defended his education bona fides.

But Ernaut had an even better idea, one that flashed like a lightbulb above his head as he flew down to the meeting in Rogich's office with his old friend, Ferraro. "It hit me like a ton of bricks," Ernaut remembered. "The one thing in this campaign that breast cancer can't be an antidote for is ethics charges." Ernaut picked up the phone on the airplane and called the campaign's reliable research expert, Denice Miller. He told her to find everything that had ever been said about Jones being unethical and to fax it all to Rogich's office in Las Vegas. When he arrived at the meeting, the information was there, including two perfect quotes—one from Supreme Court Justice Charlie Springer and one from Gov. Bob Miller. The quotes, coincidentally, were the same ones ex-City Councilman Steve Miller had put in that faxed news release during the primary as he sought to damage Jones.

The consultant cadre did not immediately buy Ernaut's premise. But he pushed and pushed, and they finally agreed. Wark also made his pitch, with Ernaut's support, to get money not just for TV but for his integrated plan. Everyone agreed. Ernaut told Rogich to go out and raise $300,000; Wark stayed behind for an hour or so to watch as Rogich barked out names to his secretary to get on the phone so he could twist arms for more cash.

Ernaut jumped into a car and headed down to Laguna Productions in the shadow of the Strip to produce the spot.

On the way, he wrote the commercial on his laptop. He cribbed a line Rogich had coined early in the campaign: that Jones had appeared before the Ethics Commission more times than any elected official in history. Ernaut wasn't sure that Rogich was right; in fact, he figured it was probably his trademark hyperbole. But what was Jones going to do? Claim she was only in second place? Ernaut also came up with the signature line for the ad: "Integrity Matters."

On a roll, the Jones campaign couldn't help but push the envelope. Jones and McCue were quietly courting Aaron Russo, who had not gone back to California. Instead, he'd continued to dabble in state politics. He'd already endorsed Republican contenders for Congress, U.S. Senate, and attorney general. McCue figured that if she could get Russo, who hated Guinn, to embrace Jones, some of the far-right and fringe types might actually vote for her. It was a gargantuan logical leap. Russo had the highest negatives of any political figure in Nevada, but Jones was willing to sell—or at least rent—her soul to him for the last two weeks of the campaign. She even went so far as to endorse his four litmus tests—questioning whether the county's voting machines produced real results, reducing exorbitant car registration fees, going to the Supreme Court to stop the nuclear-waste dump from being placed in Nevada, and going to the high court to stop the IRS from taxing tips. Jones had made a Faustian bargain, and she'd made it with a defanged devil to boot.

By this time, both candidates had emptied their war chests and were having to write significant personal checks to finish the race. Guinn put in $450,000 to complete his TV buy, while Jones eventually put in close to $300,000.

Guinn seemed to be getting more bang for his own buck as the last week of the campaign began. "Integrity Matters" appeared to be doing just what the campaign had hoped.

Guinn's internal polling showed him moving ahead by anywhere from three points to double digits. In all of the turnout models, with Wark pinpointing who would vote and advocacy calls being made by an expert in Washington named John Grotta, the Guinn campaign knew its voters. Jones' grass-roots strategy had never really materialized. She and her team had jousted with the coordinated Democratic Party campaign, which she saw was set up to be a Harry Reid vehicle, pure and simple. There was no room for anyone else.

And the newspapers began weighing in, too, lending to the perception of Guinn momentum. The *Las Vegas Review-Journal*, whose conservative bent had guaranteed Guinn would be endorsed from Day One, was first on Oct. 18, saying Guinn is "a better fit for Nevada." The *Las Vegas Sun*, whose personal connections to Guinn had assured the nod from the moment the first announcement was made in February 1996, endorsed Guinn on Oct. 25, saying, "This newspaper has waited for Kenny Guinn to run for governor for over 20 years." That same day, the *Reno Gazette-Journal* chimed in, writing Guinn "knows much more about us" than Jones.

Jones put on a new ad that last week, featuring endorsements from Gov. Miller and Sen. Richard Bryan. Her timing was astonishing. Jones had waited the entire campaign to use two of the state's most popular figures, which probably suited them just fine because both knew all about anointments. They had been invisible since Jones filed in May. And now, acting as if she had rummaged around in her jewelry box and found a pair of buried diamonds, Jones put Bryan and Miller on display.

Ernaut was ecstatic. He knew endorsement ads didn't do much; he had expected another breast cancer spot. However, Guinn's reaction was markedly different. Never had Ernaut seen Guinn, who had helped Miller and Bryan and couldn't fathom their partisan obligations, more angry. "Kenny was never more pissed and I was never more happy," he said. (Even after the election, Guinn's fury did not abate, and he confronted Bryan at a dinner about the ad.)

The polling numbers, despite Jones' campaign insisting its tracking showed a dead heat, clearly were moving. Another gaming survey released Oct. 27 and conducted by national expert Doug Schoen, with a 1,600-voter sample, showed Guinn leading by five points. A survey by Ensign's polling firm, Public Opinion Strategies, and another by ex-presidential pollster Fred Steeper showed similar margins. Less than a week before the balloting, Guinn had stanched the bleeding.

Reversing momentum in the last week of a campaign is almost impossible, barring a cataclysm. But Jones' camp was in denial. The mayor and her enabling staff believed that she could still win the race if Democratic turnout was high. Her internal polls also showed a five-point Guinn lead, but it seemed surmountable. She obviously didn't believe the race was over or she wouldn't have put in the $270,000 she reported on the final campaign disclosure. That brought her just under the $2 million mark, while Guinn reported $5.3 million in donations, including his own check for $450,000. Guinn's total was unprecedented in a Nevada race. Gov. Bob Miller's $3.2 million in 1994 had set the previous record.

Guinn's extraordinary amount of money had closed the door on Jones, unbeknownst to her. Without that cash, he never would've been able to fund the far-reaching grass-roots program that was masterminded by Steve Wark. Working with a general election budget of close to a half-million dollars, Wark had been able to do everything he had always wanted to do. He had even been able to see that mail pieces went into the Hispanic and black communities—bastions of Democratic support—to undermine Jones. One that went to Latinos contrasted Guinn's childhood picking cotton in

California's San Joaquin Valley with Jones having been born "with a silver spoon in her mouth." Another portrayed Guinn, who had in 1996 said he was pro-choice, as pro-life and opposed to same-sex marriages, and Jones as having the opposite stands. That kind of approach also helped in the African-American community with pastors, who had sway over their parishioners. Wark did not miss a trick, thanks to all of that campaign cash.

A sizable percentage of that money—close to half—had come in early, thanks to the efforts of the powers who anoint. Ironically, Guinn's anointment by a powerful group of insiders had produced the grass-roots operation, reaching across demographic groups and creating a variegated coalition. They had identified enough voters and had such an extensive Election Day plan that it was impossible to reverse with only a few days left.

However, Wark—and others—knew by this time that their organization wouldn't be much help to John Ensign in his Senate race against Harry Reid. In fact, many voters they turned out would be ticket-splitters, Guinn-Reid voters, especially in the heavily Mormon areas of Southern Nevada. But their job wasn't to help Ensign: He would benefit in other traditional Republican areas by the higher turnout Guinn would generate, though at least some of those voters would turn to Reid as well.

The polls, at least the public ones, belied what was happening in those final days. A *Review-Journal* survey, published on the day of the last debate, Friday, Oct. 30, showed that the race for governor was, in bookie's terms, "pick-em." It only enhanced Jones' view that victory was within her grasp. No one in her campaign, including veterans Behr and Lewis, believed anything other than that they had a chance.

The last debate was held in Reno at a public TV studio. It generated little excitement, matching the first couple of debates. Jones was not as dynamic as she can be, but she was clearly more focused than Guinn. *Review-Journal* reporter Ed Vogel described Guinn as "calm, but undemonstrative." Ernaut simply wanted to avoid anything catastrophic, and Guinn, although he was as disjointed and rambling as he had been all year, seemed almost to be coasting, barely on the stage. His campaign again split over his performance, but all of the consultants believed, based on their polling, that it didn't matter. Rogich was now confident Guinn would win by 10 points; others were not so sanguine, but thought at least five.

Team Guinn camped out on Election Night at Luxor Hotel, a Strip resort-casino owned by Circus Circus Enterprises, which had given that $300,000 donation, the largest recorded in Nevada history, two years earlier. All the reports from the field were fine. Wark's operation was moving heaven and earth to get Guinn voters to the polls. Fourteen phone banks in all were whirring away under Wark's command. He refused to let anyone leave the headquarters early for the Luxor party before the last phone calls had been made.

By mid-afternoon, the national returns started rolling in from exit polling. Ernaut was sipping whiskey and watching what appeared to be a Democratic tsunami, a backlash against the Republicans and their handling of L'Affaire Lewinsky.

About 5 p.m., Vassiliadis called to tell Ernaut he knew exactly how he was feeling. Four years ago, as he waited for returns in Miller's re-election against Jim Gibbons, Vassiliadis had watched the opposite trend. The Republican Revolution was rolling across the country toward Nevada. This time, it was the Democratic resurgence. "Everything's going to be okay," Vassiliadis reassured Ernaut. After all, Miller, then the Anointed One, ultimately bucked the GOP tide and won the election by 10 points.

Ernaut, as he remembered it, was "fit to be tied for hours." The campaign that he had taken on, the campaign that couldn't be lost, the sure thing no longer was so sure. Could it really slip away after all he'd been through?

Ernaut was beside himself until the early-voting and absentee-ballot numbers were posted shortly after 7 p.m. Guinn was ahead in Democratic Clark County, where Jones needed to defeat him by a significant margin, by seven points. "I jumped five feet in the air," Ernaut recalled. "I knew it was a landslide coming." Guinn was on a plane flying down to Las Vegas from Reno with Ferraro. Even before they'd heard the early results, they were drinking champagne. Ferraro had brought a bottle of Dom Perignon on board; he saw no reason to wait for the official numbers. He knew Guinn would win.

They kept calling Ernaut from the aircraft to get the results, but the phone kept clicking off. They finally connected and Ernaut told them, simply: "It's over."

The celebration began soon afterwards. Wark, who'd become a media star and would be much sought after because of his grass-roots choreography, was beaming. As he celebrated, he was surprised when a large man he had never seen before hugged him and yelled, "We did it!" Wark asked someone nearby who it was. He was told it was Harvey Whittemore, a Democrat who once headed Clinton's Nevada campaign and who actually hadn't signed onto the Guinn effort until late. But Whittemore, one of the more influential men in Northern Nevada and perhaps the best legislative lobbyist in the state, wanted to be with a winner.

So did a lot of other people who began showing up at the Luxor that evening, faces that none of the Guinnites had seen in Campaign '98 until those early returns were posted on TV.

Jones had been depressed the previous day, feeling a sense of doom, even though her campaign staffers were convinced she had a chance. She was angry, mostly at herself, because it was 1994 redux. She had expended a lot of time, energy, and money and she wondered, "What the hell did you do this for? Just to piss these guys off again?"

On Election Day she went to lunch with her close friend, George Togliatti, an ex-FBI agent turned executive at Caesars World. As they were dining, gaming lobbyists and Guinn supporters Richard Bunker and Whittemore strolled by and said hello. Behr called her on her cell phone intermittently with reports of early exit polling, which seemed favorable. She left lunch feeling more optimistic and went home to get dressed to go to the MGM Grand Hotel, where her party was scheduled for Election Night.

She was pulling into the MGM shortly after 7 when she called McCue to hear the Clark County early-voting numbers. "You're down by seven," McCue told her. Jones remembered that McCue was "trying to be upbeat, but that was it for me. I knew I was going to lose. I knew it was over."

Tears flowed that night in that room at the MGM. Lindsey Lewis broke down, believing until reality pounced that Jones might have won. Her precocious, pre-teen daughter, Katie, couldn't stop crying. She told her mother she was just so angry, angry that she lost because she was a woman.

The final numbers added up to the landslide that Ernaut predicted earlier in the evening, exactly what Rogich had forecast days before the election and, ironically, the numbers that Miller pulled when he defeated Gibbons: 52 percent for Guinn, 42 percent for Jones, 6 percent for minor candidates. After many moments of drama and some unexpected twists and turns, the anointment had been consummated.

(Ensign was not so lucky. He grabbed Guinn's coattails, but they didn't stretch far enough for him. Jones may not have defeated Guinn, but she helped Reid vanquish Ensign. And the senator needed every bit of help. The election would not be decided until a recount was performed—and Reid eked out a 428-vote win.)

Everyone involved had a different explanation for why Guinn won—and so decisively. Rogich, as he repeated several times during a post-election interview, insisted that the rural-county strategy was the key. Yes, the so-called cow counties only have 15 percent of the vote. But Guinn's assiduous attention to and Jones' refusal to visit those areas, Rogich asserted, made the difference. Rogich had prepared spots that ran late in the cycle telling rural voters that Jones was the first Democratic candidate for governor in history who did not come to ask for their vote. The truth was she had written off rural Nevada because of time, concentrating on the urban areas. And, of course, Guinn's smashing victory in Clark County rendered the rural results irrelevant. Guinn could have broken even in the rurals and still crushed Jones.

Ernaut still believes that it was the money he put behind Wark and the grass-roots program that ensured they could not lose. "It was a universe of twenty-five thousand voters and we constantly blasted them with something," he recalled afterward. "We never let up on that little universe of people, almost all in Clark County." But the grass-roots were planted far and wide. In fact, Guinn's machine had such breadth, he lost only one county—Mineral—by 61 votes. "They had the union deal, but we had an army of volunteers in every county," he said. And, as Ernaut pointed out and was borne out by the candidate's activity in the early going, Guinn was one of the hardest-working contenders the state had ever witnessed. As Ernaut put it, comparing him to the man most famous in Nevada for his affinity for rubber chickens and shaking hands, "[Guinn] makes Dick Bryan look like a guy who sits on a couch."

Jones was convinced her media campaign was better—
it was. She also contended that her campaign didn't make
any mistakes—her team made few. Anecdotal evidence and
conversations later persuaded her that blue-collar men, many
of them Democrats and union workers, just didn't vote for
her. Culinary operative D. Taylor, who had advised her in
1997 not to get into the race because she would lose, told
her that they didn't like Jones because they were threatened
by her smarts. There might have been another reason, too.
As one Democrat confided after attending a focus group
during the campaign with working-class men, all they could
do was talk about her legs. When asked what kind of animal they would compare her to, they said a racehorse. Why?
Great legs.

Jones also knew she had been hurt by her financial dis-
advantage and her own unwillingness early on to write a
blank check. She never thought she would raise $2 million—
but she did, thanks to Lindsey Lewis and her own resource-
fulness. She felt let down by Emily's List, believing the national women's group had not come through for her, had
not considered her race as one of its priorities. She didn't
even have enough money to do any mail pieces that helped—
one, in fact, landed at homes after the election.

Roy Behr added one other post-mortem to Jones' loss.
Democratic turnout was much worse than anticipated. His
projection, and others, called for a one-point gap between
Democrat and Republican voters. It turned out to be five
points—a testament to Wark's machine. That accounted not
for the loss, but for the landslide. Behr also pointed out the
difficulty of electing female governors. And with Jones' flamboyant style, contrasted to Guinn's blandness, especially in
a state where people were skittish about the future, Guinn
was the logical choice. Even though the campaign tried to
spread wispy tales of unethical behavior to the media in the
waning days, no one, not even those who liked him the
least, was going to believe Kenny Guinn was venal.

Most of these analyses makes sense. But the real reason

Guinn won had been set in motion back in February 1996 when Rogich decided to bring this candidacy into stark relief and basically announce Guinn was the Establishment's man. The strategy paid off. Guinn, like Jones, was far from a perfect candidate; he never acclimated to the public part of the campaign, often speaking incoherently. But the anointment had worked despite his poor performance. The anointment begat money, which allowed Guinn to buy the best talent and grass-roots operation. Jones made them pay a little more, but she got in way too late because of the anointment and she, ultimately, had too much baggage. Still she made it interesting, partly because of some Guinn campaign miscues. But in the end, money and grass-roots will out. And they did.

The day after the election, Guinn and his wife, Dema, went to Guinn Junior High School, the eponymous tribute to the former schools superintendent in western Las Vegas. There he apologized to the principal and faculty for the ugliness of the campaign. They then went over to Southwest Gas and told executives and workers he had not intended for the company to be so reviled in TV ads. These were signature gestures from a man whose warmth and sincerity had acquired him plum jobs, plenty of friends, and chits that he cashed in when he sought the governorship.

The headlines that followed said it all, if not intentionally. "Business Leaders Cheer Nevada Election Results," announced the *Las Vegas Sun*. Even more tellingly, in the *Sun* the next day was, "Major Changes Not Expected After Guinn's Election."

Indeed, the status quo had been preserved. That, fundamentally, was what the balloting was all about. Like Bob Miller before him, Kenny of The 1,000 Days, with a little help from his men, had ensured that the state would be led by a steady and predictable hand. And in an uncertain world where extra-Nevada threats to gaming were multiplying, certainty at home was paramount for the casino industry and its operatives.

So Kenny Guinn, the man who wanted to be the state's chief executive because it was his time, the candidate who was willing to let his advisers take him there, was now governor of Nevada. You can almost imagine him turning to Rogich, just as he did during that interview way back in 1996, just as Robert Redford did as the vacuous victor in *The Candidate* right after he had been elected, and ask, "What do we do now?"

EPILOGUE
ECHOES FROM THE PAST

Joe Neal, the obstreperous state senator and forgotten man of the 1998 governor's race, was determined to find another way to exact a pound of flesh from the gaming industry, which he blamed for squashing his candidacy. A few months after the election, he proposed in the Legislature a two percent increase in the gross gaming tax. It was a purely symbolic act. The bill received a perfunctory hearing, then lawmakers, lobbied by the likes of Billy Vassiliadis, Greg Ferraro, and Harvey Whittemore, entombed it.

But the issue of taxing the casinos had been raised again, at a time when the state's economy was expanding, but not enough to keep pace with the infrastructure demands of its astronomical population growth, especially in Southern Nevada. The industry wasn't worried, though. It had invested a lot of money in the new governor, Kenny Guinn. And so far, he was reciting the lines directly from their script. At his first session, in 1999, Guinn held the line on spending and taxes. He received rave reviews for his fiscal conservatism and for proposing a plan, the Millennium Scholarships, to allow every 'B' student in Nevada to go to a state school for free, paid for courtesy of the tobacco settlement.

Yes, Guinn was performing just as his financial backers had hoped he would. And he was much more comfortable as governor than he was as a gubernatorial candidate. He remained a woeful orator—he mispronounced words and tended to wander into uncharted rhetorical territory. But he became known as the people's governor, much in the mode of one of his friends and role models, ex-Gov. Mike O'Callaghan. Occasionally, unlike most governors, he sauntered over to the Legislative Building, which had been off-limits to most chief executives. He sat down with Democrats, with lobbyists, with janitors.

The casino bosses couldn't have been happier with his first session. Not only didn't he raise taxes, but Guinn privatized the troubled workers' compensation system, which the casinos had feared would go belly up, leaving them to pay the freight. Like Miller before him, Guinn was advised by the same people who had helped elect him, especially Rogich and Ernaut. Indeed, shortly after the election, Ernaut naturally had been named the new governor's chief of staff. Ernaut was the political mind of the governor's office, the yang to Guinn's yin when it came to strategy. Vassiliadis, Ferraro, and Whittemore also had access to the governor, and, of course, to Ernaut. They persuaded the governor and his chief of staff not to interfere as they rammed through the Legislature a bill that changed the casinos' contractual relationships with slot manufacturers they felt were taking too big a cut. It was an astonishing power play, but Guinn signed the bill. As usual, the session ended with the industry securing its entire agenda: no new taxes, no workers compensation bill to pay, and a restructuring of their slot agreements by legislative fiat.

Guinn came out of Session '99 with high popularity numbers based on a foundation of the Millennium Scholarships and his gubernatorial bearing. However, unlike Miller before him, Guinn emerged from the session determined to expend his political capital. He continued hinting, which he'd begun during the session, that he was going to do something about the state's tax structure. Indian gaming, slowed only temporarily by legal hurdles, was going to spread in

California. Because the competition to the west would surely reduce tax revenues from Nevada's casinos, Guinn's intuition and the numbers he had seen had persuaded him that state government could not keep pace with its own population explosion. He had to do something. The gambling industry knew it, too. But most of the casino leaders weren't willing, at least initially, to be part of the solution. Most believed that this anointee, like their previous one, would hold the line on gaming taxes and insist someone else pay. Guinn didn't fundamentally disagree. And exactly 10 years after Miller had quietly put together a broad-based business tax, which dovetailed with the industry's agenda, Guinn was talking about stretching the tax base.

But with Neal insisting a gaming tax be put on the ballot and the teachers' union similarly trying to qualify a business-profits tax, Guinn knew no one could be spared from the restructuring. Even if he thought the industry was paying its fair share, politically he could not do what he had to do without the casinos' participation. By mid-year, Guinn had made the case in a public forum for more money and he was looking for a solution. Ironically, the man consecrated with gaming's holy water was whispering about including the resorts as part of a tax solution. It looked as if the casinos would have to pay up—at least that was the plan.

At first, Jan Jones was bitter about her loss to Kenny Guinn. She would never see the money—$300,000—she had invested. Harry Reid didn't raise it back for her, as he'd promised. She had done her job for him but her usefulness to him ended on Election Day. In a way it was even more galling when President Clinton called Jones the day after the balloting and told her that Reid couldn't have won without her in the governor's race. She was angry with a lot of people, but most of all herself. She wasn't sure whether she would run for mayor again. She flirted with a top job at the Democratic National Committee. Then she bowed out of the 1999 mayor's race to take a cushy, amorphous contract with the Nevada Resort Association and the Las Vegas Convention and Visitors Authority, which, of course, Vassiliadis helped arrange.

In fact, the powers that anoint were paving the way for Jay Bingham, a former county commissioner, to take Jones' job until he became ill with a heart condition. Guinn was on board—if you can't kick an opponent after you've vanquished her, when can you kick her? And so were his men—they were advising Bingham until his health became an issue and he abruptly dropped out. Without a fallback position, the powers who anoint had to sit on the sidelines and watch as a former mob attorney named Oscar Goodman became the state's newest political celebrity. Goodman reveled in being aloof from the political power structure, using his charisma and TV savvy to destroy an inept field of competitors. He was an anomaly in Nevada politics—getting elected to a high-profile position without the help of the power elite. But, as they well knew, and Jones had realized and Goodman would soon discover, the mayoralty has much rhetorical power, but not much real power.

Jones' stint as the high-priced NRA-LVCVA mouthpiece didn't last long. Her friend, Phil Satre of Harrah's, recruited her to become an executive at the company, which she gladly accepted. She couldn't help but chuckle as the year went on. At NRA meetings, she listened as her new colleagues in the industry—the ones who had a few months earlier hastened her political demise—talked about the man who had beaten her, the man anointed by the casinos and now thinking of taxing them. She remembered that story about how the Strip executive chastised his subordinate for even lunching with her, because she might tax the industry. It was a delicious irony, Jones thought.

❖ ❖ ❖

Others involved in the election also reaped the fruits of their toils. One Jones aide harvested the true bumper crop. Susan McCue, Jones' press secretary and de facto campaign manager for most of the general election, was rewarded by her ex-boss Harry Reid. The senator, who had brought McCue back from the Department of Housing and Urban Development to ensure Jones stayed viable long enough to boost his candidacy, tapped her after the election to be his chief of staff. It was a plum plum, especially since Reid had been elected the assistant minority leader, the number two position among the Senate Democrats.

Team Guinn's key elements also thrived. Sig Rogich, seen as the mastermind of Guinn's election win, was sought after by those who wanted the governor's ear. He promised appointments to some, and delivered on many. For example, he supported Amy Ayoub, the ex-Democratic fundraiser and Jones confidante, to become the first woman on the Nevada State Athletic Commission.

Vassiliadis and Ferraro were the lead gaming lobbyists at the Legislature; their company, R&R Advertising, continued to prosper. Vassiliadis was seen as arguably the most powerful man in the state, while Ferraro became known as a go-to operative in Northern Nevada.

Steve Wark was a much-courted grass-roots expert in local races—a couple of which he either lost or barely eked out. But he received his real payoff with a lucrative regional contract with the National Republican Senatorial Committee.

Frank Schreck and Mike Sloan, the Democratic money men who quietly helped Guinn, continued to be prime players. Sloan, as chairman of the Nevada Resort Association, pushed the industry's tax policy, while Schreck, especially after his friend Bill Bible became the president of the NRA (courtesy of their mutual pal, Sloan), began to receive more business from gaming's lobbying arm.

It was too early to judge whether the anointment had paid off for the state's most important industry—the tax man would cometh, but how much he would taketh away was still not clear. Still, those who had acted on behalf of the casinos saw their net worths continue to grow under the Guinn administration.

On Thursday, Feb. 18, 1999, one of the more stunning announcements in Nevada political history was made. Sen. Richard Bryan, the former governor who had imagined a career in politics almost from his time in a high chair, announced he would not seek a third term. No one saw it coming. So, after an election cycle during which the first open governor's seat was contested in 16 years, the first open Senate seat in 14 years was there for the taking. The next day, 25 hours later to be exact, John Ensign, the ex-congressman who'd only a couple of months earlier demanded and lost a recount in his race against Reid, announced his candidacy. John of the 600 Days was born.

The dominoes quickly fell.

Ex-Gov. Miller, despite having been vaccinated for Potomac Fever, was courted by local and national Democrats, including President and Hillary Clinton. Only Miller, who left office on a popularity crest, could beat Ensign, the Democrats declared. And he could have. But one month later, on March 16, Miller, ready for private life and with no interest in Washington, announced he would not run.

Attorney General Frankie Sue Del Papa soon became the focal point of the Democrats' attentions, despite her aborted gubernatorial run in 1997. That was an eternity ago, the Democrats felt, and a pro-choice woman with a statewide persona would give Ensign fits. Del Papa, who still maintained a house in Washington from her days working on the Hill for former Sen. Howard Cannon, declared her candidacy on June 1. Polls had shown a Del Papa-Ensign race to be very tight. But Del Papa lasted an even shorter time as a Senate candidate than she did as a gubernatorial contender. In August, already frustrated by fundraising, she told labor leaders in Reno, who had questioned her commitment, that they could find another candidate if she wasn't good enough. Word of Del Papa's behavior filtered back to Reid in Washington, who cut the legs from underneath her candidacy. On Aug. 3, Del Papa gamely insisted she was "in it to stay." But five weeks later, she announced she was quitting the contest, using almost the same verbiage she had when she was forced out of the governor's race in late 1997.

Reid was quietly telling people he thought the race was over. His first choice to fill the void was *Las Vegas Sun* Editor Brian Greenspun, whom Reid believed could pour millions of dollars into the campaign and might even defeat Ensign. His second choice was one of two other millionaires musing about the contest—Ed Bernstein, a personal-injury attorney, or Steve Cloobeck, a shopping-mall heir who ran a time-share outfit on the Strip.

Greenspun, who would have had to switch parties, decided not to run. And Bernstein, who had thought about public office before, announced that he was interested. But the Washington punditocracy dismissed his chances fairly regularly, and by mid-year, polls showed Ensign ahead by 20 percentage points.

Part of it was name recognition and Ensign's recent near-defeat of Reid. But there were other reasons, too, that he was such a heavy favorite. Ensign's father, Mike, was the chairman of Mandalay Resort Group, formerly Circus Circus Enterprises, the same company that had provided the $300,000 financial jolt for Guinn's anointment. By the end of 1999, Ensign had amassed $2 million. And he had started to assemble a team that looked very familiar.

In December 1999, Pete Ernaut announced that he was leaving as Guinn's chief of staff to helm Ensign's campaign, a hiring quietly brokered by Vassiliadis, just as he had gotten his friend hired by Guinn in mid-1997. Sig Rogich was already on board. So, too, were Greg Ferraro, and Steve Wark, the man who redefined GOP grass roots for Guinn and whose turnout model may, ironically, have cost Ensign his 1998 race because it turned out so many Guinn-Reid voters.

Even before that, though, Reid was signaling where he believed the race between Ensign and Bernstein would go. On a Reno TV show in mid-November, he was asked about the Senate race and Bernstein's chances. He sounded, almost word for word, like Miller in 1998 when he was asked about the governor's race between Guinn and Jones: "You have two very fine people. The state of Nevada is going to be served very well."

On March 6, 2000, John Ensign held a formal kick-off for his Senate campaign at the Clark High School gymnasium in Las Vegas. The event had an eerie familiarity, teeming as it was with the throng of insiders and business types of all stripes. It felt like a victory party, or at least a mass ring-kissing. The scene was much like the one about 30 months earlier at the Las Vegas Racquet Club, when hundreds had turned out for Kenny Guinn's first gubernatorial fundraiser.

Vassiliadis stood against a wall and looked on. Ernaut worked the floor, making sure everything was choreographed correctly. Wark organized the ground troops, who wore Team Ensign shirts that looked strangely similar to the Team Guinn shirts from 1998. Elected GOP leaders assembled on a riser behind Ensign.

Finally, Kenny Guinn strode to the microphone and briefly gushed about Ensign, whom he called "a man of honesty and integrity," and, of course, "the next senator from Nevada." It looked like a torch-passing: the Anointed One of 1998 to the Anointed One of 2000.

It had begun anew.

CHAPTER NOTES

This book is indebted to various sources. Many of them provided me with contemporaneous information during the period from February 1996 to November 1998. Those interviews provided the bulk of a journal I kept during the governor's race.

In addition, interviews—some on the record, some for background—that I conducted immediately after the election proved invaluable to fill in gaps and add color. They also provided me with a more textured perspective of how Kenny Guinn became governor.

Of course, this story could not have been told without material published during the campaign, not just by myself, but by numerous reporters for the state's newspapers. I also kept an extensive file of faxes, e-mails, press releases, speeches, polls, and other documents. That assisted me in creating a comprehensive chronology of events, which proved essential in reconstructing what happened.

The notes below provide general descriptions of where information was gleaned. I have followed the common practice of not repeating citations already included in the text. The *Las Vegas Review-Journal* is referred to as the *R-J,* the *Las Vegas Sun* is the *Sun* and the *Reno Gazette-Journal* is the *Gazette-Journal.* *TRR* refers to *The Ralston*

Report, my biweekly political newsletter.

PROLOGUE

This was written from news accounts of Brian McKay's announcement, and interviews conducted before and afterward with knowledgeable sources. McKay, then an executive with International Game Technology, also consented to an interview as this book was being written. Billy Vassiliadis also provided some of the information in a post-election interview. The announcement of Kenny Guinn's appointment as the co-chair of Bob Miller's re-election campaign came from an *R-J* column I wrote on Oct. 12, 1989.

CHAPTER 1—KENNY OF THE THOUSAND DAYS IS BORN

The interview with Kenny Guinn and Sig Rogich took place on Feb. 29, 1996.

The background on Rogich came from interviews with Rogich after the November balloting, numerous sources close to him (and observers from a distance), and many published reports. The anecdote about the first meeting on the race between Guinn and Rogich came from interviews with both men.

Guinn provided extensive details of his Las Vegas career. Observations were also provided by those who have watched him during his four decades in Southern Nevada.

Details of Guinn being romanced to run for the U.S. Senate in 1994 came from a column I wrote on Nov. 3, 1994 and subsequent follow-up pieces.

The recollections of early 1996 by Rogich, Guinn, and others were invaluable in reconstructing how the anointment began.

The encapsulation of Bob Miller's gubernatorial career came from my observations and a variety of news sources. The thumbnails of other possible candidates came from my observations and well-established facts.

The account of Guinn's role in championing a justice bond was derived from news stories of April 9, 1996. The story about Guinn accepting the award from the American Jewish Committee was reported in the *Sun* on June 5, 1996.

The details of Guinn's visit to Secretary of State Dean Heller and Jan Jones' poll were published in *TRR* on Oct. 18, 1996; details were also gleaned from interviews with the principals—both at the time of, and after, the election.

The recruitment of Frank Schreck and Elias Ghanem was reported in *TRR* on Oct. 3, 1996. Guinn's speech at the Nevada Development Authority breakfast was first reported in the Oct. 18 edition of *TRR*.

Chapter 2—The Powers that Anoint

The portrait of Jim Joyce was culled from a variety of sources, personal recollections, and published reports. I witnessed the incident with Bob Coffin. I was also present at the UNLV forum when the incident with Lori Lipman Brown occurred.

The portraits of the powers that anoint were put together through interviews, years of observation, and numerous published reports. The reports at the beginning and the end of Rogich's strategy came from interviews with him and others in the incipient campaign.

Chapter 3—Playing the Money Game

The opening vignette was written with the assistance of knowledgeable sources.

The strategy employed by Guinn and Rogich laid out here came from interviews with both men and those who were both privy to and subjected to their strategy.

Details of the contributions were obtained through extensive study of campaign contribution reports. The new donation regulations were detailed in a number of newspaper reports, including a column I wrote on Nov. 3, 1996. The account of the rush by Rogich & Co. to get contributions came from interviews with him and Guinn, as well as dates obtained from public records of donations. The motivations of Steve and Elaine Wynn were taken from interviews with both of them at the time.

The study of campaign contributions in 1988 was conducted by myself and published in the *R-J*. Heller's comments about disclosure were published in a column I wrote on Dec. 22, 1996.

CHAPTER 4—THE SHORT, UNHAPPY CANDIDACY OF FRANKIE SUE DEL PAPA

The Del Papa/Joyce Christmas story was told to me by those who were there.

Much of the information about Del Papa's thoughts and motivations emerged in an extensive interview I conducted with her immediately after the election and conversations with her confidants. The story of her traveling to Washington came from a column I wrote in the *R-J* on Jan. 19, 1997. The story of Del Papa being wooed by two legislators was first reported in a column I wrote on Feb. 3, 1997 in the *R-J*.

News of her exploratory committee broke in a column I wrote on Feb. 26, 1997. *The Cook Report* evaluation of the race was first reprinted in *TRR* on April 4, 1997. The finding that Guinn was relatively unknown was published in *TRR* two weeks later. That same issue contained the poll of insiders on who would be the next governor.

The bill that would limit donations was reported May 6, 1997 in the *R-J*. Two days later, the *Sun* reported Aaron Russo's interest in the race.

The background on Pete Ernaut came mostly from him, via some interviews and personal observations. His courtship by the Guinnites came courtesy of a variety of sources, including him, Rogich, Greg Ferraro, and Vassiliadis.

Steve Wark and Ernaut were interviewed on how Wark came to be hired. Guinn's insertion as the keynote speaker at the AFL-CIO convention, as well as Del Papa's first fundraiser, were reported in a column I wrote on Aug. 27, 1997. The information about the convention and the maneuvers came from interviews conducted at the time and notes from my journal. Some were also published in stories and columns.

Steve Wynn's decision to contribute to both candidates was revealed in an interview with him on Sept. 11 and repeated in a column written that day. The information about Kent Oram's decision to go with the Guinn campaign came from contemporaneous interviews and post-election reflections from knowledgeable sources.

Speeches by Guinn and Del Papa at the labor convention were reported in several stories in both major Las Vegas newspapers during the meeting that began Sept. 16, 1997, and an issue of *TRR* published shortly thereafter.

CHAPTER 5—HER HONOR TAKES A PASS

The background on Jan Jones' interest in the governor's race was written with her help and from various published reports and interviews at the time, and after the election. The vignettes about her appearances at the Andre Agassi event and the Democratic convention were culled from interviews with knowledgeable sources.

The story of Rogich's offer to be on the Gaming Commission came from interviews with all three participants in the meeting. Accounts of her contacts with Vassiliadis came from interviews with both of them.

Jane Ann Morrison's piece on the party's prospects without Jones appeared in the *R-J* on Oct. 18, 1997. The background on Reid was developed from interviews with him, his advisers, and others.

The account of Jones' decision-making process came from interviews with her, those who talked to her, and published reports, including an *R-J* piece on Oct. 23, 1997, concerning her canceling a fundraiser for her mayoral campaign.

Jones related her conversation with Vice President Al Gore. She also talked about her conversation with D. Taylor, which he confirmed.

The meeting between Guinn and Jones at the Desert Inn was pieced together after interviews with both, and those they talked to afterward.

The story about Guinn riding in the Nevada Day parade appeared on Nov. 1, 1997, in the *R-J.* The Russo-Salinger announcement came on Nov. 6, 1997. Joe Neal first floated his candidacy in the *Sun* on Nov. 7, 1997. Dini put his name aloft on Nov. 11, 1997.

The Guinn fundraiser was reported in my column on Nov. 17, 1997. Miller's decision not to become ambassador of Mexico was reported in several media outlets during the first week of December. Guinn's first mail piece was reported by me in the *Gazette-Journal* on Dec. 8, 1997.

Guinn's law-enforcement event was reported in the *R-J* on Dec. 18. The first report of a paycheck-protection initiative appeared in my *R-J* column on Dec. 9.

CHAPTER 6—THE MAKING OF A RACE

The genesis of paycheck protection came from interviews at the time with those involved, including John Mason, Chuck Muth, and George Harris. I obtained the reaction of Team Guinn to the initiative in interviews with the candidate and his advisers.

Jane Ann Morrison wrote about Guinn's contributions on Dec. 31. I subsequently tallied the numbers myself and wrote about them in the first *TRR* of 1998.

Neal announced his candidacy in media reports on Jan. 5, 1998. The interplay between Heller and Ernaut over

Guinn's war chest was first reported in the *Gazette-Journal*, then put together from interviews with the players.

Reid's machinations to recruit an alternative to Neal were uncovered by interviews with knowledgeable sources. Hammargren's decision-making process was related to me by him and those advising him.

Guinn's statement on paycheck protection was first reported in the *Sun* on Jan. 27, 1998. The details of the meeting at the Airport Plaza were obtained from interviews with several of the participants at the time, then later reported in my *R-J* column on Jan. 29, 1998, and followed up on in that week's *TRR*. News stories and columns in the next couple of weeks detailed the GOP's stop-and-start campaign on the union-dues initiative.

Russo's education plan was reported in the *Sun* on Feb. 17, 1998. Hammargren's congressional courtship was reported in the *Sun* that same day and details were obtained through interviews at the time.

I put together Heller's exit vignette from an interview with him and others. The meeting of the Guinn inner circle came from interviews with several of those who attended.

Events at the Clark County convention were reported to me in interviews conducted at the time and after the election. News reports and columns detailed some of the activity during the weekend of March 27.

The first poll was reported in the *R-J* on March 29, 1998. Neal's reception by the Democrats at their conventions was reported in my column on April 14, 1998. Numerous news reports and columns detailed the state GOP convention during the last week of April.

CHAPTER 7—THE FLY IN THE ANOINTMENT

The story of Jones' discovery of her breast cancer emerged from an interview with her and news reports at the time. The run-up to her decision to file for governor came from interviews with her and those close to her at the time and after the election.

The story about her appearance on the radio was published in the *Sun* on May 8, 1998. The reactions of the Guinn team to her musings came after interviews with his advisers at the time and after the election.

I heard the story of the Guinn-Jones encounter at Steve Wynn's dinner party from knowledgeable sources. The account of Reid's wooing of Mike Schneider came from interviews at the time. Both participants related the story of the Vassiliadis-Jones dinner.

I obtained a copy of the poll Celinda Lake conducted for Jones. Jones and others also related the events leading up to her announcement after the poll was done. Reid's efforts to generate phone calls that final weekend before the end of filing came from him, and those close to him. Jones told of the events, including the Wynn phone call, the weekend before she filed.

Stories of Jones' and Hammargren's filing appeared in all major newspapers on May 18. The analysis of Jones' motivations for filing, that appear at the end of the chapter, were pieced together from interviews with many sources, including Jones, familiar with how it was made.

CHAPTER 8—A FISHY BEGINNING

The story of Clyde Turner's meeting with Richard Schuetz was taken almost entirely from transcripts of an Ethics Commission meeting in which the encounter was described by Schuetz.

Dina Titus' comments about Guinn's team were quoted in a May 24 *R-J* story. Jones related the assembling of her team, and Schuetz' role, in an extensive interview. Others who talked to her at the time also contributed.

The detailing of the thought process of Team Guinn after Jones' announcement was gathered from extensive contemporaneous and post-election interviews. Reid's activities in helping Jones were related by the senator, and others familiar with the events. Jones and Dan Hart also provided information about how Denise Rawles was hired.

CHAPTER 9—MANAGING THE LABOR VOTE

The story of Jones' 1994 AFL-CIO experience was recounted with the help of news clips from the time. The overview of the convention outlook in 1998 came from interviews at the time and afterward with campaign insiders and labor leaders.

I read copies of the two candidates' speeches to the convention. News stories and columns that first week in June 1998 were also helpful.

The events leading up to the erasure of paycheck protection from the ballot were first reported in an extensive piece I wrote for the *R-J* on June 21, 1998. Much of it was reprinted here.

The *R-J* poll was published on June 14.

CHAPTER 10—ANOINTMENT LOST

The letters on the power company merger were first published in the *R-J* on June 20, 1998.

The statement from Jones' doctor was issued in a news release. The account of the TV buys came from interviews and news reports during June.

Interviews with Guinnites provided the mayoral news conference background. The Guinn poll taken in mid-July was first published in *TRR*.

Jones' kickoff was reported in the *R-J* on June 11, 1998. Jones' Chamber of Commerce encounter came from interviews with knowledgeable sources. A campaign news release announced her endorsement by the state employees on July

17, 1998. Stu Rothenberg's assessment was also repeated in a Jones campaign news release. Jones' appearance before the Ethics panel was reported in all the major newspapers—I wrote a column about it on July 26, 1998.

The *R-J* poll showing Russo within 7 points ran on Aug. 7. My column ran two days later, the same day Russo called me in the vignette described herein. Interviews at the time, and afterward, with various Guinnites revealed the story of how the spot attacking Russo was conceived.

Jones' exoneration by the Ethics Commission was reported in the major newspapers on Aug. 17, 1998.

CHAPTER 11—ANOINTMENT FOUND

The Jan Jones 1991 events were well-documented.

Reid's primary-night comments were reported in my Sept. 3, 1998, column in the *R-J*. The developments inside the Jones campaign were culled from various inside sources. Jones later related the story about trying to raise money from the gaming industry.

The Guinn campaign's post-primary strategy percolated from interviews with campaign players during that period and after the election.

The accounts of debate strategies were gathered from interviews with campaign aides to both candidates. Jones' environmental initiative was reported in several news outlets, including my e-mail publication, on Sept. 9, 1998.

The report of the AFL-CIO convention was written with the help of interviews conducted at the time and afterward, as well as news accounts in the *R-J* and *Sun* on Sept. 15-16, 1998.

The story of the Guinn campaign meeting after the convention came from various sources at the confab. The subsequent strategies were also extracted from Guinn campaign sources.

The subsequent polls were reported in my e-mail publication and in the general media in the first week of October. Vice President Al Gore's appearance for Jones was reported in the *R-J* on Oct. 3, 1998.

The story about Guinn preparing for the debates was confirmed by two campaign aides. The reports of the debates were gleaned from news accounts, my own notes, and interviews afterward with key players.

The account of the Team Guinn meeting in Rogich's office in mid-October came courtesy of several attendees. The Election Day accounts were augmented by recollections of the candidates and their aides. The analysis of why Guinn won was gleaned from extensive interviews with the campaign teams after the election.

EPILOGUE

The summary of the 1999 Legislature came from well-documented events. So, too, with Sen. Richard Bryan's retirement announcement and the subsequent chain of events. John Ensign's Senate campaign kickoff was reported in the *R-J* on March 7, and later in my column.

INDEX

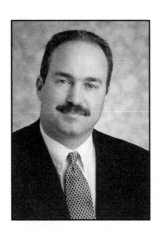

Jon Ralston has covered politics in Nevada for 14 years. He writes columns for two major state newspapers, produces a daily political briefing and a biweekly newsletter and hosts a weekly television show. He lives in Las Vegas with his wife, Sarah, and daughter, Madeline.

About Huntington Press

Huntington Press is a specialty publisher of Las Vegas- and gambling-related books and periodicals. To receive a copy of the Huntington Press catalog, please call 1-800-244-2224, go to www.huntingtonpress.com, or write to the address below.

Huntington Press
3687 South Procyon Avenue
Las Vegas, Nevada 89103

These acclaimed books from Huntington Press are available at a bookstore near you:

The Art of Gambling Through the Ages
by Arthur Flowers and Anthony Curtis
(ISBN 0-929712-90-0)

*No Limit: The Rise and Fall of Bob Stupak
and Las Vegas' Stratosphere Tower*
by John L. Smith
(ISBN 0-929712-18-8)

On the Boulevard: The Best of John L. Smith
(ISBN 0-929712-69-2)

*The First 100: Portraits of the Men and Women
Who Shaped Las Vegas*
edited by A.D. Hopkins and K.J. Evans
(ISBN 0-929712-66-8)

*Fly on the Wall: Recollections of Las Vegas'
Good Old, Bad Old Days*
by Dick Odessky
(ISBN 0-929712-62-5)

Hiking Las Vegas: 60 Hikes Within 60 Minutes of the Strip
by Branch Whitney
(ISBN 0-929712-21-8)

Hiking Southern Nevada
by Branch Whitney
(ISBN 0-929712-22-6)

*Cult Vegas: Everything "In" and Outrageous About
the Swingin'est Place on the Planet* (December 2000)
by Mike Weatherford
(ISBN 0-929712-71-4)